IMAGES
of America

ROCKLAND

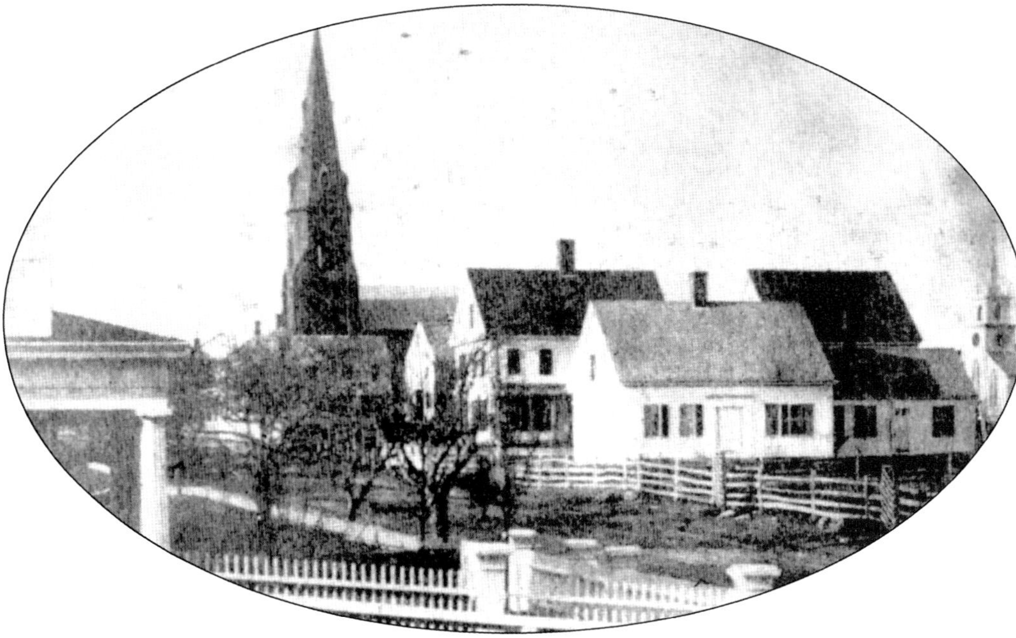

Since its laying out in 1815, the heart of Rockland has been Union Street. These 1860s views show more of a rural setting than exists today. Before the full effect of the Industrial Revolution, East Abington, the village that in 1874 became Rockland, was rural in character. However, just outside of this scene, shoemakers are hard at work building a reputation for the town, a community soon to be awakened by the arrival of a railroad, enormous factories, and big business.

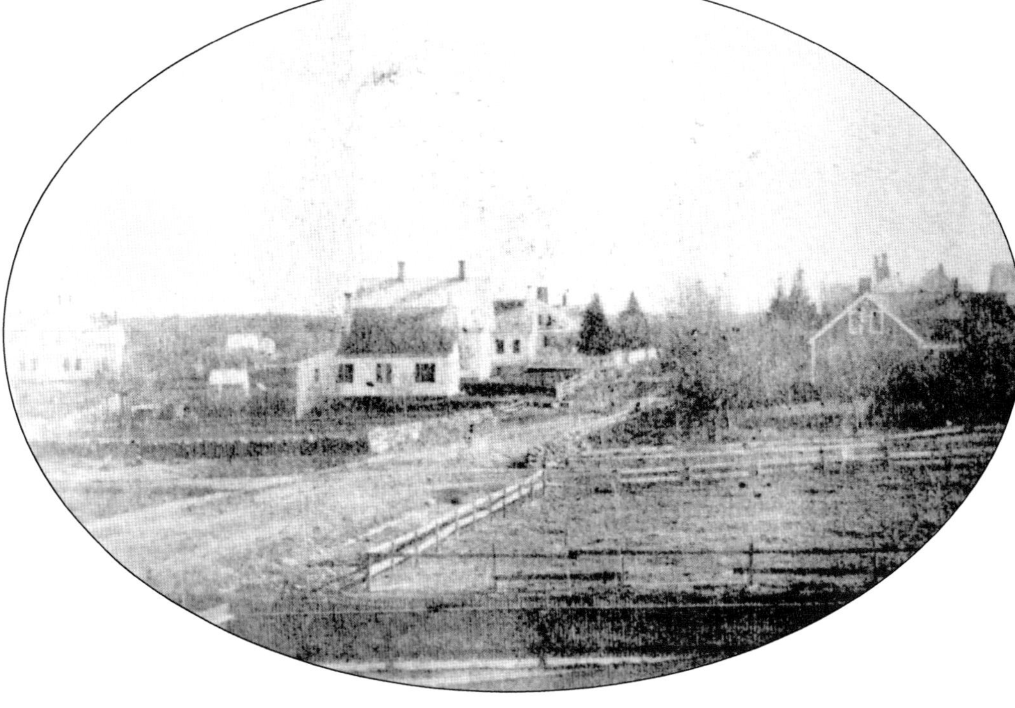

IMAGES
of America

ROCKLAND

Donald Cann and John Galluzzo

ARCADIA
PUBLISHING

ISBN 978-0-7385-1248-8

Published by Arcadia Publishing
Charleston, South Carolina

Printed in the United States of America

Library of Congress Catalog Card Number: 2003106112

For all general information contact Arcadia Publishing at:
Telephone 843-853-2070
Fax 843-853-0044
E-mail sales@arcadiapublishing.com
For customer service and orders:
Toll-Free 1-888-313-2665

Visit us on the Internet at www.arcadiapublishing.com

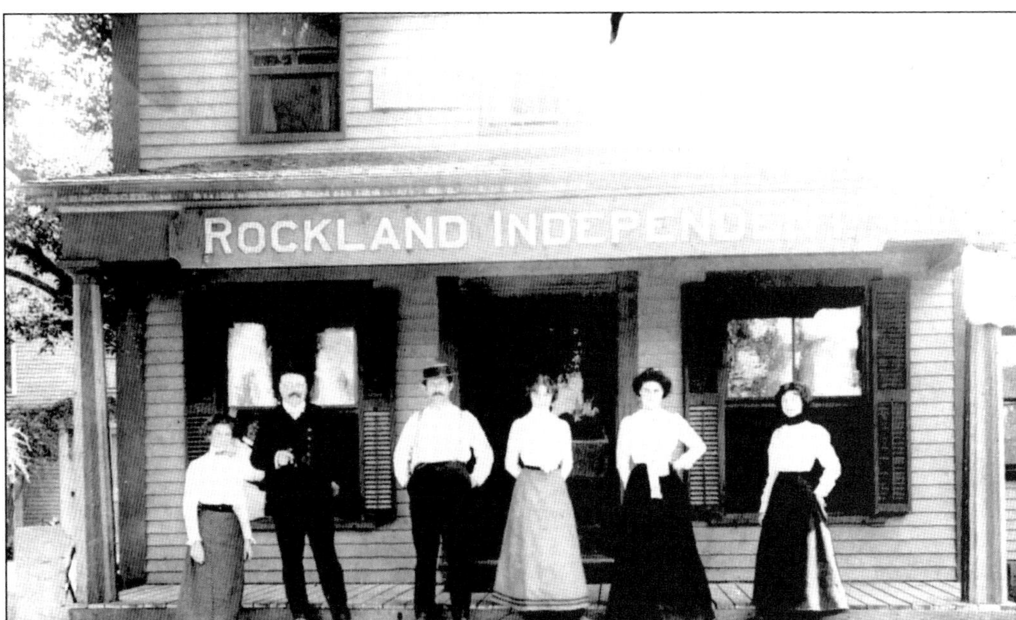

There could be no better name for a newspaper in Rockland than the *Independent* to reflect the nature of the community after its split from the town of Abington in 1874.

Contents

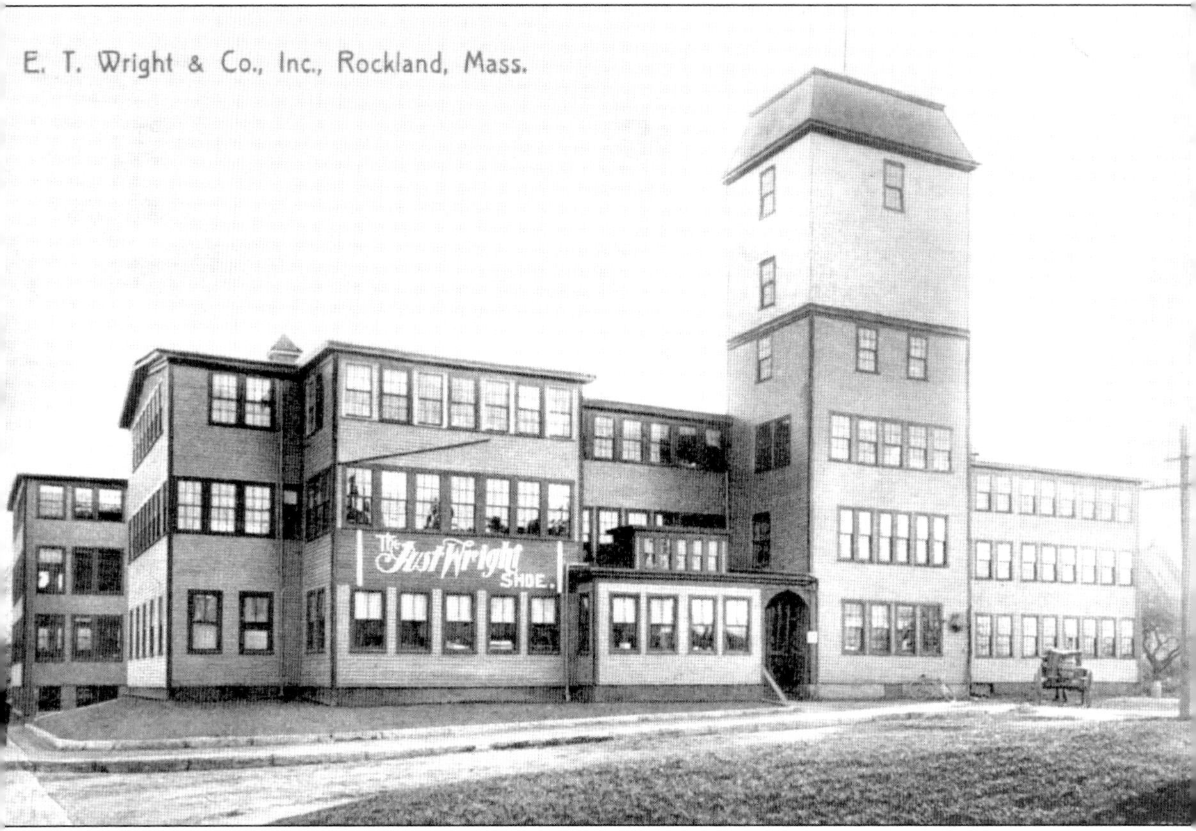

By the 1880s, it became apparent that the shoemaking industry was "Just Wright" for Rockland. Factories grew and expanded on spots once occupied by "ten-footers," backyard shops where early shoemakers carried out their process from the raw materials to the final products.

Introduction

Commotion, Massachusetts.

It may be hard to believe it today, but when the Divisionists, George Clapp, Washington Reed, and the other East Abingtonians who wanted to break their village away from the larger town of Abington and incorporate as their own community, met in January 1874 to decide the name of the new town, two people stood up and voted for Commotion. Others voted for Aberdeen, Highland, Albion, Glenwood, Rock, Benton, Alton, Underwood, and Aalberg. One person even voted to keep the name East Abington. In the end, 19 people voted for Andrew, 69 chose Hatherly, and 114 selected Rockland. When the Divisionists filed their petition to the state to form the new town on January 21, 1874,—the same day that the people of South Abington filed a petition to form their own town, Whitman—the name on the document was Rockland. Just over two months later, on March 10, 1874, Rockland was born.

The distinctive history of East Abington began well before the village's separation from the rest of the old town. The earliest settlers of the area that eventually became known as Rockland took advantage of the selling off of the Hatherly grant, the nine-square-mile tract of land deeded to merchant adventurer Timothy Hatherly and others in 1656 in compensation for problems with another tract of land in Cohasset. The land delineated as the Hatherly grant made up two-thirds of today's Rockland, and the northern section of town still retains the neighborhood name.

Those first settlers of the Hatherly land and Cornet Robert Stetson's purchase to the south, cut down the virgin timber stands that covered the area and sold the lumber to end users such as the great shipbuilding yards on the North River. Produced in these yards were the well-known vessels *Columbia*, the first ship to circumnavigate the globe under the American flag, and *Beaver*, of Boston Tea Party fame. The Thaxter family came from Hingham in 1703 to build a sawmill on Cushing Pond on East Water Street. Stephen French constructed and operated a mill on Market Street two years later.

When the trees disappeared, the local settlers looked out across the vast expanse of cleared land and began their transition into the next logical vocations, herding and farming. Out in those fields, the seeds of Rockland were planted. In 1712, the General Court recognized the incorporation of the town of Abington. The village of East Abington began to grow as Weymouth residents moved over the northern border and settlers of West Hanover moved in from the east. Farming remained the major industry of East Abington until Thomas Hunt arrived with a handful of tools in 1793.

Hunt, a traveling shoemaker, established a shop in the northern section of the East Abington village. From this simple act grew the spirit of a community. By 1832, six full-fledged factories were producing twice as many shoes as neighboring Brockton. By 1865, East Abington shoe manufacturers produced $3.5 million worth of shoes and boots, employing nearly 3,000 people. By 1874, when a fight arose between Center Abington and East Abington over the spending of tax dollars on local schools (the central village's school cost twice as much as those built in East and South Abington), the people of the eastern village were ready to strike out on their own.

In 1886, the town of Rockland adopted the Hatherly family coat of arms as its official town seal. The people of Rockland never looked back.

Rockland is not the complete history of East Abington and Rockland. This book is a pictorial record of the town. The authors were constrained only by the selection of photography available. Certain wonderful anecdotes did not make it into the main text of the book, such as the P.T. Barnum balloon that crashed in town and the tale of the Confederate soldier who hung around the Grand Army Hall but was always asked to disappear when cameras appeared. Since there was no photography to be shown, those stories could not be told at length.

On the other hand, several residents responded to the authors' requests for imagery with local photographs pulled from family albums. These photographs reveal forgotten times from Rockland's past. Through the book's eight chapters, which focus on Union Street, Union Square, Rockland's historic houses, churches, events, people, factories, and municipal buildings, the stories of Rockland come to life. Included are the fabulous Sweeney sisters outside their millinery on Union Street, Judge George Washington Kelley's parade, the arrival of Rockland's "movie queen," and the rebuilding of landmark structures after destructive fires brought them to the ground. The authors' desire is that you view this as Rockland's family album.

Dozens of people contributed to the production of this book, which the authors hope will be regarded as a community history and not just the work of two historians. So join the authors, now, as they take their first steps up Union Street into Rockland's past.

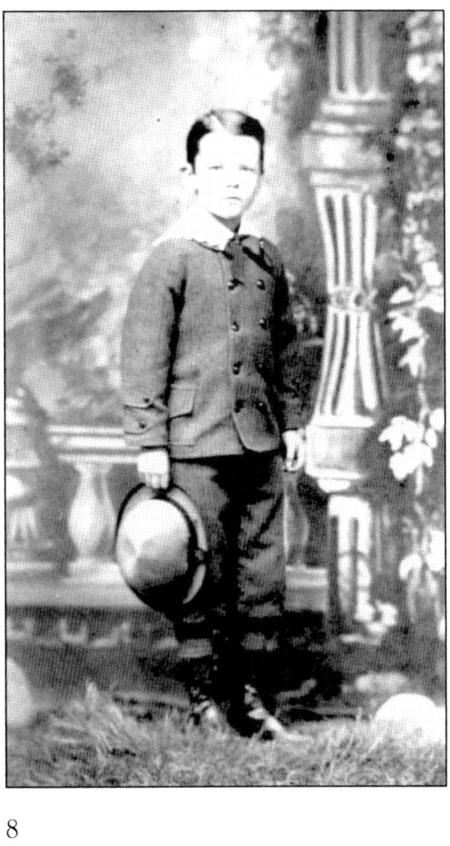

On March 10, 1874, Rockland received good news and bad news. The bad news was that ex-President of the United States Millard Fillmore had died. The good news was that Rockland was finally its own town. That same day, George Rockland Hunt, the first child born in the new town, had arrived, forever gaining fame as the "first citizen of Rockland."

One

The Hill

Rockland's Business District

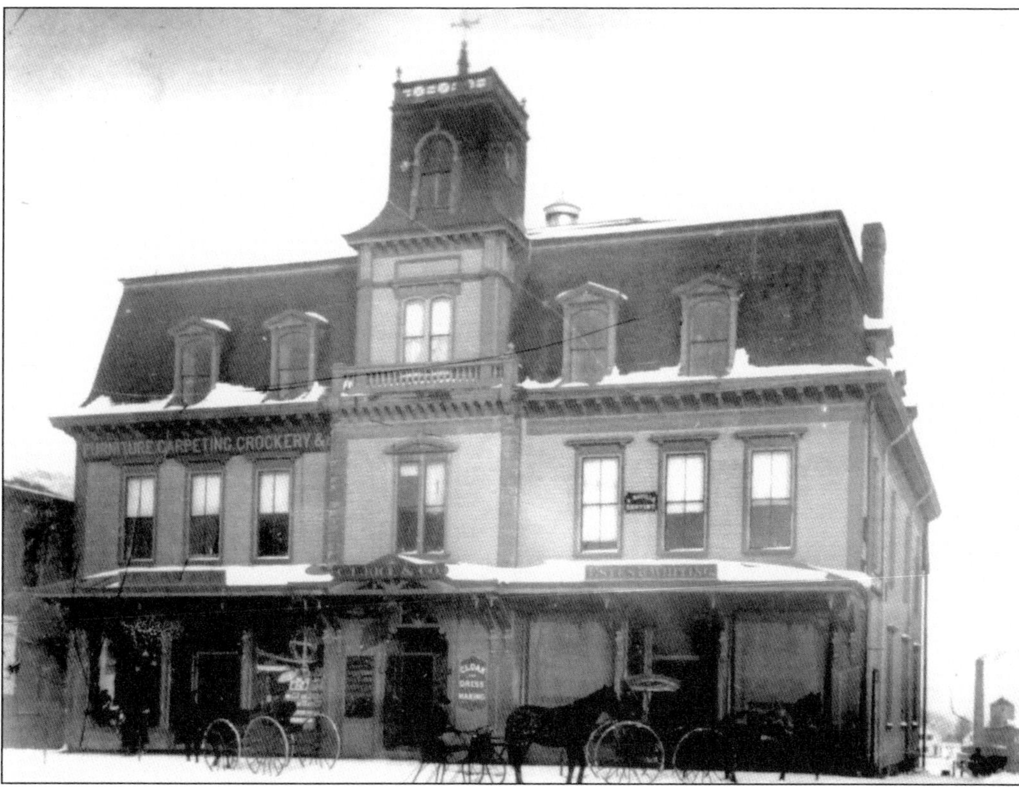

The businesses that later made Rockland famous had been established on Union Street in the retail district known as the Hill long before East Abington became Rockland. The Phoenix Block, built in 1869, in the French Second Empire style, became a symbol of Rockland as an independent town. The first town meeting was held on the hall's third floor on March 19, 1874. John A. and Charles L. Rice had their store in this building after the Civil War.

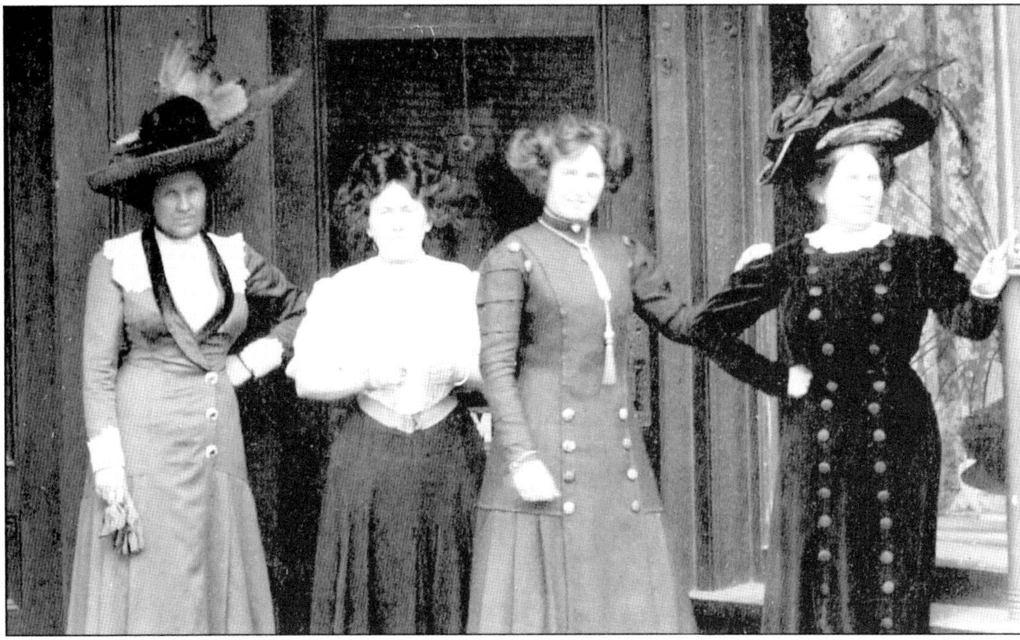

Although Rockland was always known for its shoes, other businesses thrived here as well. The Sweeney sisters had a millinery and furrier shop at 221 Union Street. This photograph, taken c. 1905, shows the sisters and their niece outside the shop. Seen here are, from left to right, Sarah Sweeney, Anna E. Sweeney, Helen McCarthy, and Susie Sweeney.

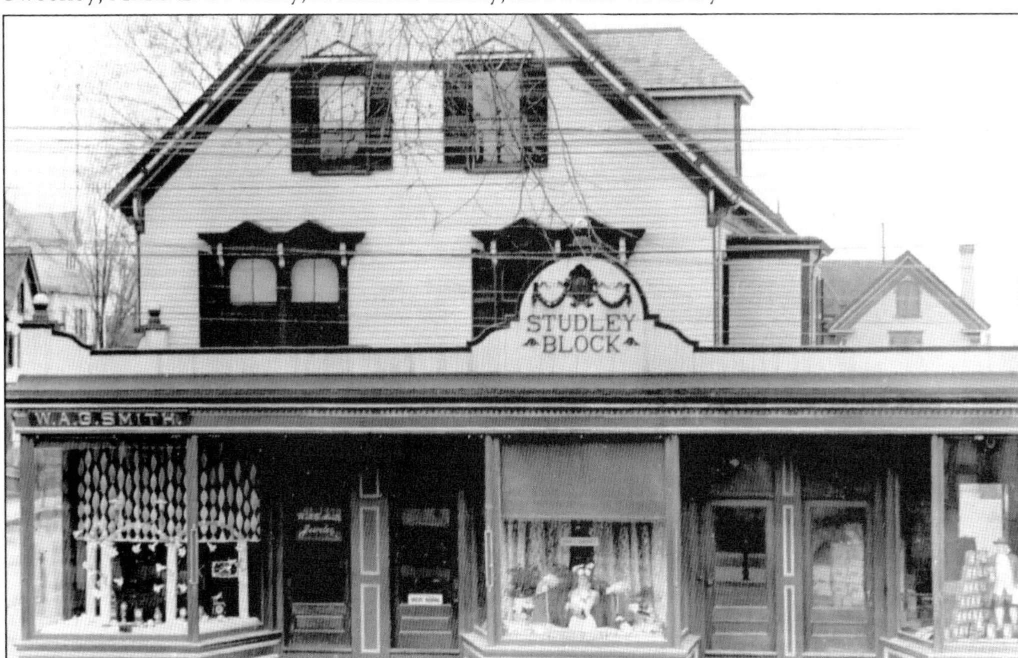

The Studley Block stood on the corner of School and Union Streets. The Sweeney's shop is in the center. The shop on the left, W.A.G. Smith, is a jewelry store, and the one on the right is a grocery store. You can see the Quaker Oats man in the window. The building on the left with the flagpole is the Grand Army Hall, which was located on School Street.

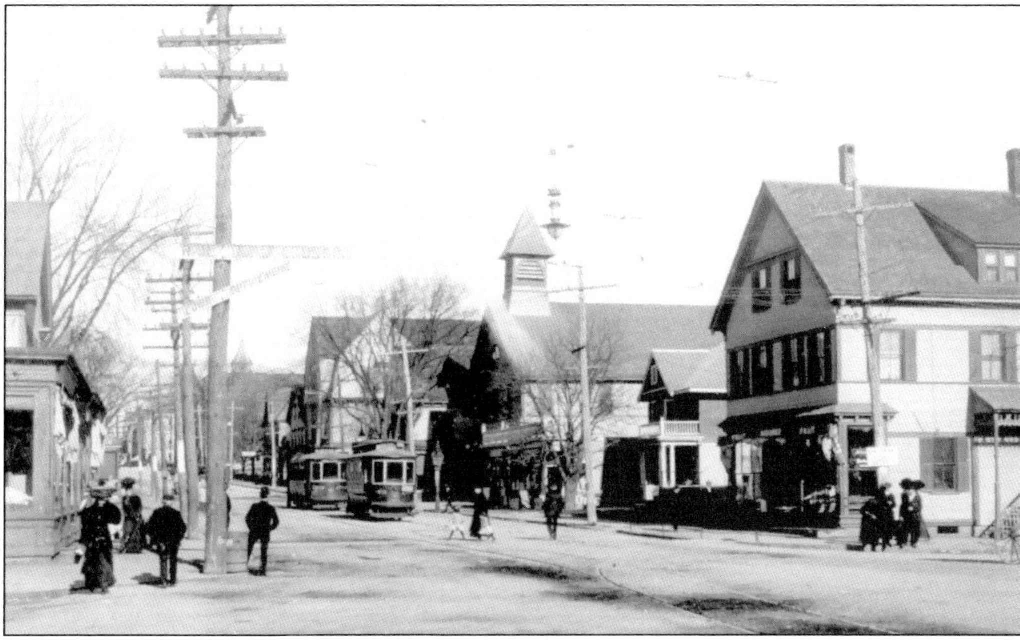

This view, looking north from Union Square, shows the Temperance Building, the building on the right with the cupola. Most of the buildings in this view have disappeared. The second building on the right is a home that remains today, and the Congregational church stands in the background. There are two trolley cars on the street. The trolleys came with electric lights in 1892. This service provided transportation to surrounding towns and to Nantasket Beach. The last trolley ran to Brockton in 1931.

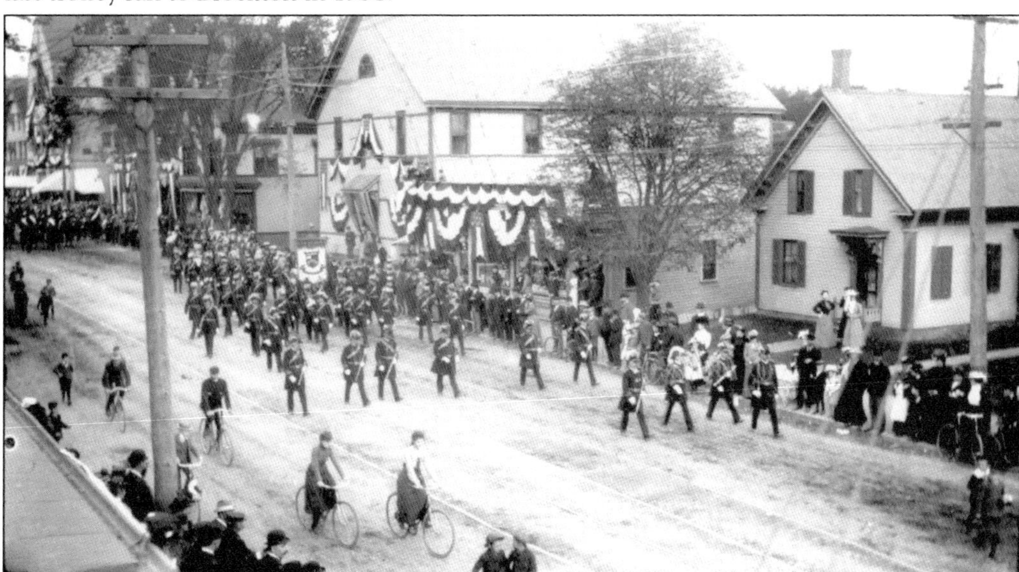

The parading unit passes in front of the Temperance Building. The St. Alphonsus Total Abstinence Society built this building in 1882. Father Rathkey of St. Bridget's parish organized the society in 1870. The purpose of the society was to give aid and understanding to the victims of alcoholism and to prevent further addiction. This hall was later remodeled into the Strand Theatre.

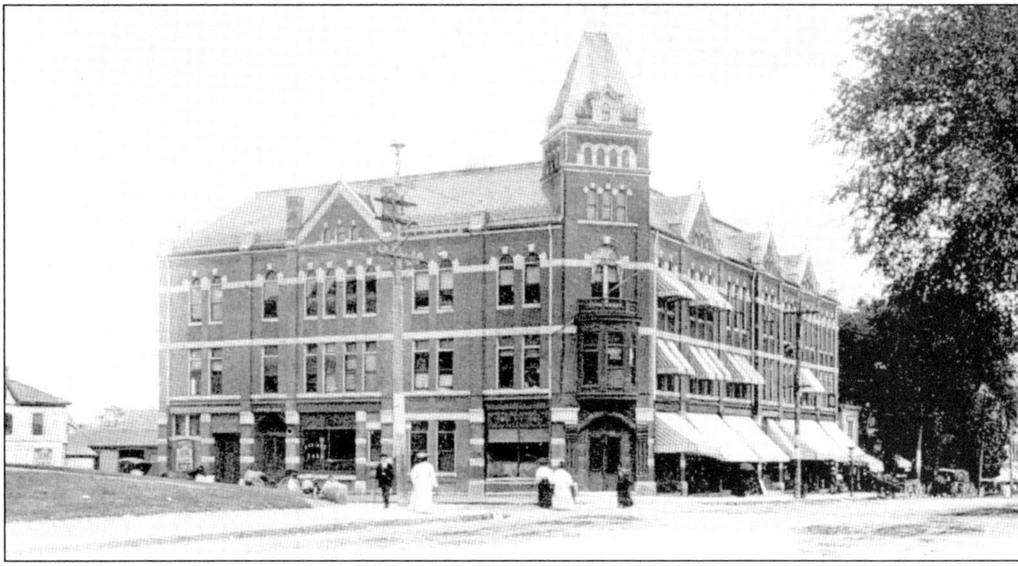

The Rockland Savings Bank building was the Hill's biggest and most elaborate building. This structure replaced an earlier one, the Underwood Building, after the Brown Church fire of 1890. On the street floor were the Rockland Savings Bank (now the South Coastal Savings Bank) and the First National Bank of Rockland, which became the Rockland Trust Company. The Howland Insurance and Amos Phelps Insurance Companies had offices on the second floor. The rest of the building held a hall called the Opera House and space for a social club, the Union Glee Club. The upper floors were removed in 1965.

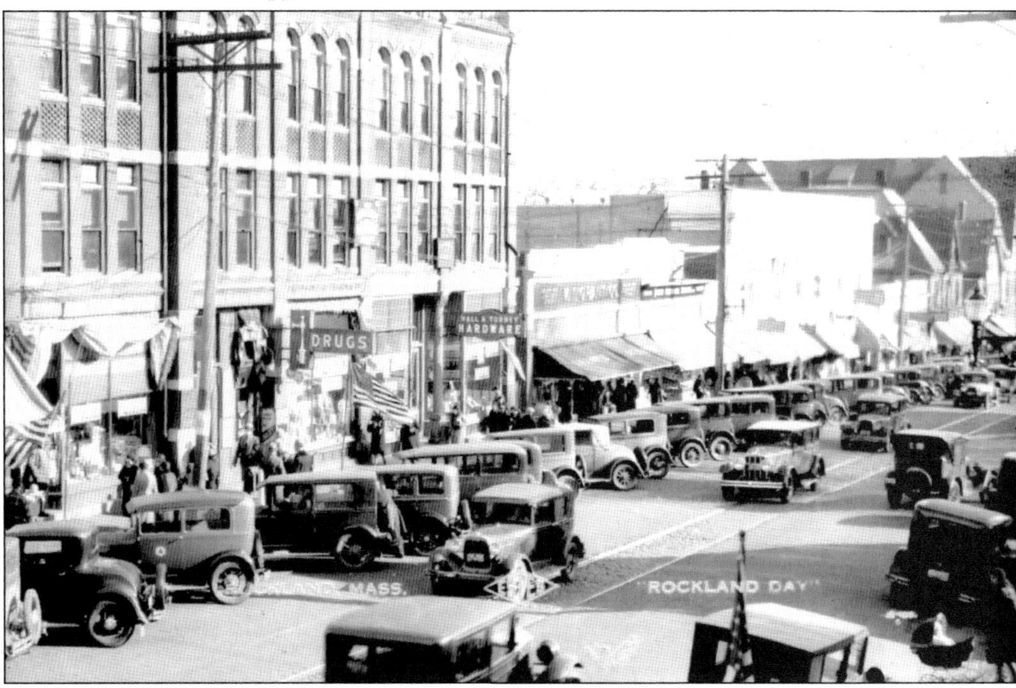

On this busy day *c.* the mid-1920s, you can see the Amos Phelps Insurance sign on the second floor of the bank building. The automobile has certainly made an impact on Union Street. By this time, both local business and chain stores were located on the Hill.

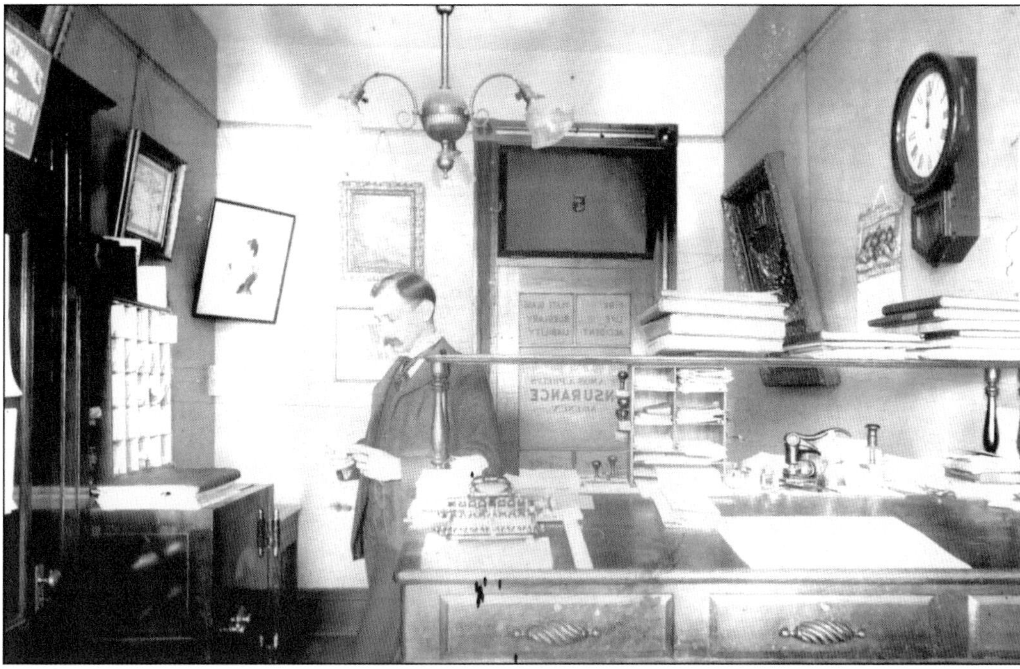

Insurance man Amos Phelps poses in his office on the second floor of the bank building in 1904 (note the clock and the calendar on the wall). No doubt these rooms are right behind the company sign we saw in the previous photograph.

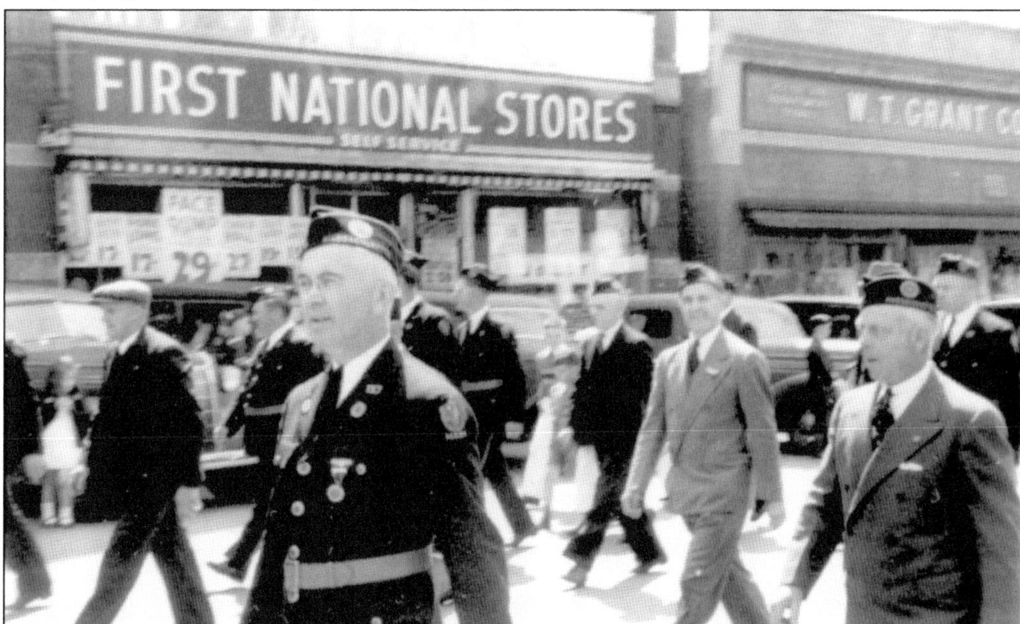

The man facing the camera is Russell Osgood, one of the twin sons of Dr. Gilman Osgood. These marchers are veterans of World War I. The stores in the background are just south of the savings bank building. The prices in the window of the First National may be competitive by late 1930s standards, but look like a steal by contemporary standards. Fire destroyed the Grant building in 1941.

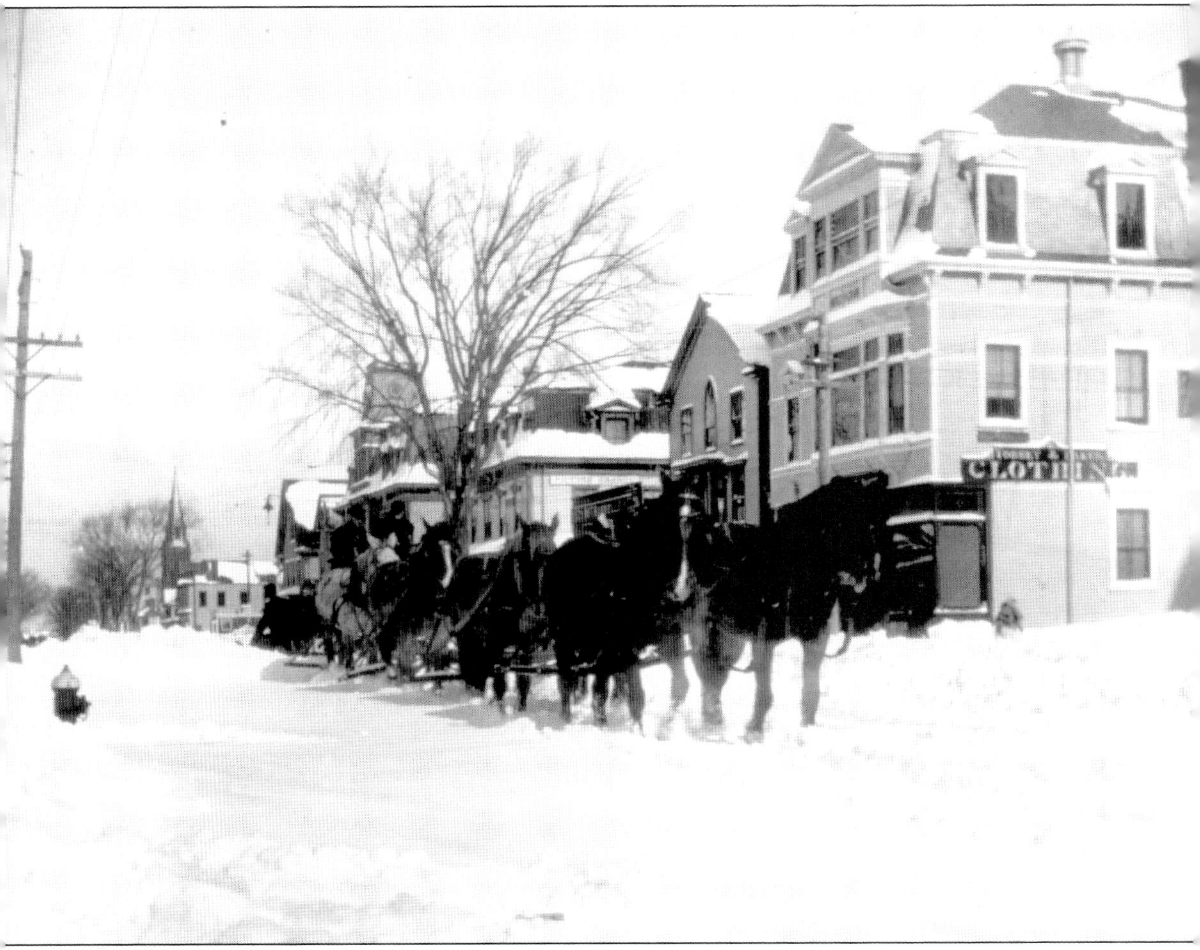

The first building on the right is the Webster Building. Next to that is the Gibbs Building, before a full third story was added. Down the street are two other mansard-style buildings. The one with the cupola is the first Phoenix Building. The next one is the Standard Building. The horse-drawn snowplow was working some time before 1914, the year the first Phoenix Building burned.

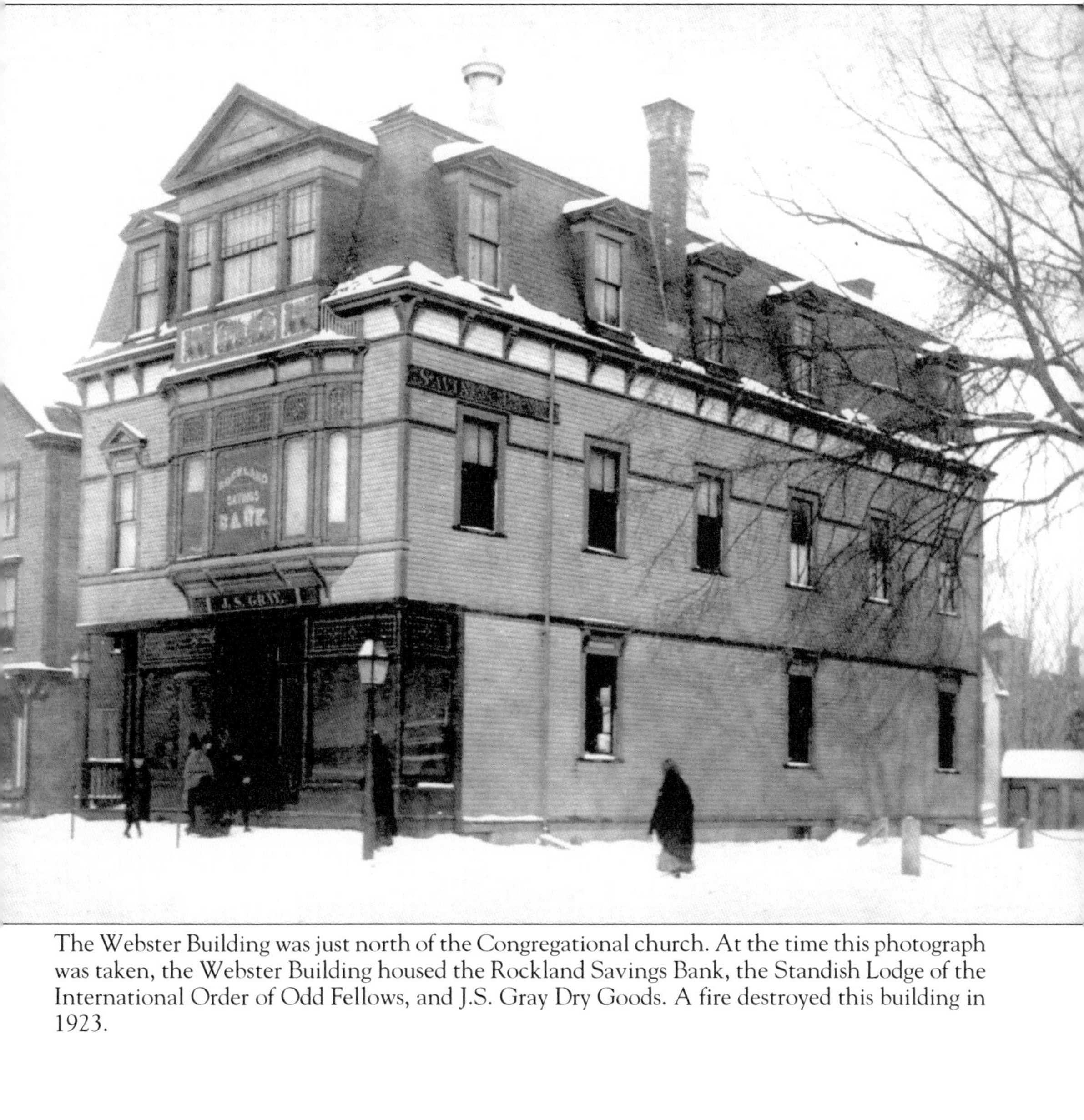

The Webster Building was just north of the Congregational church. At the time this photograph was taken, the Webster Building housed the Rockland Savings Bank, the Standish Lodge of the International Order of Odd Fellows, and J.S. Gray Dry Goods. A fire destroyed this building in 1923.

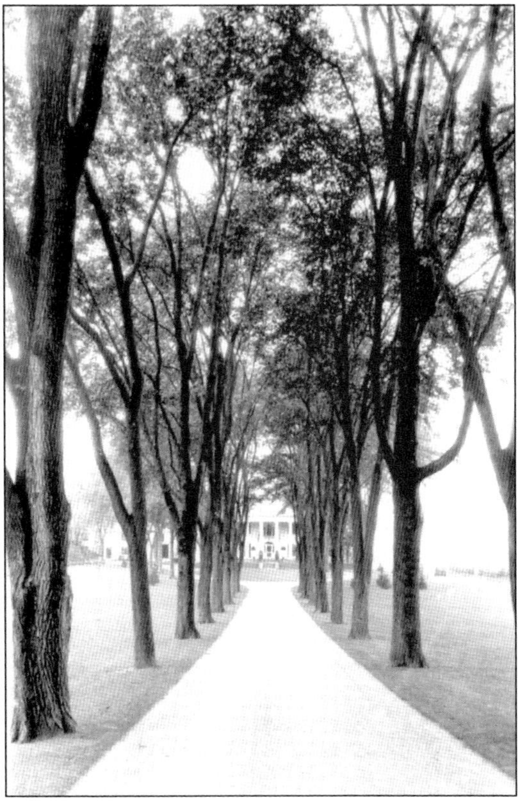

The estate of James W. Spence was a showplace of Rockland and the South Shore. Its tree-lined entrance drive was on Union Street, and the house was built where the high school stands today. Washington Reed developed the estate in the 1850s. Reed was in the shoe business and pioneered outlets for his shoes in Boston and New Orleans. He also initiated the use of buffalo hides to make fur-lined boots. Reed made large profits during the Civil War on government contracts and was a prime mover in establishing the town of Rockland. Spence bought the estate in 1913 and remodeled the house.

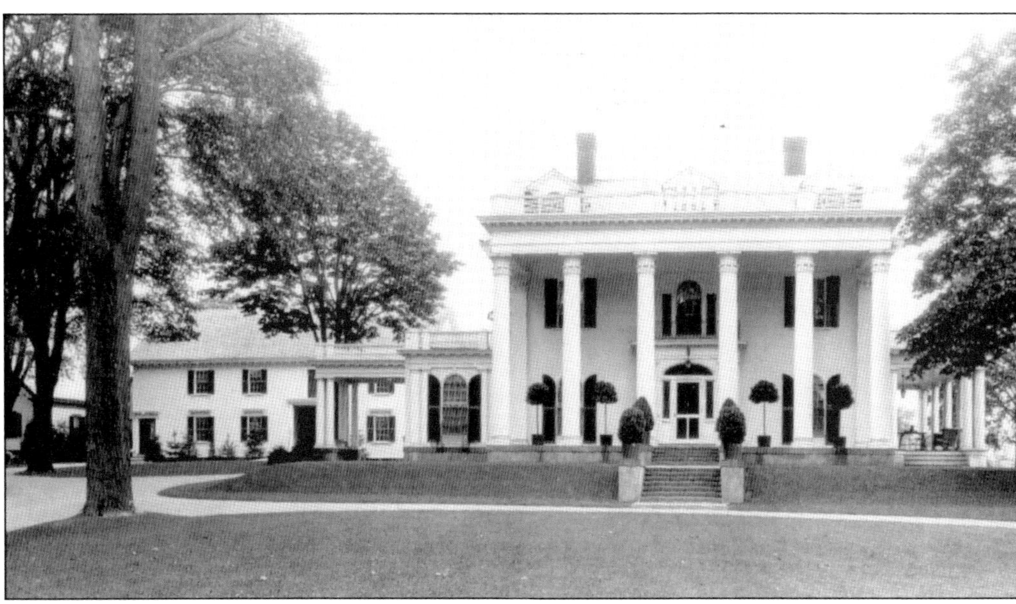

After remodeling, the Spence estate was a home that looked like it would be happier on the banks of the Mississippi River than the banks of Union Street in Rockland. The house is a revival of styles popular in the first half of the 19th century.

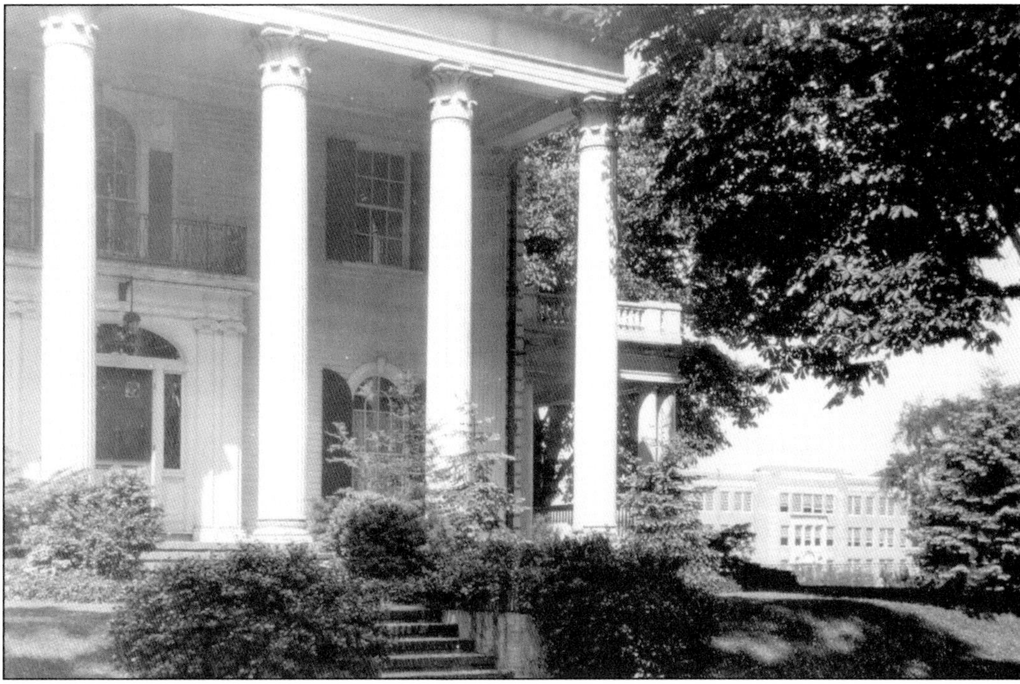

The building on the right was built as the high school in 1927. It is now the John Rogers Middle School. For more than 30 years, Rockland students passed this fabulous bit of historic architecture on the way to school. In 1960, the town acquired the Spence estate, razed it, and built the current high school.

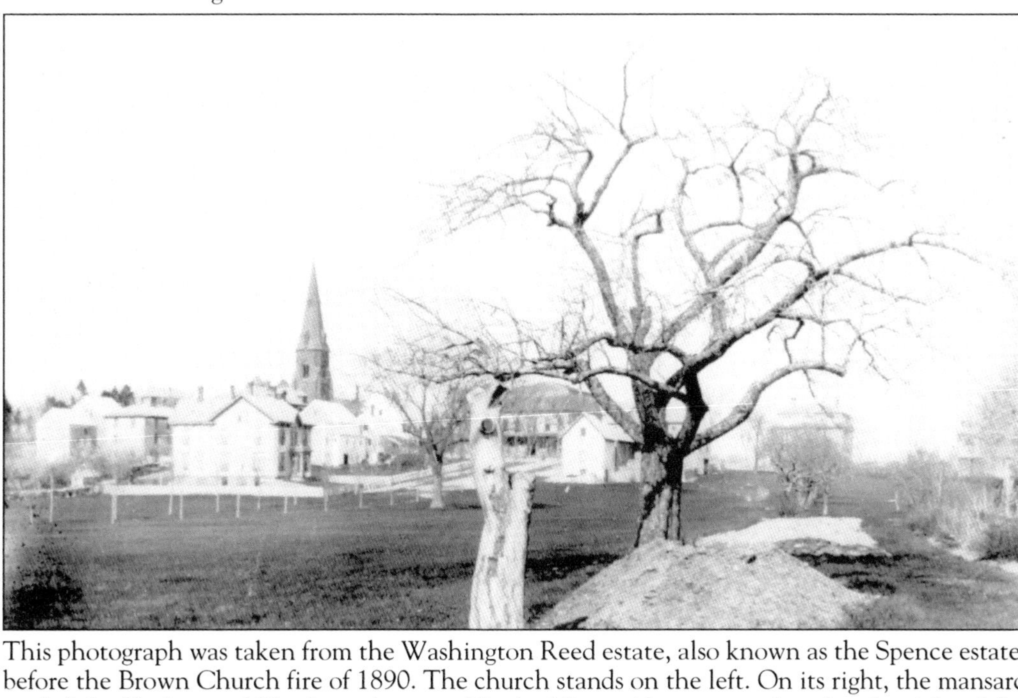

This photograph was taken from the Washington Reed estate, also known as the Spence estate, before the Brown Church fire of 1890. The church stands on the left. On its right, the mansard roof of the Underwood Block can be seen. The building with a mansard roof to the right of the apple tree is not the Hotel Thomas, but more likely a home.

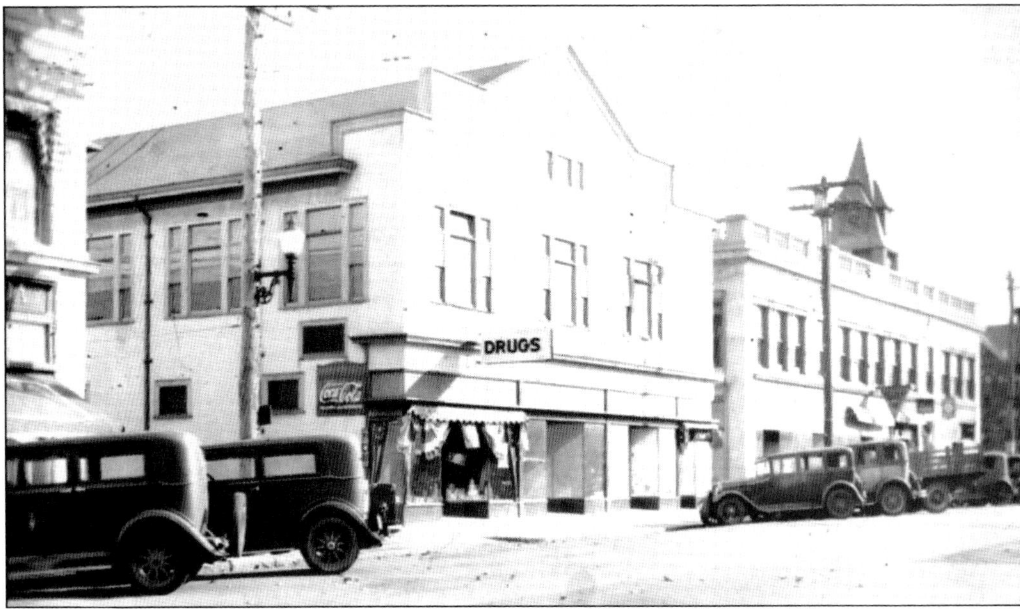

This building was on the corner of Park and Union Streets. The Bigelow Building to the right, as well as the new Phoenix Building (the corner of the building is on the left) are good examples of the Neoclassical style. Both buildings, built in the 1920s, use concrete for their façades and have balustrade at the roofline. The tower of the Congregational church is seen above the Bigelow Building.

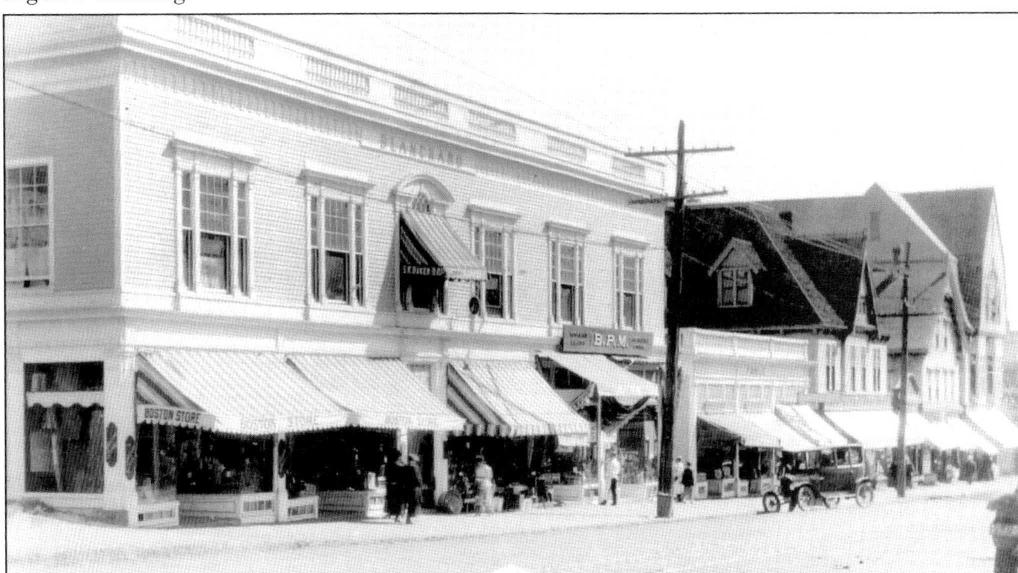

The Blanchard Building, originally located at 255 Union Street, is gone, as well as all the other buildings in this photograph. Kelly's Bar was located in the one-story building to the right of the Blanchard. Looking down the street, the Payson Block is next, then a small store with an interesting curved roofline. The next building is the Grace Building. The last on the right is the Torrey Block, where Newbury's five-and-ten was located. The Grace and Torrey Buildings were destroyed by fire in 1935. The Rockland Federal Credit Union, organized in 1921, takes up most of this block at the present time.

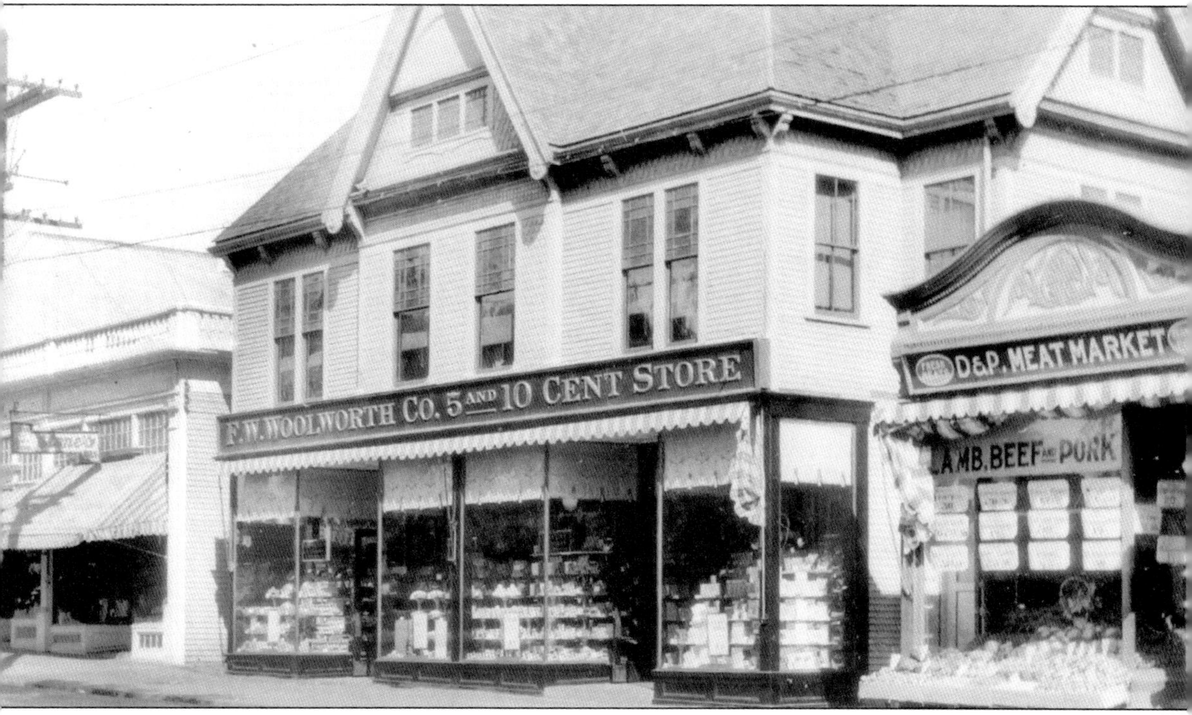

E. Payson Torrey built the Payson Building in the1880s. It was the biggest building in Rockland at that time. The Commercial Club was located here. The building was lost in the fire of 1957. The Hill's smallest commercial building, which housed a meat market and grocery store, was next door.

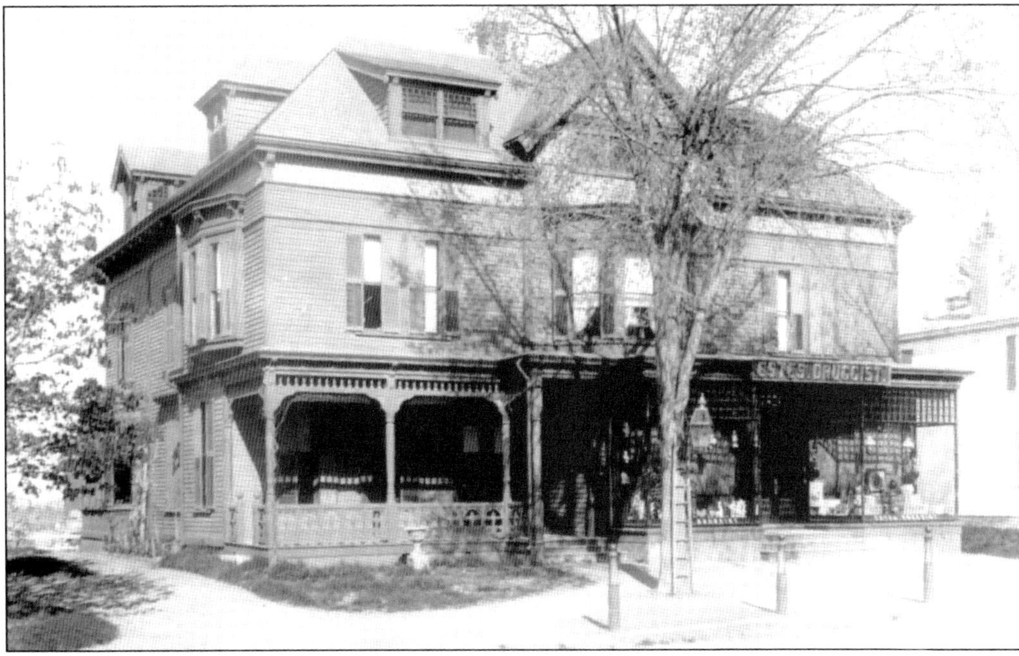

Joseph Jocelyn Estes built this house about the time of the Civil War. Estes was a druggist and a perfumer. The ground-floor shop can be seen on the right side of this photograph. The ladder resting on the tree is no doubt for a lamplighter. Burton O. Estes, Joseph's son, continued the business in the family name. He also added photography to the business. Most of the photographic record of Rockland is the work of Estes. Nathan Ranney remodeled the building in 1923 for his clothing store. Rome Brothers Hardware also moved into the building in the 1920s. Rockland Trust acquired the building and used it for offices in the late 1980s, then took it down in the late 1990s.

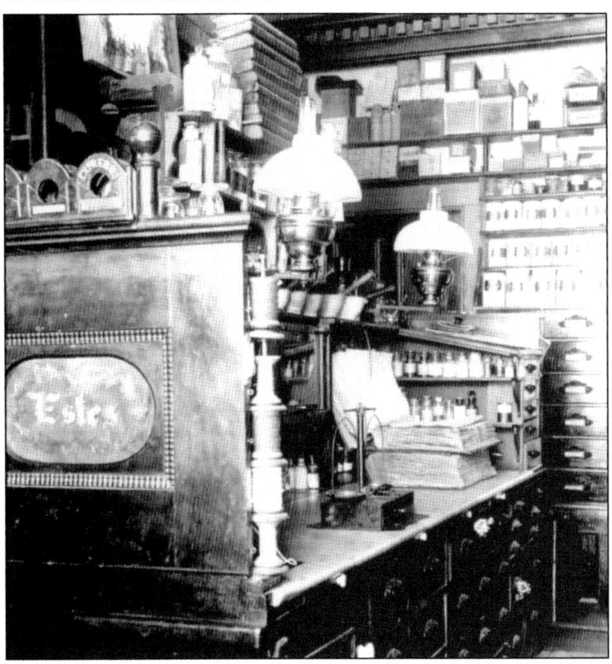

Estes knew what his customers wanted. This photograph gives some idea of the variety of merchandise he stocked. If a clock was not what you wanted, then perhaps it was a cough syrup, or an ice-cream sundae made to order.

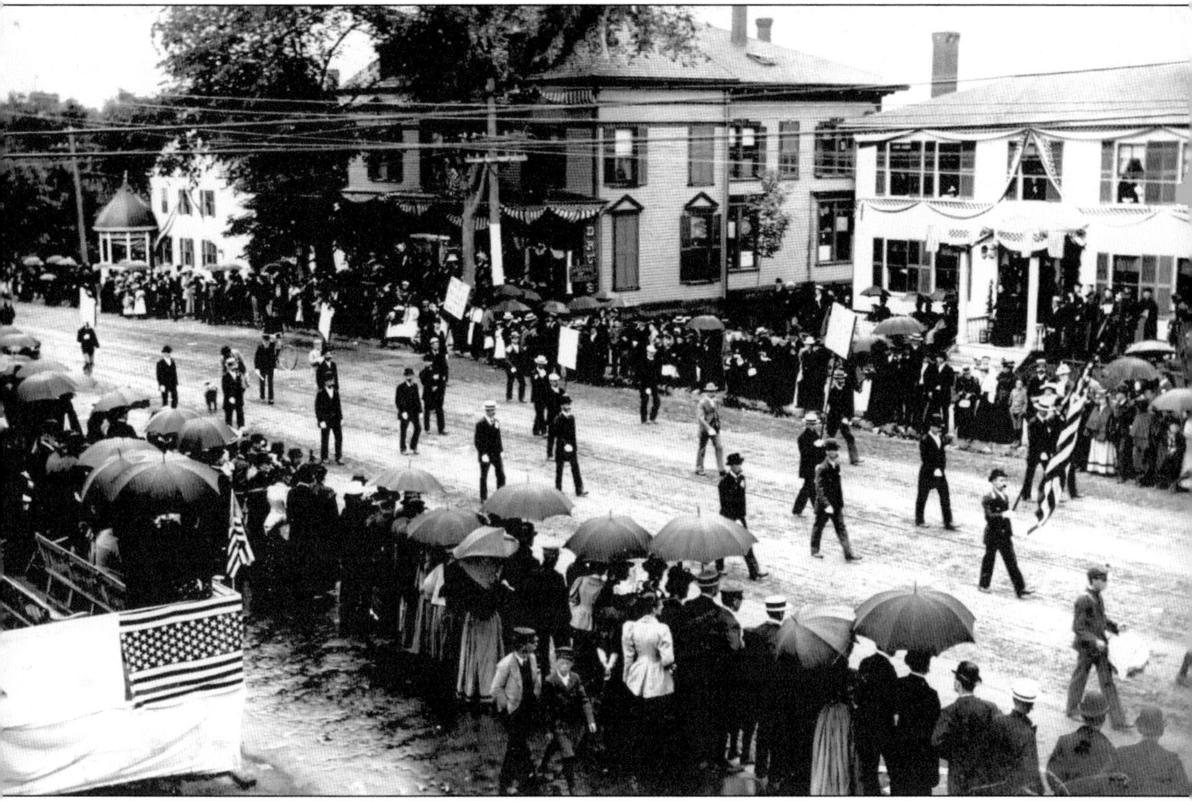

This is most likely the Fourth of July parade in the 1890s. This marching unit seems to be a labor organization. The reviewing stand is on the lawn of the Congregational church. Across the street to the left is the Gleason house. The house was built in 1845 for Dr. Alonzo Chapin, who was a medical missionary in the Sandwich Islands. In 1854, Rev. Horace Walker purchased the house and spent 14 years there. In 1875, Dr. Jubal Gleason bought the house, and it stayed in his family until it was moved and then taken down in 1961. To the right is the Estes Building, and to the right of the Estes Building is the Rev. Samuel Colburn's house, which he built in 1814, across the street from the church, before there was a road. As he was moving in, the house caught fire and burned down. It was replaced in 1815 with the house pictured here. That house was taken down in order to build the Rockland Trust Company in 1917.

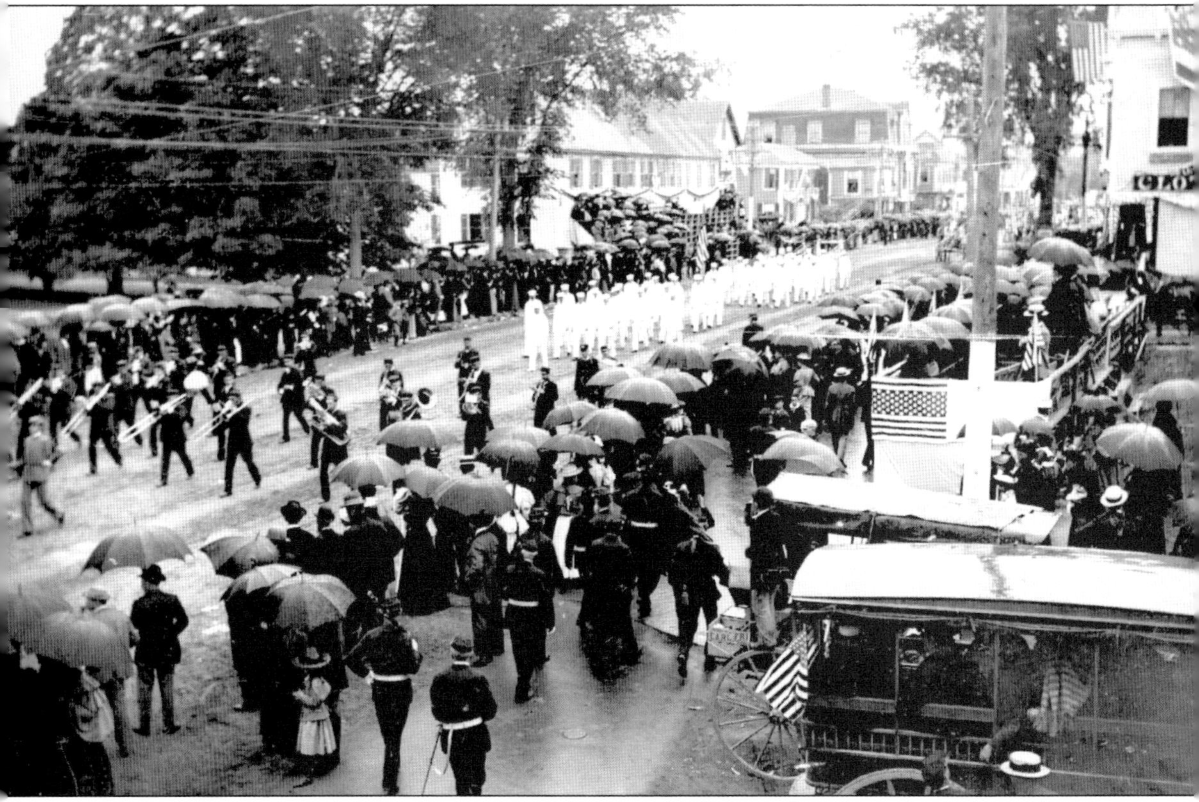

It is the same rainy day, but in this 1899 photograph, the parade is going back down the street. In the foreground are horse-drawn vehicles. The building that has a clothing sign on it is the Webster Building. Across the street, the open space is the front lawn of the Ira Blanchard home, built in 1856. The building with the viewing stand in front is known as the Lincoln Block. This was the shoe factory of Ira Blanchard. The building remains today. Storefronts were added in the late 19th century. The next building, the second house built on the Hill, was built by Thomas Reed III in 1815. In 1921, a storefront was added, and Abraham Lelyveld opened a shoe store. The building with the mansard roof is the Daly-Stevens Block, also remaining at the time of the publication of this book.

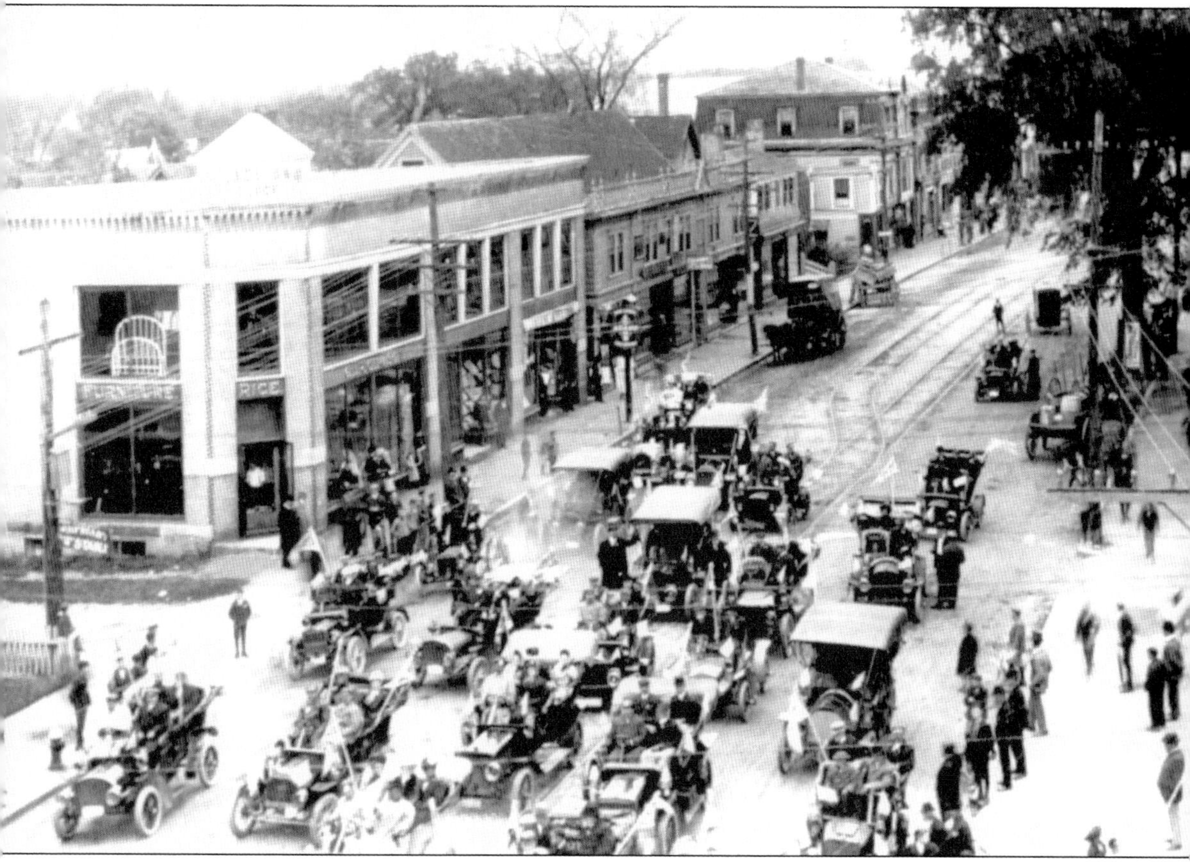

By the time this photograph was taken, approximately 15 to 20 years later, things had changed. A house still stands on the south side of Taunton Avenue, where a lawn and fence are visible. In 1900, the Gladstone Block, named after British prime minister William Gladstone, was completed, and C.L. Rice moved his furniture store into space specially designed for him. Storefronts were added to the Lincoln Block in the late 1800s. The dome of the Rockland Memorial Library, built in 1905, peeks over the rooftops. An automobile club appears to be starting a rally.

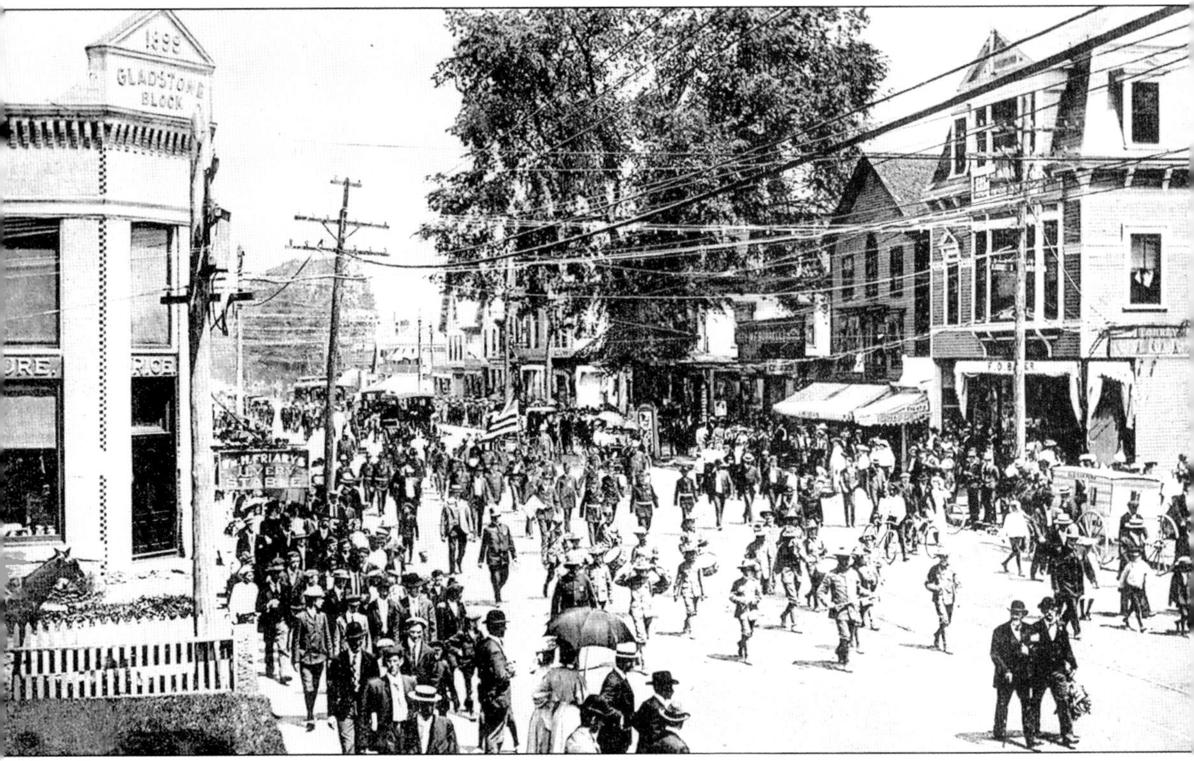

This July 4, 1905, parade was controversial. The Massasoit Fife and Drum Corps of Plymouth, made up of boys 10 and 12 years of age, was hired to march in the parade. But the local union bands refused to march with the nonunion boys. Judge George Kelly, upset with the union, held his own parade with the boys and the citizens of Rockland. The photograph shows the boys followed by the police department.

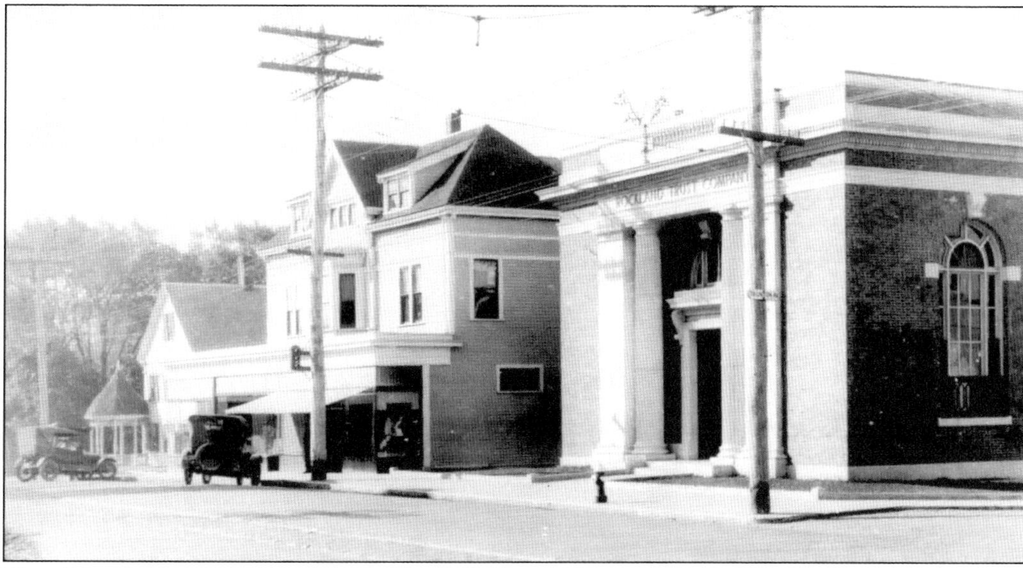

The First National Bank of Rockland became the Rockland Trust Company in 1907. In 1917, the Rockland Trust built its new headquarters on the site of the Colburn house, on the corner of Union Street and Taunton Avenue. Storefronts had by now been added to the Estes Building.

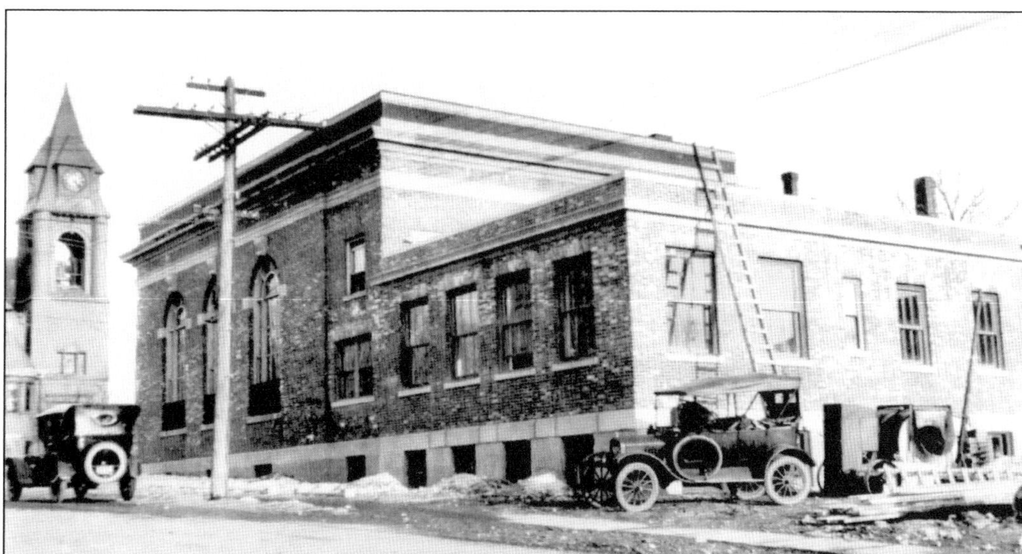

By the 1920s, the first addition was added to the bank. Built in a Georgian Revival style, the Rockland Trust building has been a landmark on the Hill for nearly a century. This building is listed on the National Register of Historic Places.

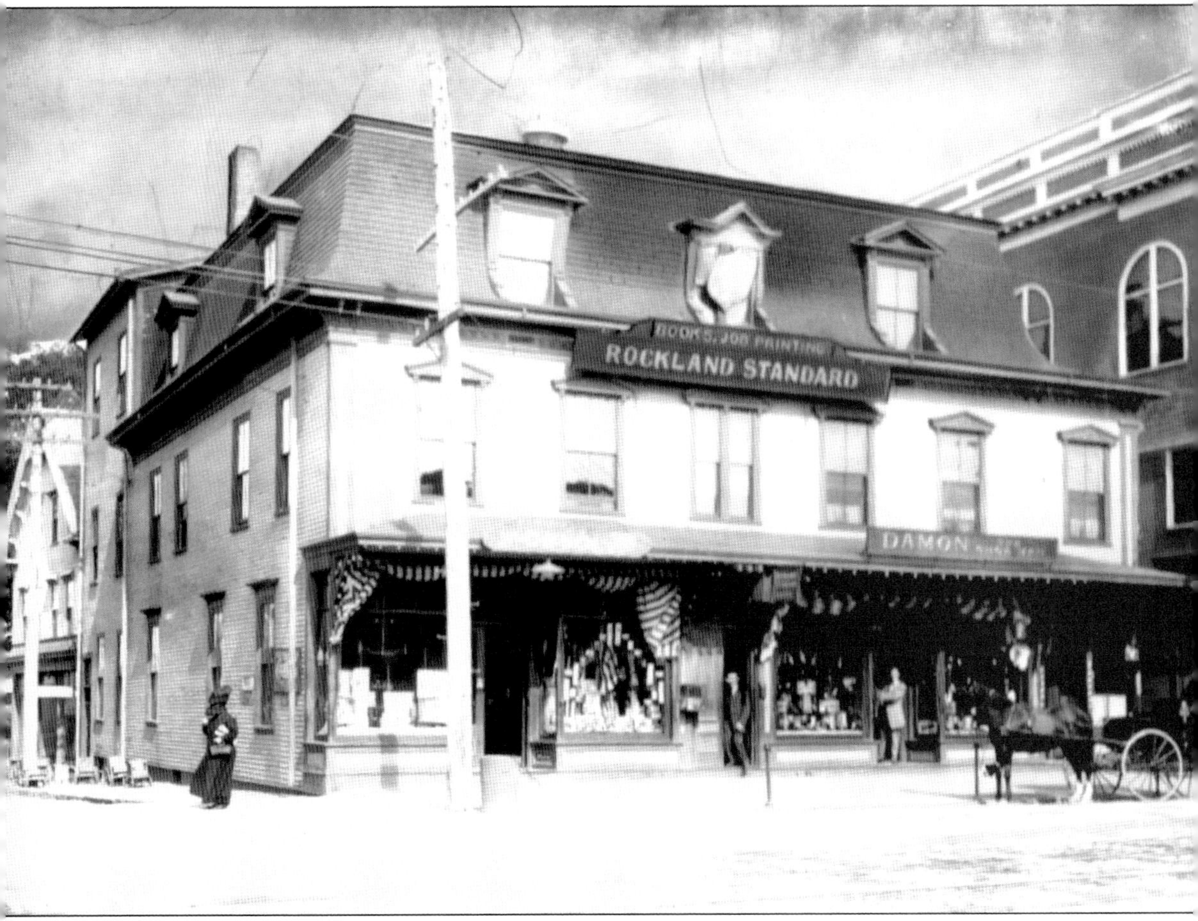

The *Rockland Standard,* originally titled the *Abington Standard,* was established in 1854. It became the Rockland paper in 1874, with the formation of the new town. The Standard Block (1871) once stood on the southeast corner of Union and Park Streets. The paper was on the second floor, and the rest of the building was rented to other businesses. Damon's shoe store moved in *c.* 1900. In 1929, fire burned this section of town, taking the Standard Building down. The Bemis Building and the second Phoenix Block were built on this site. The corner of the Bigelow Building can just be seen in this photograph.

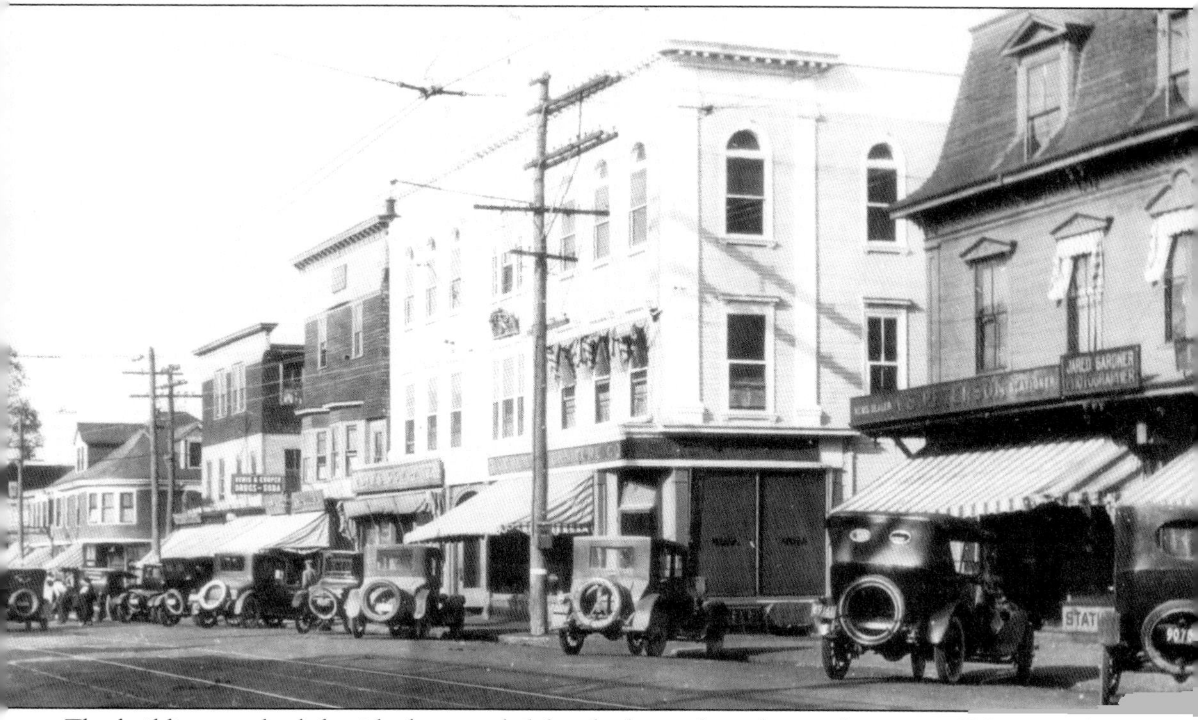

The building on the left with the rounded façade, located on the north corner of Union and Webster Streets, is the Crovo Building, built by Andrew Crovo in 1902. The next building is the Dill Block. All the rest of the buildings in this photograph were lost due to fires in the 1920s. To the right of the Dill Block is the Gibbs Block. Just after the Gibbs Block is the second Phoenix Block. Appearing last is the Standard Block.

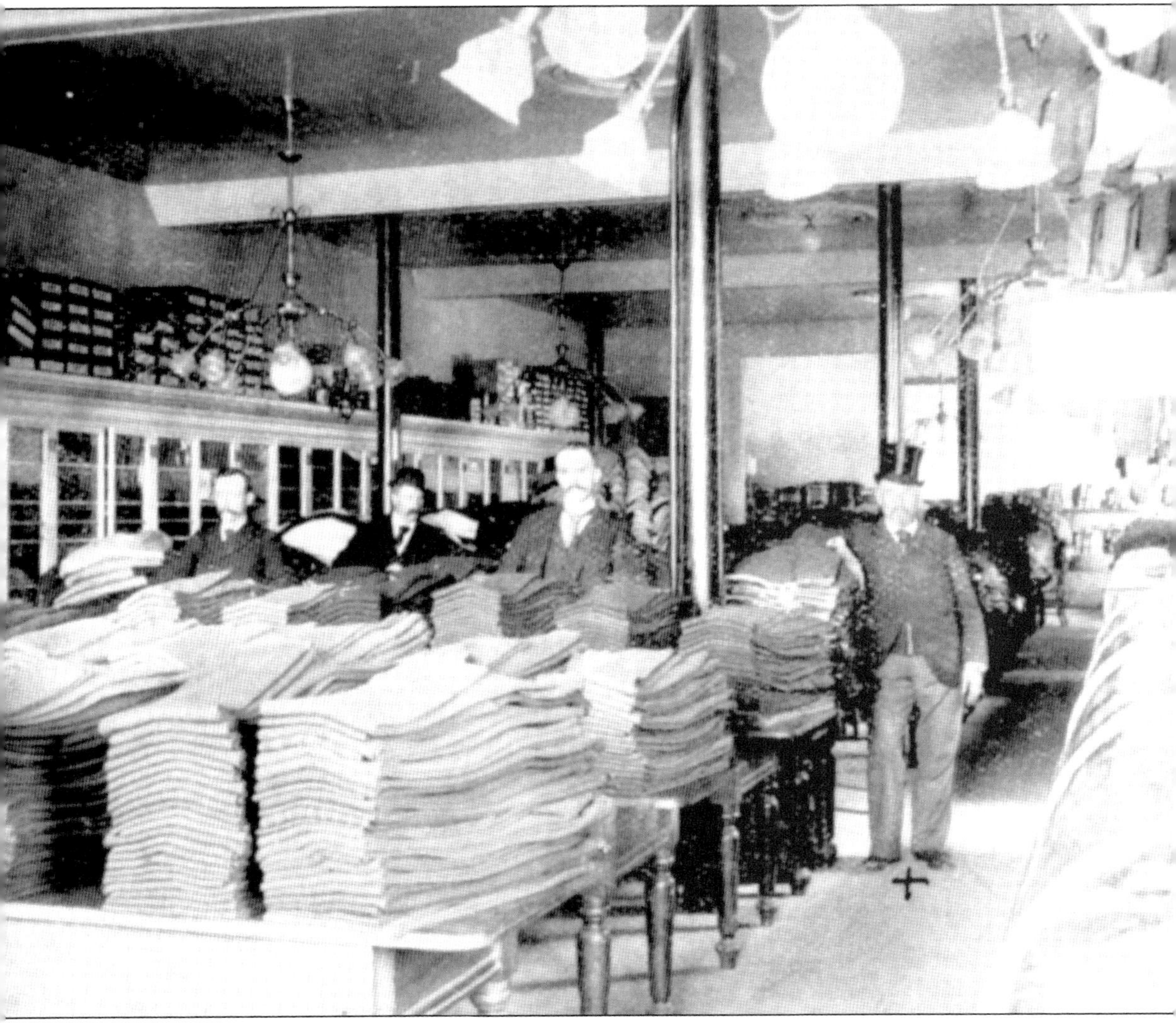

Edwin Whiting, marked by an "x" in this photo, and his staff worked in his clothing store located in the Phoenix Building (1894–1896). Our current style of pants was established by the origin of the folded crease, as demonstrated in Whiting's store. The crease was acquired when pants made in factories were folded for shipping and display. Homemade pants had barrel legs and no crease. People preferred the factory-made pants, hence why we have creases today.

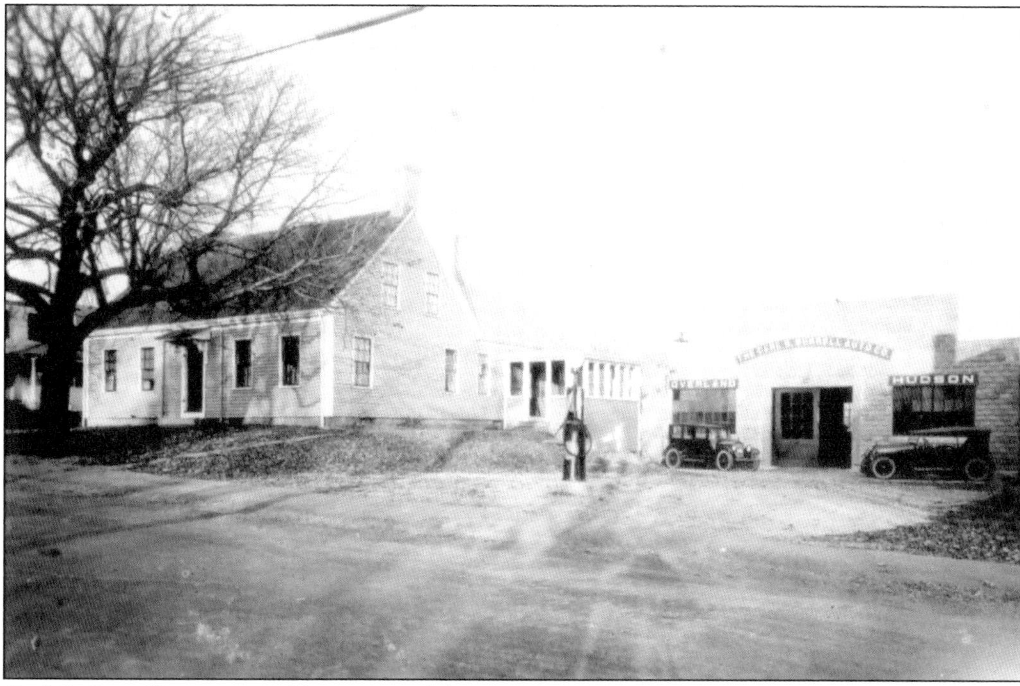

Carl S. Burrell maintained his automobile company at 45 Union Street in the 1920s. Besides the Essex, Burrell sold Overlanders and Hudsons. Although his showroom was on the Hill, his garage was located in a residential area that is the historic district of Rockland today. The adoption of zoning practices in the 1950s separated residential neighborhoods from business activities, except those that preexisted.

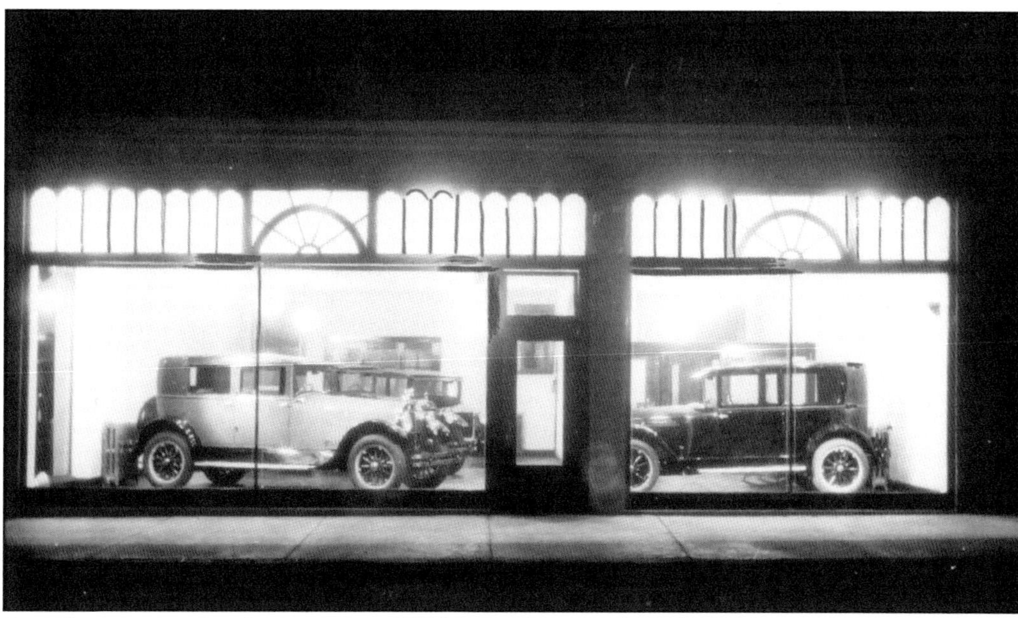

Burrell maintained a showroom at 375 Union Street, where he sold Essex automobiles. This is the last store on the east side of the street. Burrell was still in business in the 1960s, selling Oldsmobiles at his shop at 45 Union Street.

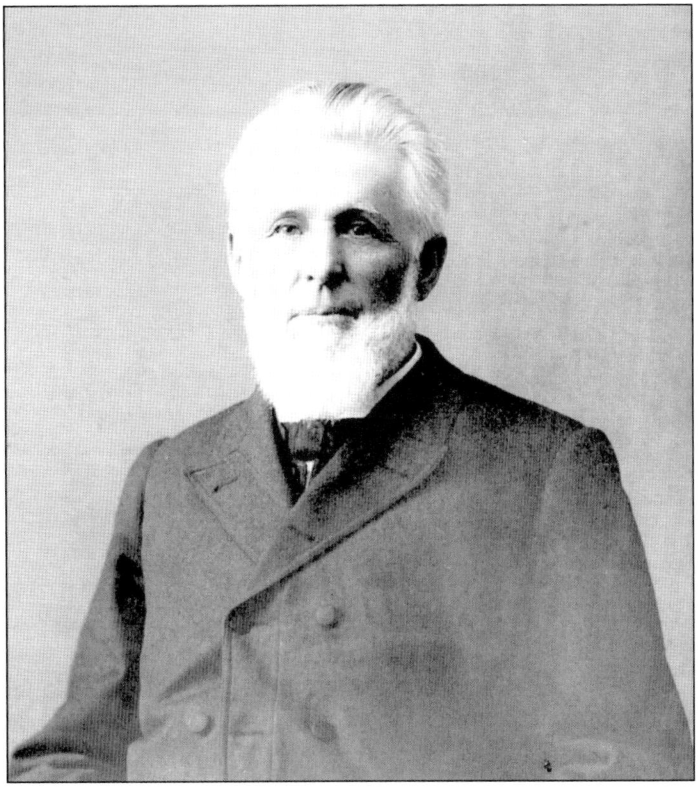

In 1851, at the age of 21, John A. Rice went out West. He returned to the East Coast and settled in Rockland *c.* 1854. He then began to work in the store of Nahum Moore. Robert Estes had established the business in 1842. By 1865, John owned the store outright. His brother Col. Charles L. Rice came to town the same year, and they entered a partnership that lasted just seven years. In 1872, the partnership split; Colonel Rice took the furniture business, and John took the dry goods.

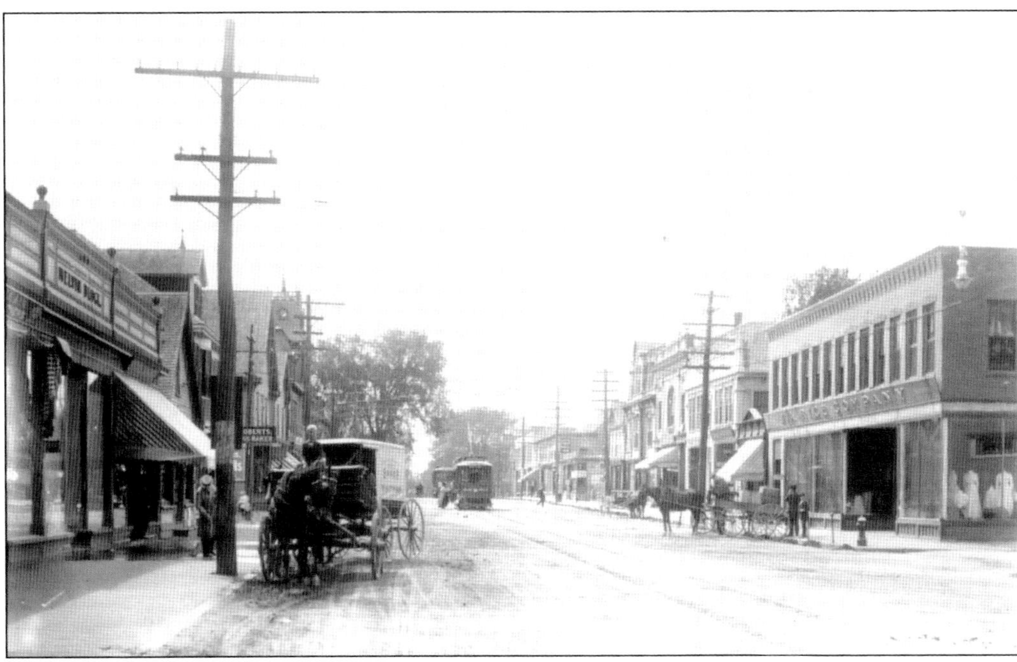

This is almost the end of the business section of the Hill. The new Rice Building, seen in this photograph, was built in the 1890s. The building on the left houses the last set of stores on this side of the street and is where Burrell had his automobile showroom.

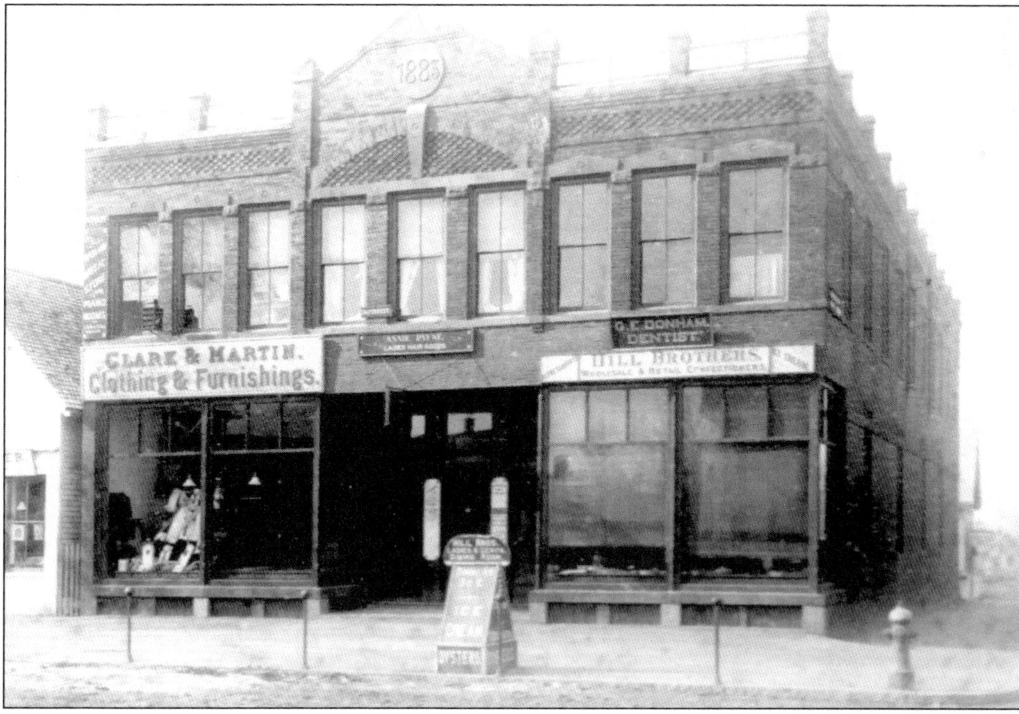

This is the southwest corner of Union and Pacific Streets. The first Rice Building was built in 1883. It was the first commercial building on Union Street to be built entirely of bricks. John Rice did not move into this building, but rented it instead. Frank B. Clark, who had been his clerk, was the first tenant.

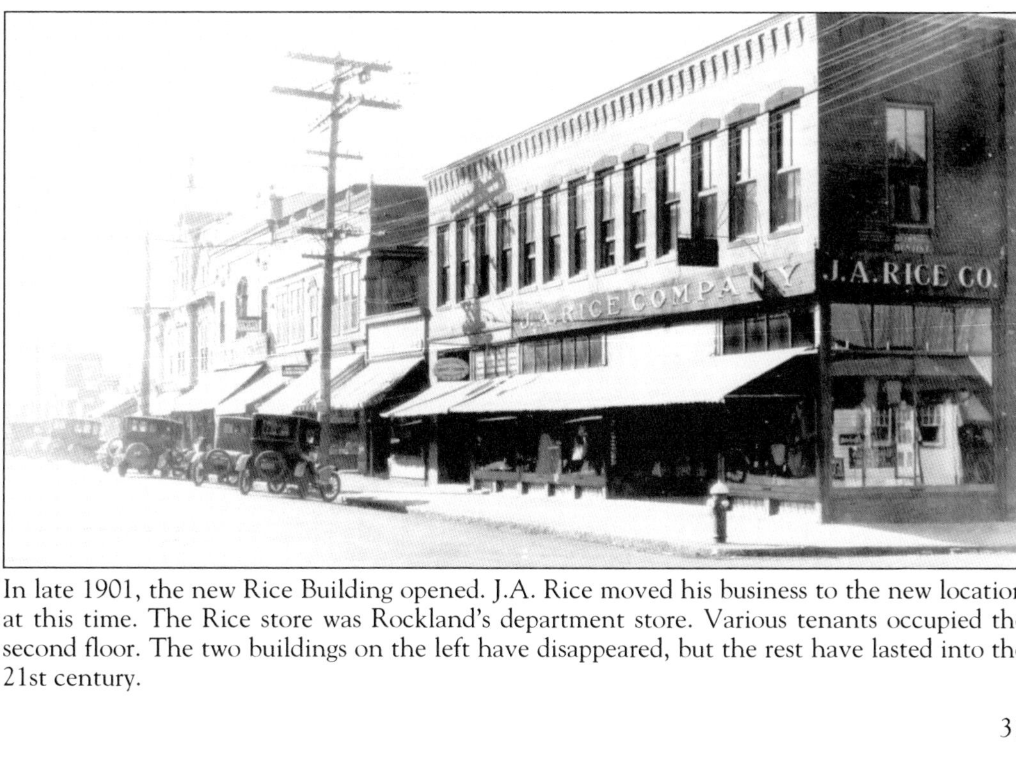

In late 1901, the new Rice Building opened. J.A. Rice moved his business to the new location at this time. The Rice store was Rockland's department store. Various tenants occupied the second floor. The two buildings on the left have disappeared, but the rest have lasted into the 21st century.

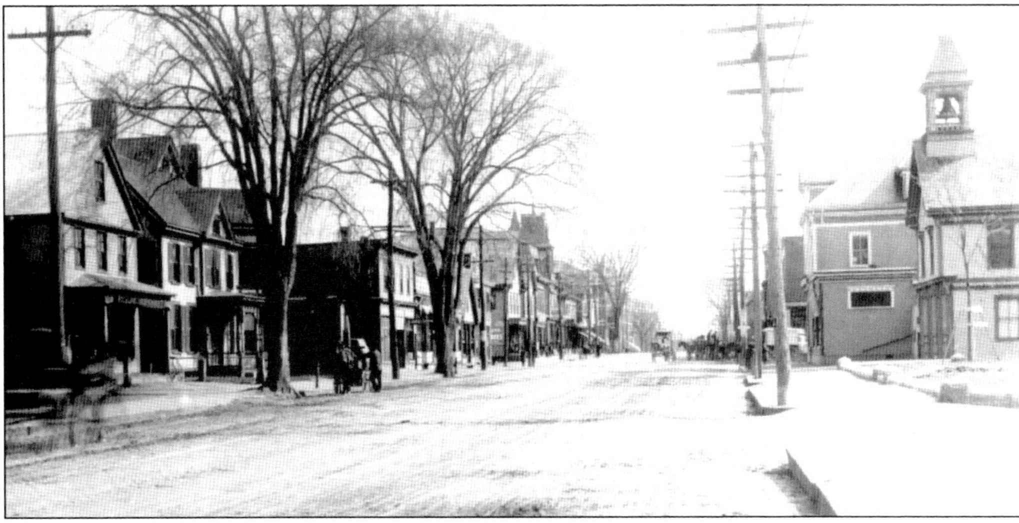

In this view before 1900, utility poles are up, but it does not look like the tracks have been put down for streetcars. The building with the bell is the fire barn. The Rockland fire station still occupies this site. The tower of the first Phoenix Building is on the left.

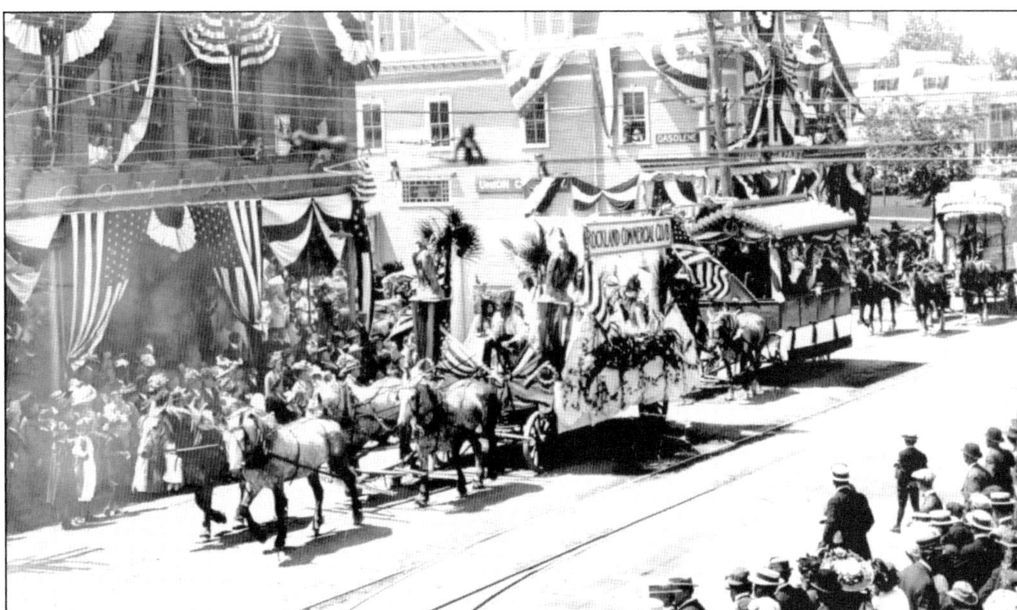

This parade section stretched from the Rice Building up toward the McKinley School (the high school in 1900). The sign that says "gasolene" on a building indicates that the automobile has arrived in Rockland. From horse-drawn carriages to bicycles to automobiles, Rockland's Hill grew and changed with the times.

Two

UNION SQUARE
ROCKLAND'S CROSSROAD

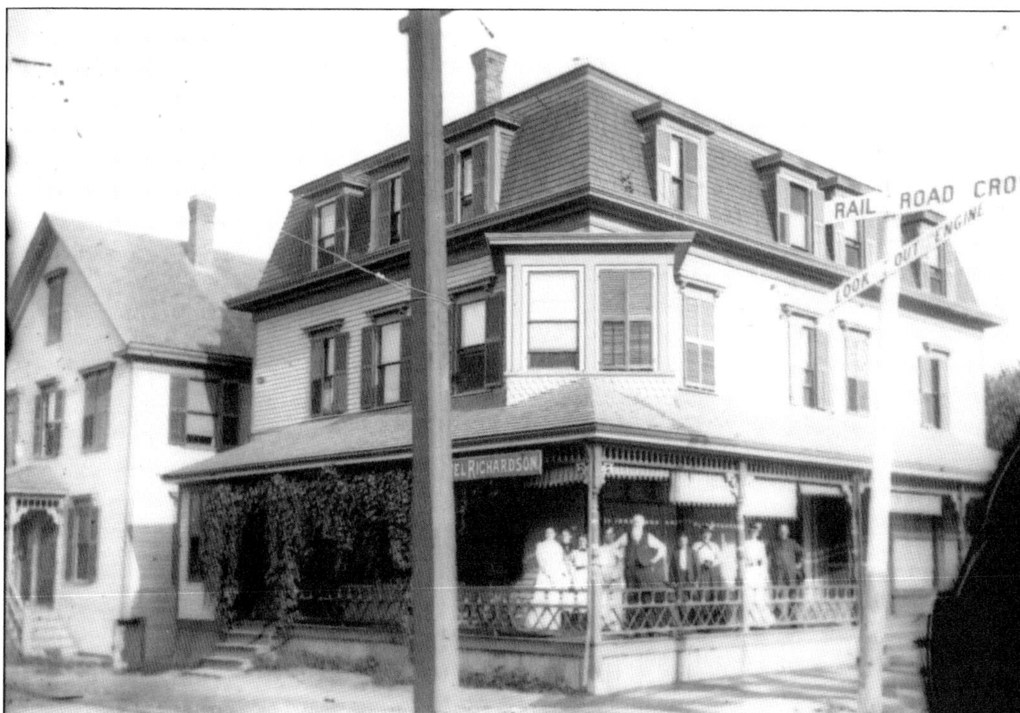

Trains carried people, goods, and information, and automatically the stations they stopped at were the foci of small communities. In the days before the automobile, an ideal place to have a hotel was next to the train station. B.F. Richardson, who moved his boardinghouse business from Vernon Street to Union Street, near the railroad station, knew this well when he built the Richardson House in 1893. Calvin Coolidge, as governor of Massachusetts, made a speech here, probably on the porch where the staff is gathered to have their picture taken. The Richardson has come to be known as the Hotel Thomas.

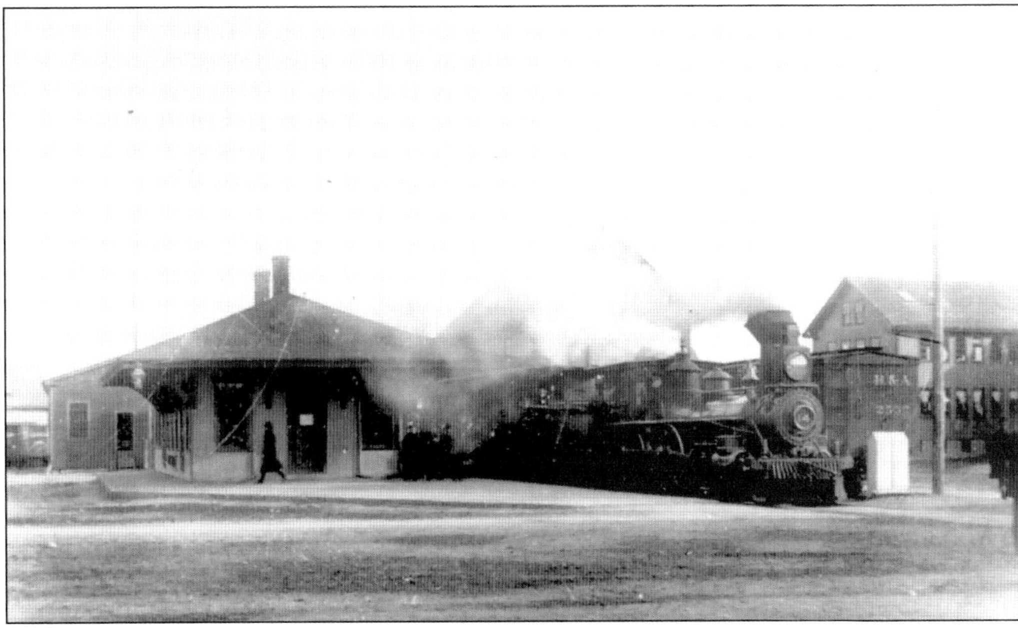

This is the Hanover Branch Railroad Company's locomotive No. 3, *Spark*. After 1887, the branch became part of the Old Colony Railroad, and the locomotive's number was changed to 14. A Boston and Albany boxcar sits on the track, and behind it is a shoe factory, probably the Rockland Company.

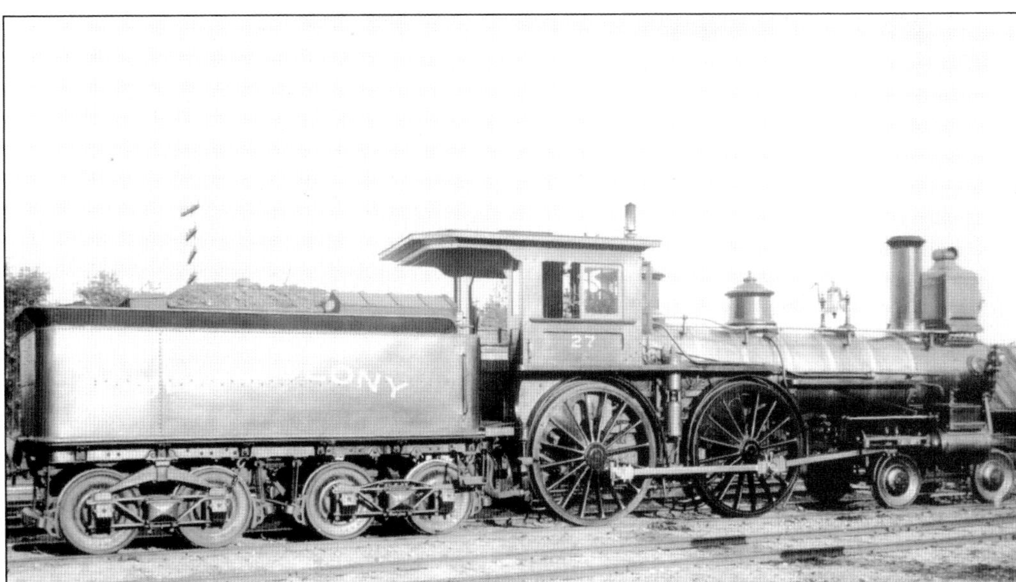

Typical of the locomotives seen on the tracks in Rockland and throughout the United States is Old Colony locomotive No. 27, put on the Hanover Branch when the branch merged with Old Colony. The locomotive was built in 1865 by Manchester Locomotive and worked on the line until 1935.

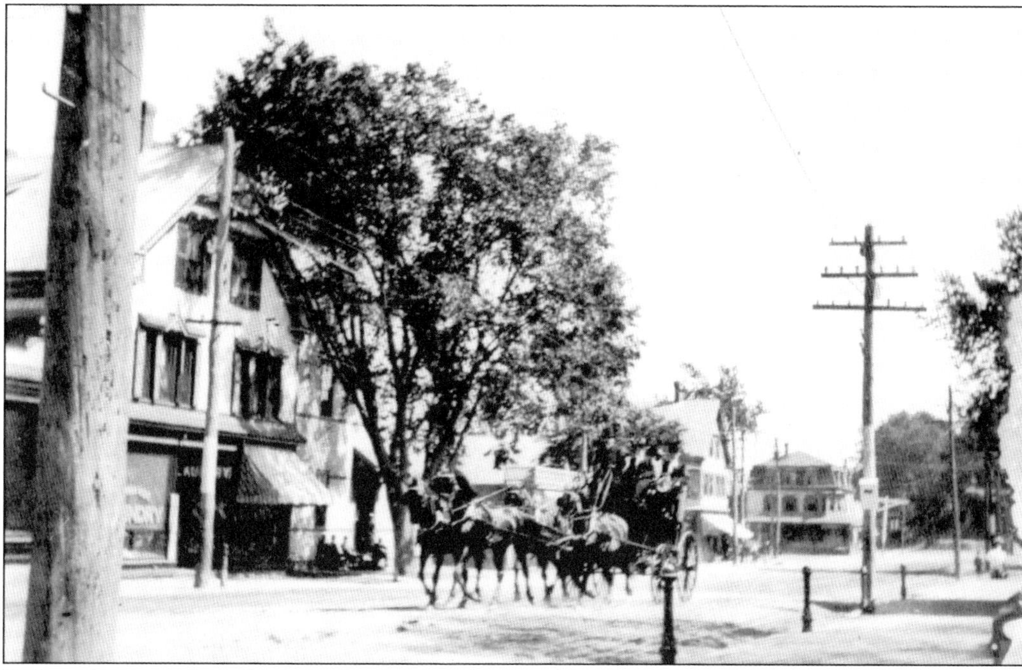

Before the arrival of electric streetcars and, after that, automobiles, stagecoaches took people from one part of town to another. This one has just left Union Square and is heading north. Its passengers may have just arrived by train. There were other coach routes in town. Factory workers who did not live within walking distance of their jobs also traveled by coach.

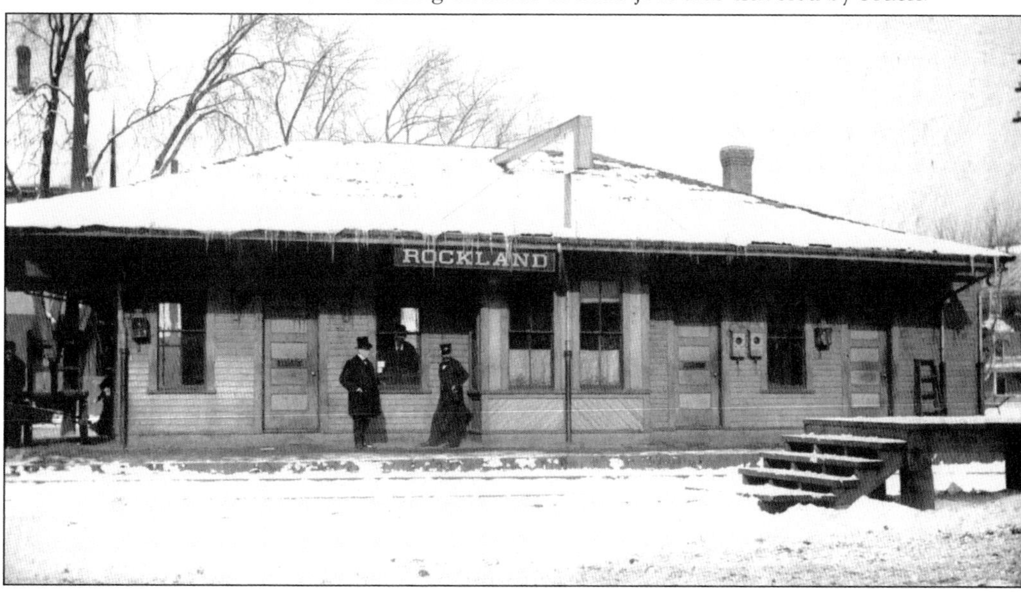

The first Rockland train station was small and built on the south side of the tracks. Banking and tickets were available in this station through Zenas Jenkins, the ticket agent. He was also the first treasurer of the newly organized Rockland Savings Bank. The station in the photograph is probably the second station and was built on the north side of the tracks. Some railroad personnel and perhaps a shoe company manager stand waiting for a train. The third station, which is the current brick building, was built in 1907.

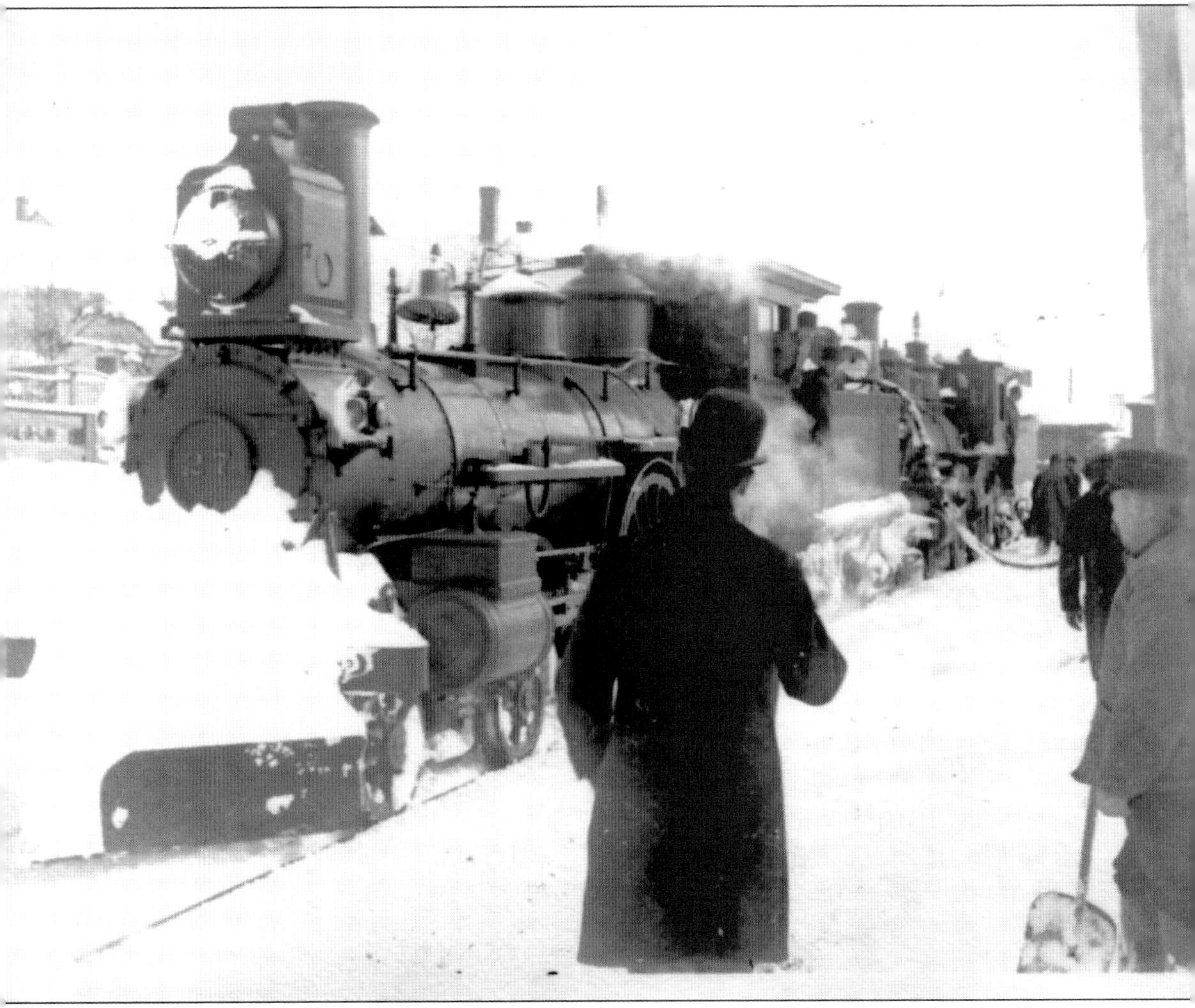

In the winter, railroad operations could be difficult. Frozen water, frozen coal, and snow on the tracks were just a few of the recurring problems. Here, Old Colony No. 27 and another locomotive running in tandem take on snowplow duty. They have stopped at the station to take on water, using a fire hose instead of the water tower. The Hanover Branch Railroad was incorporated in 1846, but did not operate until July 18, 1868. E.Y. Perry, a tack manufacturer in Hanover, was the main force in establishing the line. It ran from Hanover Four Corners and met the Old Colony line in North Abington, about eight miles away. The Hanover line's main service was freight, but it also carried passengers. In 1887, it became part of the Old Colony Railroad and was known as the Hanover Branch. The line had three locomotives: No. 1, *Brant Rock*, which became Old Colony Railroad No. 13; No. 2, *Hanover*, which became Old Colony Railroad No. 49; and No. 3, *Spark*, which became Old Colony Railroad No. 14. Other locomotives worked the branch after the merger, such as the Old Colony No. 27. By the late 1940s, the branch changed over to self-propelled cars and continued to provide commuter service until the late 1950s. Freight service lasted longer, on a limited basis, until the 1980s.

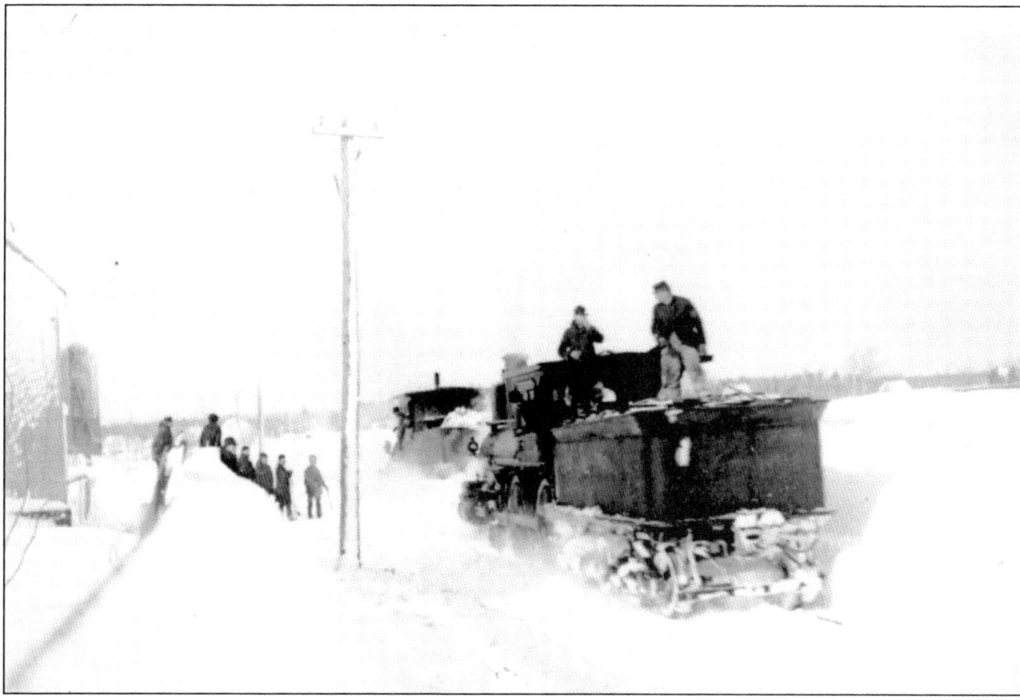

The snowplow locomotives with a crew on hand are on their way to see if the engines can get through the snow. If they cannot, the crew will shovel them out.

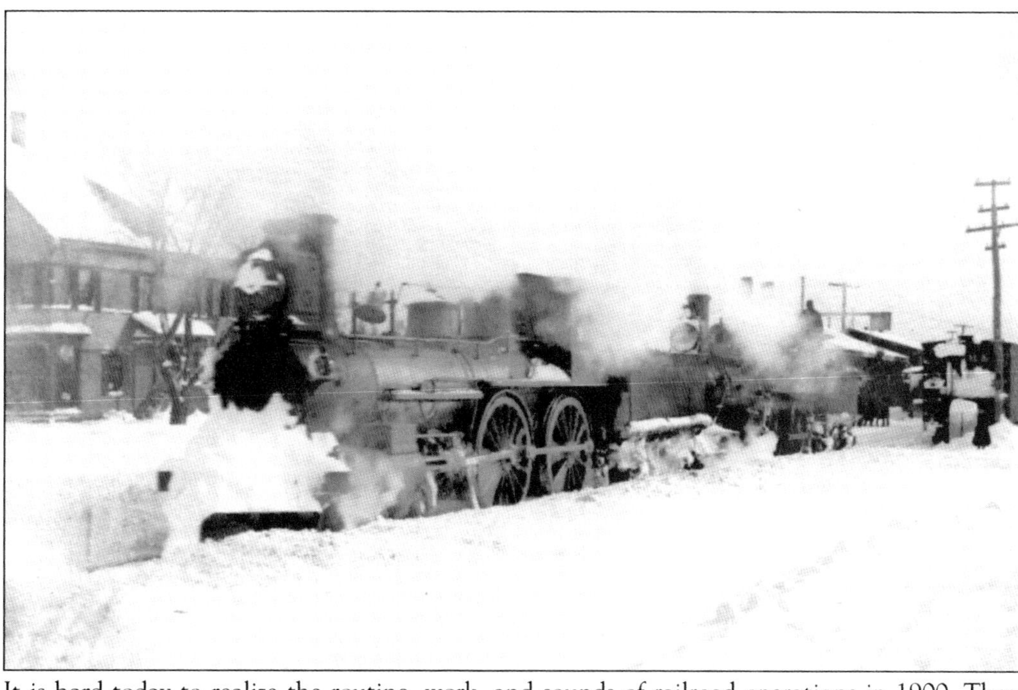

It is hard today to realize the routine, work, and sounds of railroad operations in 1900. These scenes depict the disruption of that routine on one snowy day a long time ago in Rockland.

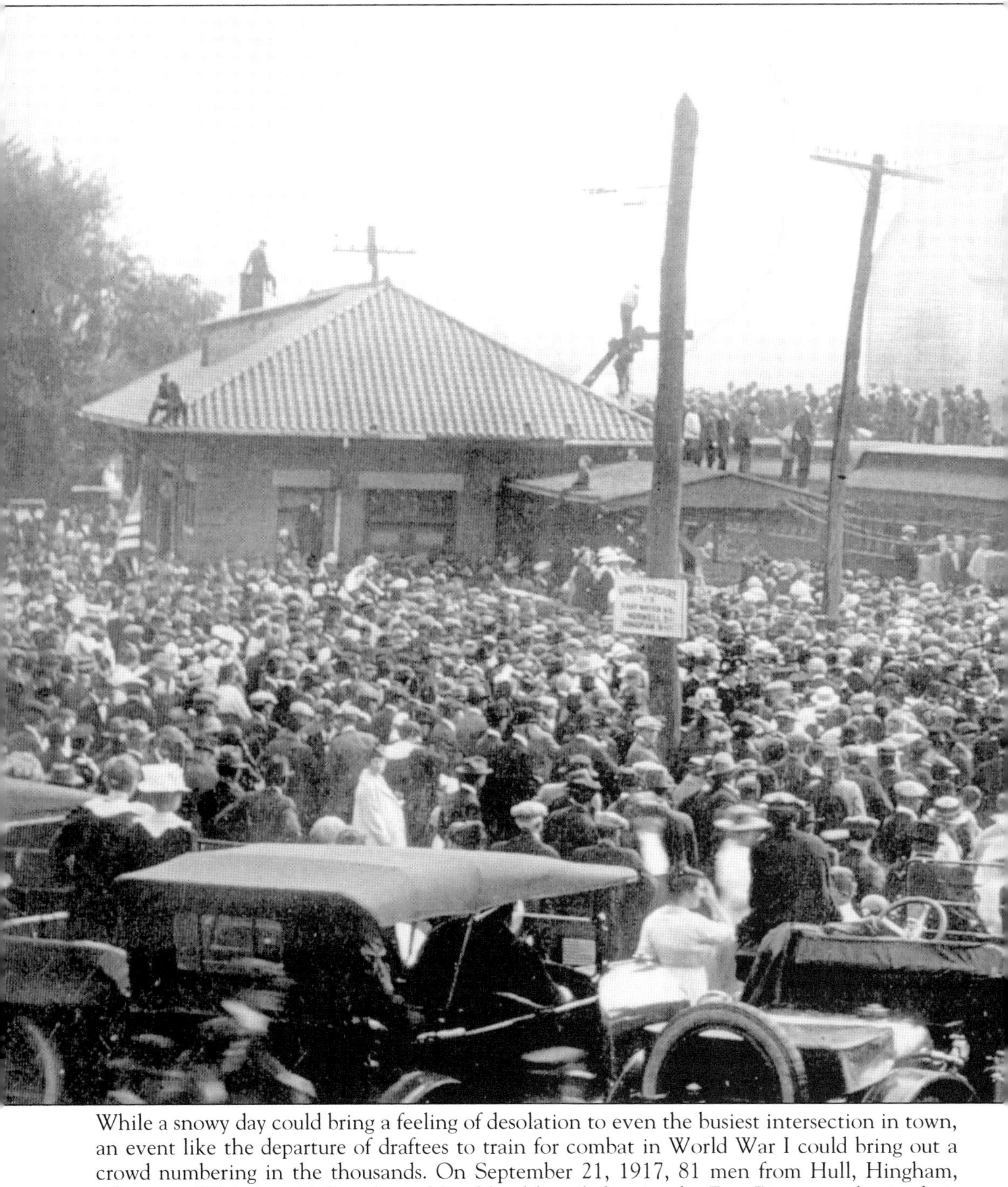

While a snowy day could bring a feeling of desolation to even the busiest intersection in town, an event like the departure of draftees to train for combat in World War I could bring out a crowd numbering in the thousands. On September 21, 1917, 81 men from Hull, Hingham, Abington, Whitman, Holbrook, and Rockland boarded trains for Fort Devens to begin their combat training. At least one, Oscar Smith Mitchell of Hull, who marched at the head of the procession, did not return. To see the boys off, Rockland cancelled school for two hours to allow local students to witness history in the making, and all of the local factories shut down as well. As 8:30 a.m. bells sounded all over town, the selectmen, the surviving members of the

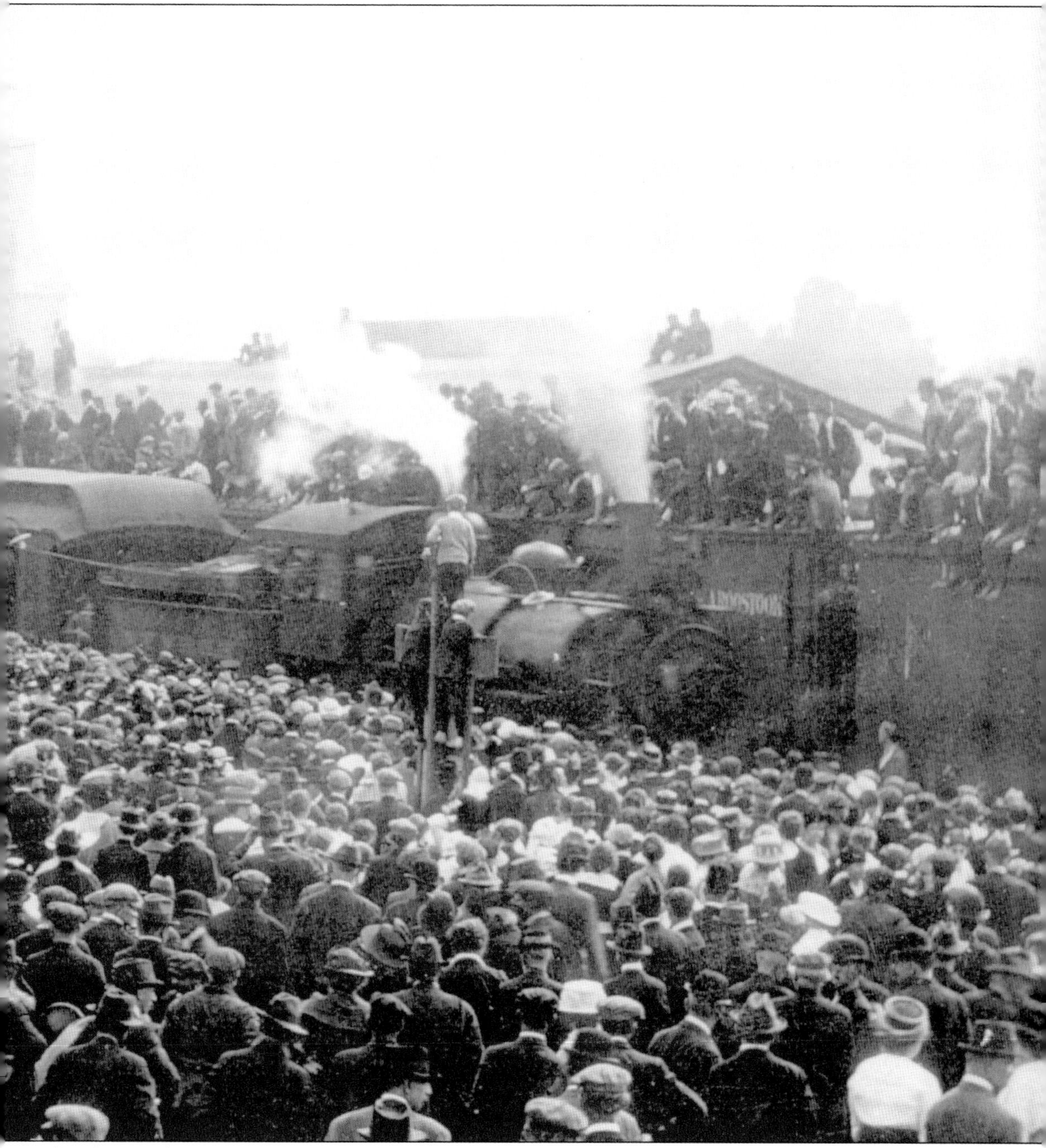

local Grand Army of the Republic posts, and the Rockland company of the Massachusetts State Guard led the parade to the station. The *Rockland Standard* reported that local knitters presented each of the 25 Rockland boys with a handmade a sweater, a muffler, a pair of socks, a face cloth, and "wristers." Local shoe man E.T. Wright gave each man shaving razors and cigars. Wright, who also served on the Soldiers and Sailors Welfare Committee, benefited greatly from the war, as did other manufacturers such as Emerson Shoe, and Rice and Hutchins, all of whom negotiated contracts to provide shoes for the U.S. Army. The Hurley factory alone received an order for 25,000 pairs of marching shoes.

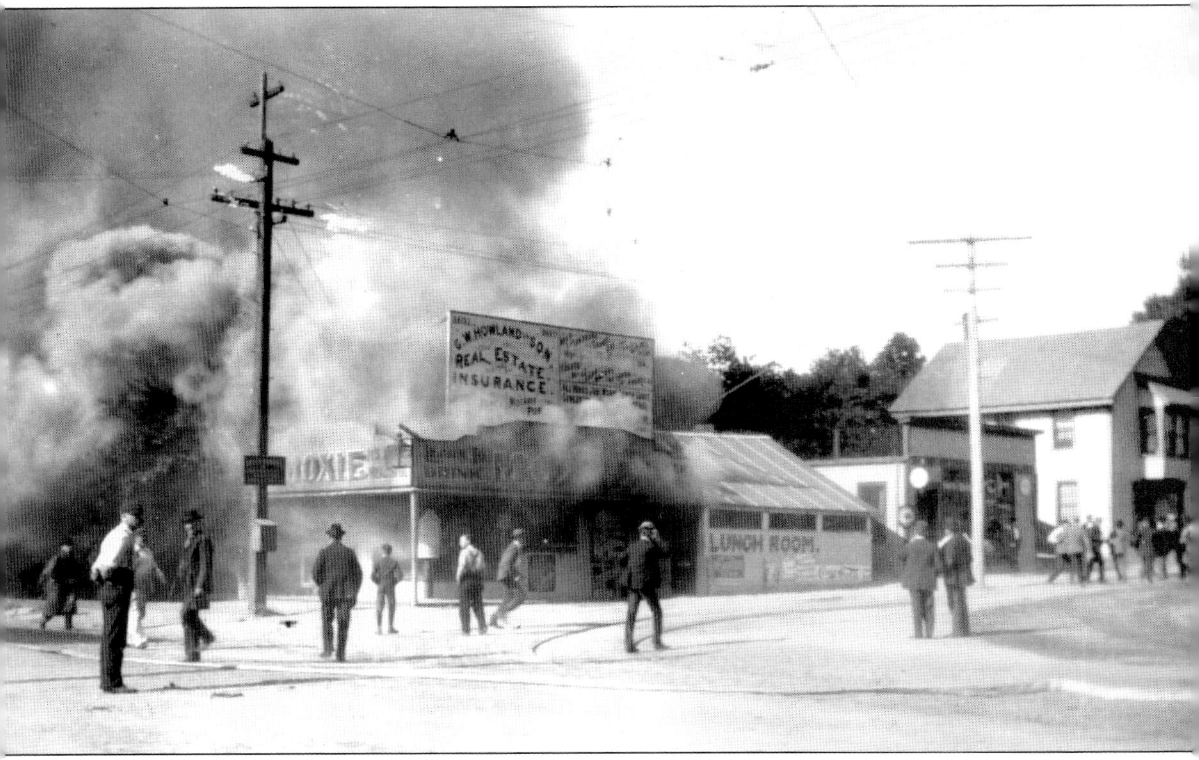

The *Rockland Standard* of Friday, June 21, 1901, reported on the fire that struck Payn's Lunchroom at the northeast corner of Union and East Water Streets. The story read, "There was a lively blaze at H.S. Payn's waiting room at Union square about 7 a.m. Monday. The alleged cause was the explosion of a gasoline stove. The department responded promptly, but the building was enveloped in flames, and although standing, is worthless. The loss is $800, with $500 insurance. Bert Hammond, Mr. Payn's assistant, had his arms badly burned in trying to put out the fire. Smith Bros.' Saloon had a narrow escape and was severely scorched." No money value was placed on the loss of revenue incurred by Charles Howland's insurance company, established in 1851 and still going strong, who advertised atop the building. A waiting room was just that, a place to wait, and hopefully spend a few dollars, until the next train arrived.

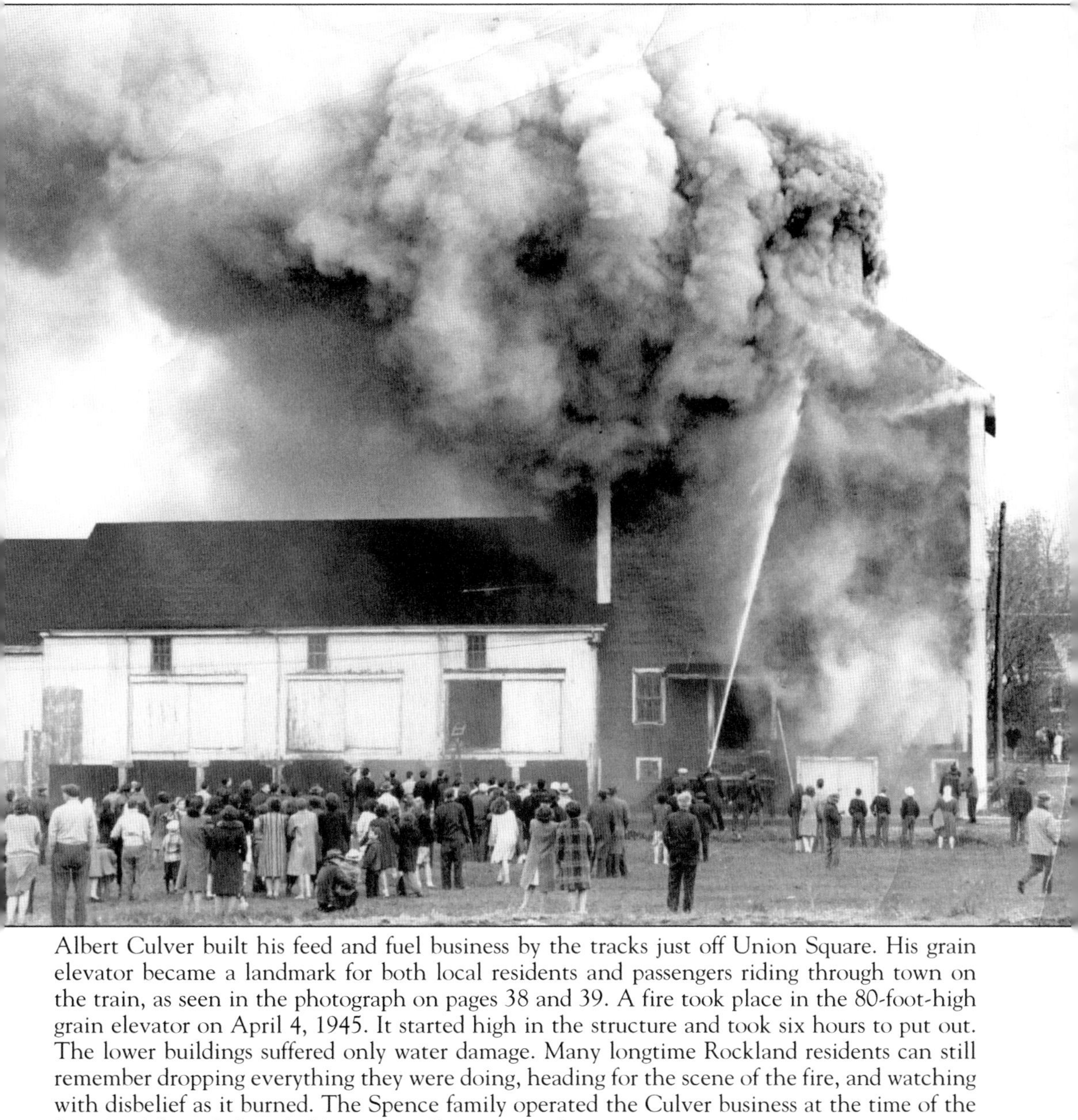

Albert Culver built his feed and fuel business by the tracks just off Union Square. His grain elevator became a landmark for both local residents and passengers riding through town on the train, as seen in the photograph on pages 38 and 39. A fire took place in the 80-foot-high grain elevator on April 4, 1945. It started high in the structure and took six hours to put out. The lower buildings suffered only water damage. Many longtime Rockland residents can still remember dropping everything they were doing, heading for the scene of the fire, and watching with disbelief as it burned. The Spence family operated the Culver business at the time of the fire. An Albert Culver fuel business still survives today.

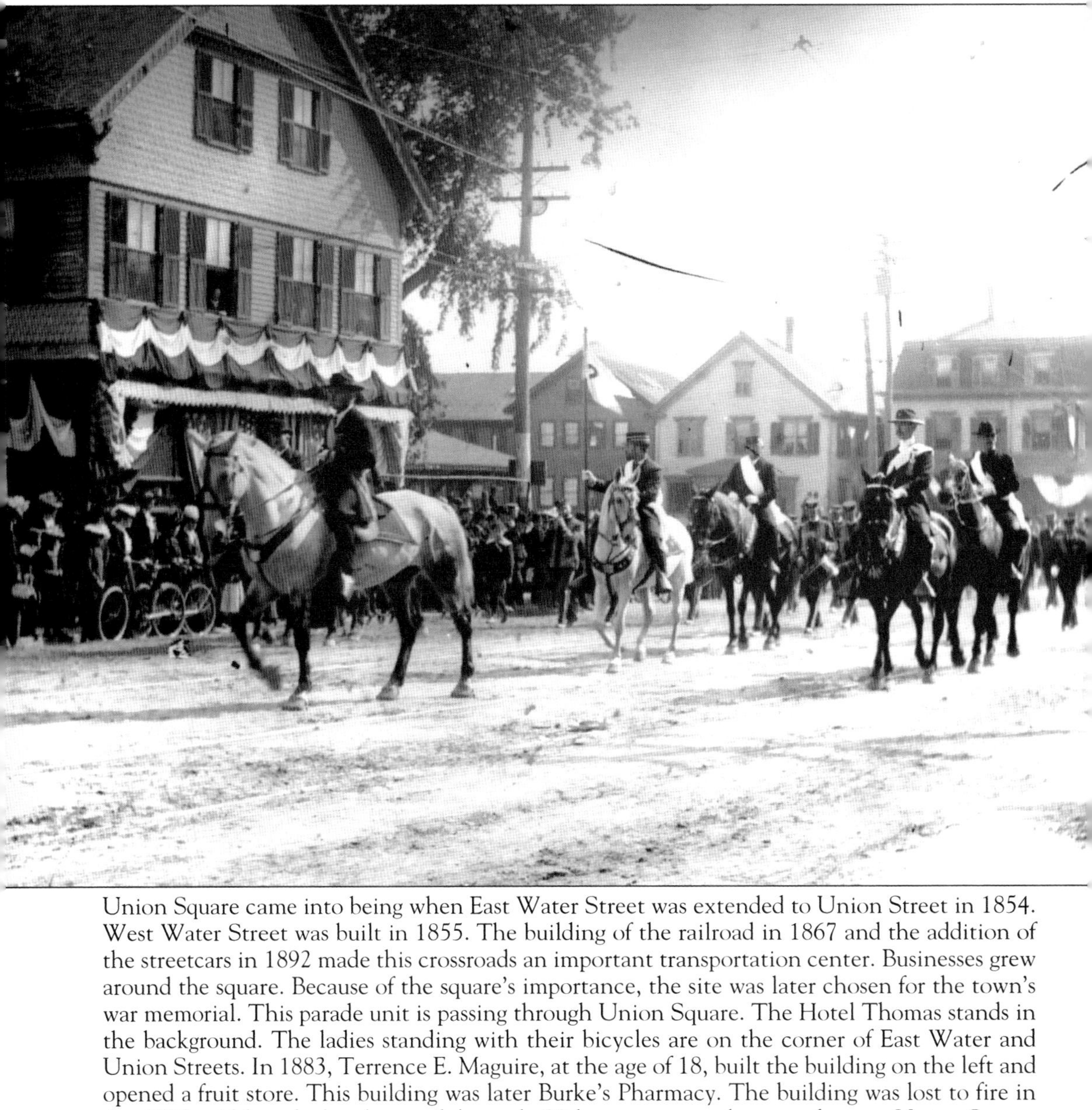

Union Square came into being when East Water Street was extended to Union Street in 1854. West Water Street was built in 1855. The building of the railroad in 1867 and the addition of the streetcars in 1892 made this crossroads an important transportation center. Businesses grew around the square. Because of the square's importance, the site was later chosen for the town's war memorial. This parade unit is passing through Union Square. The Hotel Thomas stands in the background. The ladies standing with their bicycles are on the corner of East Water and Union Streets. In 1883, Terrence E. Maguire, at the age of 18, built the building on the left and opened a fruit store. This building was later Burke's Pharmacy. The building was lost to fire in the 1980s. Although the charm of the early 20th century may be gone forever, Union Square still bustles with activity in 2003, as it did in 1903.

Three

Friendly Neighborhoods
Comfortable Homes

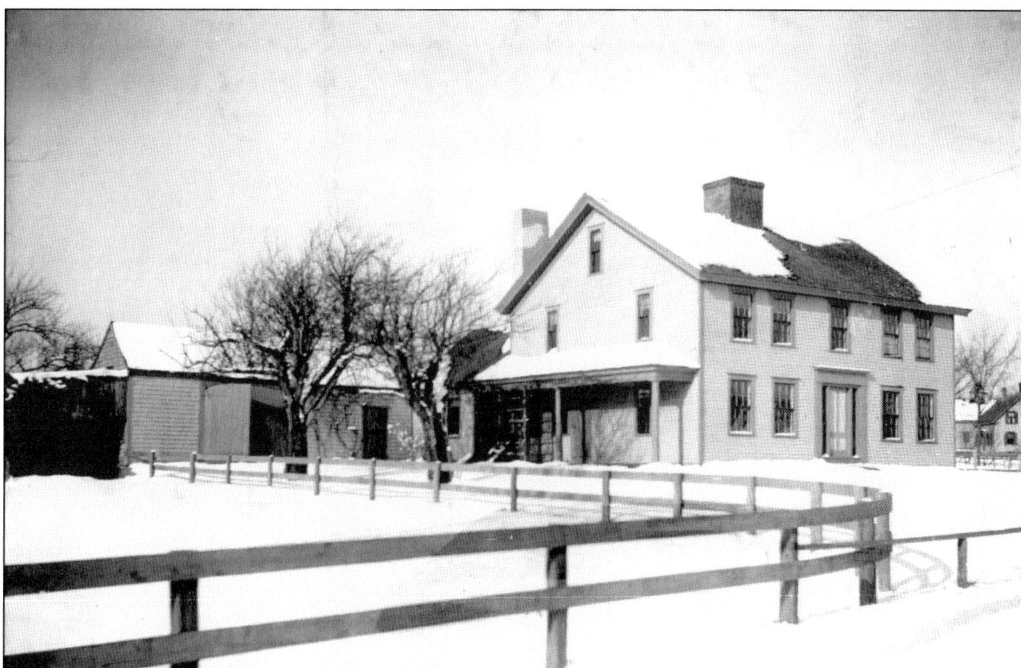

Away from the hectic crowds of the retail district of Union Street, several friendly neighborhoods grew up in Rockland, each with its own flavor. Several homes, some of which remain while others have passed into history, boasted interesting tales. The Samuel Reed house was built in 1788 and was located at 80 Market Street, just east of Reed's pond. In 1812, a meeting was held at this house to organize the Third Parish Church. Reed, an abolitionist, supposedly ran a station of the Underground Railroad at his house. Famous Boston abolitionist and publisher of the *Liberator* William Lloyd Garrison was smuggled away in a load of hay and hid out in this house after an unruly rally at Island Grove in Abington threatened his life. This house was taken down in 1970.

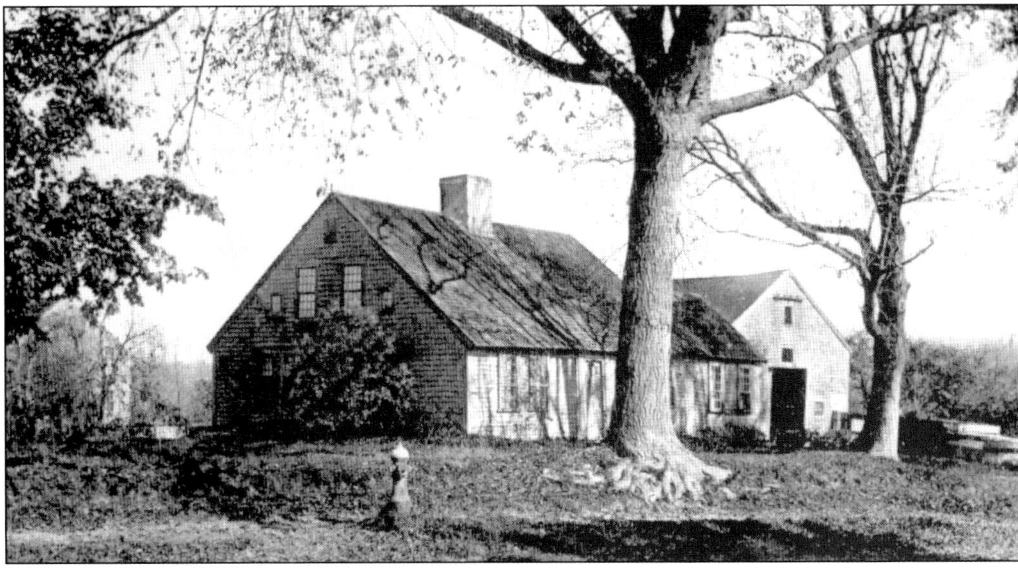

The Barnabas Stetson house was located at 620 Market Street, near Old Market Street. When the land that eventually became Rockland was open for settlement, people started to move in from other towns. Peleg Stetson was the first person to move from Hanover to East Abington, c. 1738. His house was located at 808 Market Street. He had many descendants that lived in this section of town. This house was also known as the Davis Cushing place.

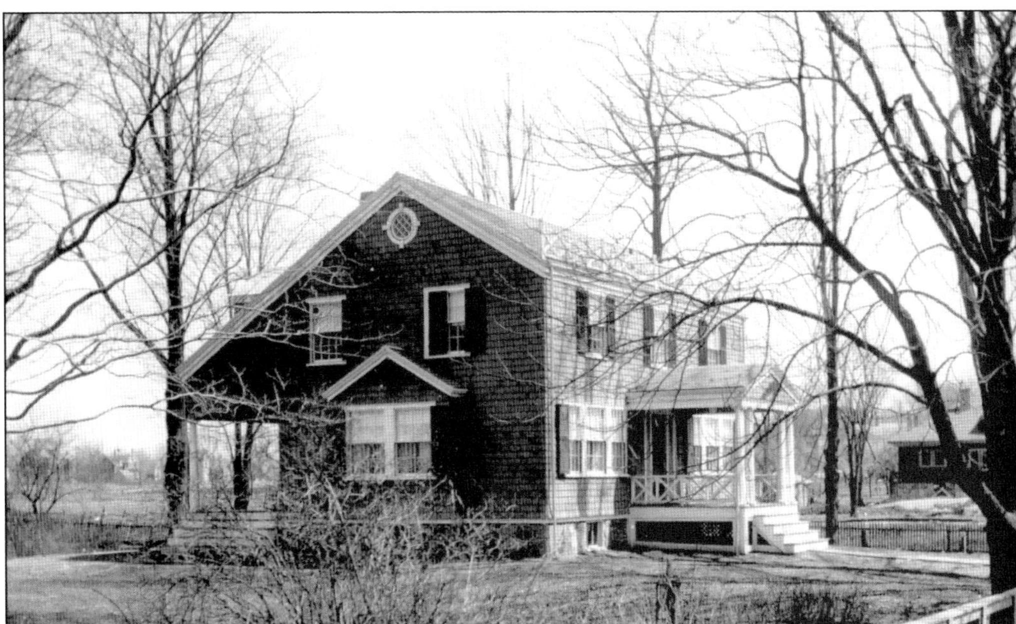

The Myra Lane house is at 242 Market Street, one house away from Union Street. It was built in the 20th century and is an example of the Colonial Revival style, a reflection of the often nostalgic and circular themes in American architecture. A revival-style home may incorporate hints of both the old and modern interpretations, which in this case unmistakably separates it from an actual Colonial home.

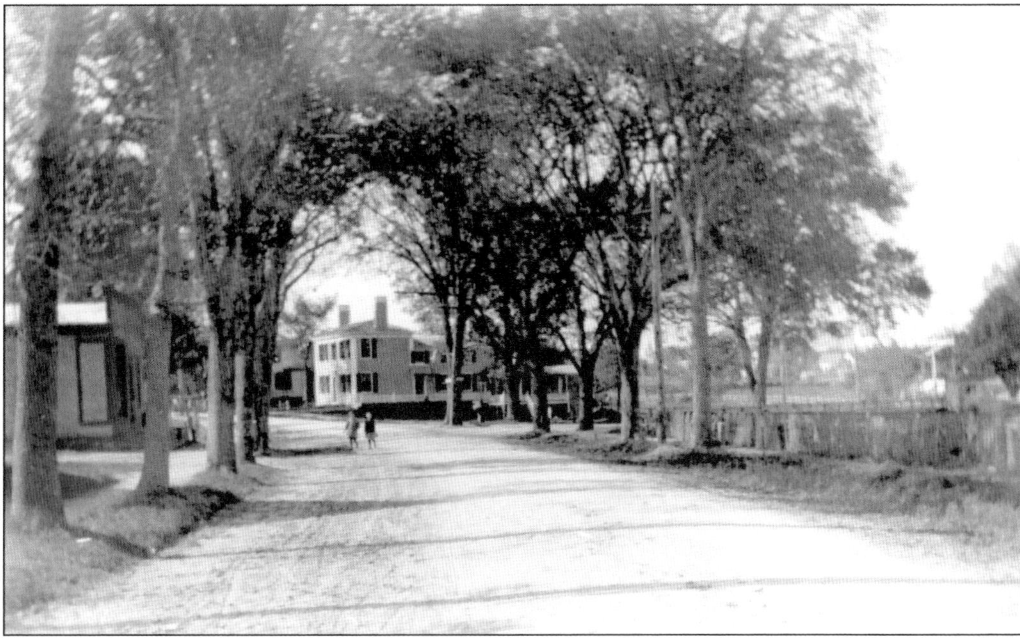

This view of Market Street, looking west, leads down to the Harvey Torrey house, built before 1830 in the Federal style. The house is at the corner of Market and Liberty Streets. This corner was known as Dog Corner because of all the butcher shops in the area.

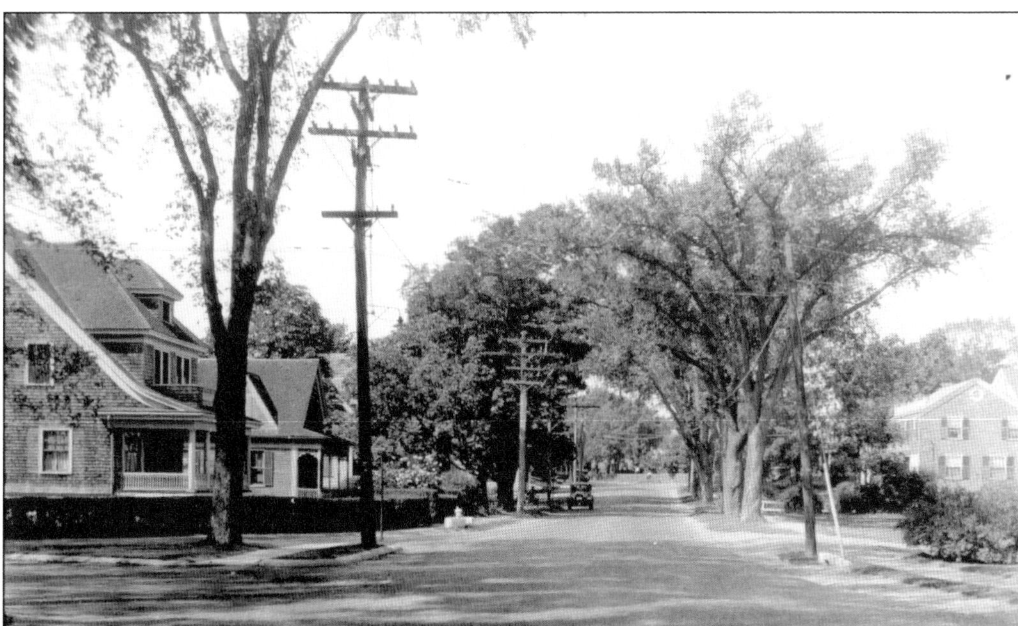

This view of Market Street looks west in the direction of the Union Street intersection. The house on the left is at the corner of Market and Concord Streets. It was built early in the 20th century. The three houses next to it have all been demolished. The house on the right is the Myra Lane house pictured on page 44.

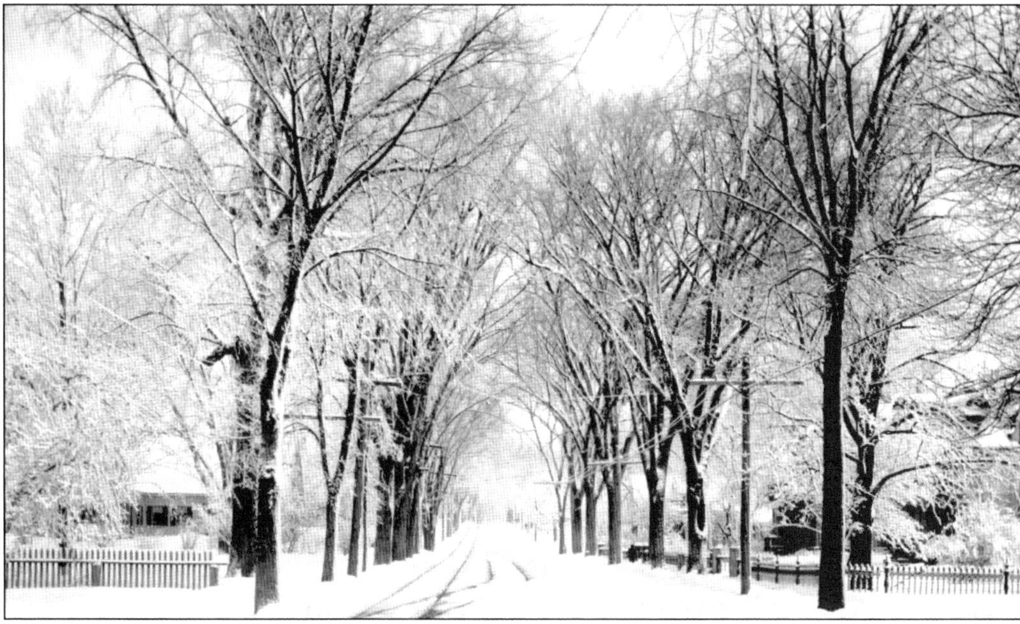

Looking north on Union Street from the intersection of Market Street after a moderate snowfall, one can see the arch of elm trees that once canopied the street. The elms disappeared under the double assault of the early 1930s Dutch elm disease and the Hurricane of 1938.

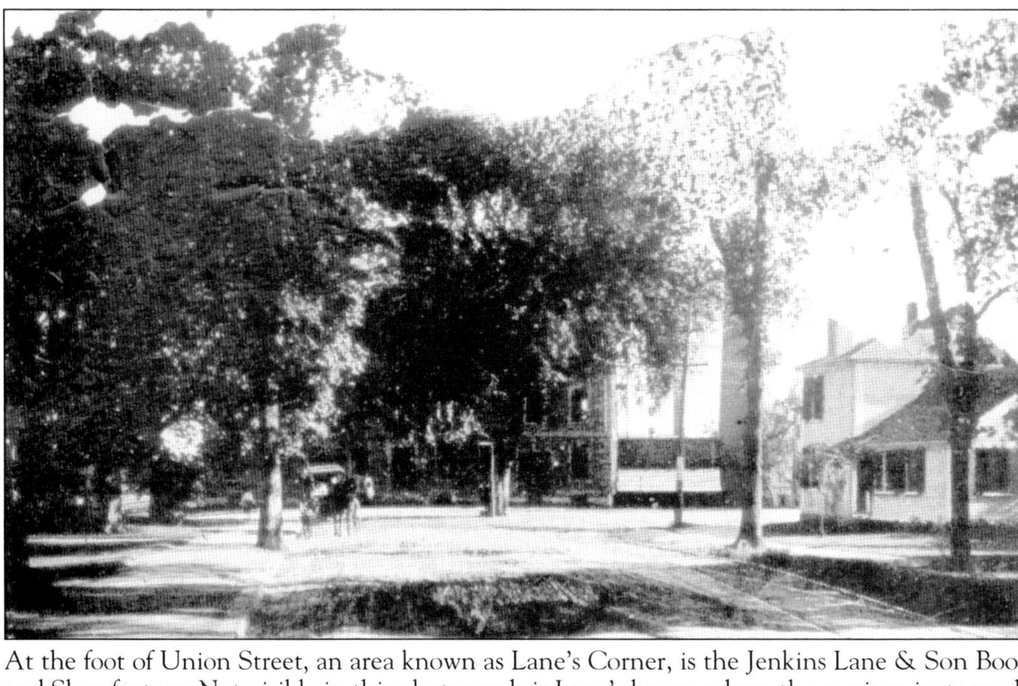

At the foot of Union Street, an area known as Lane's Corner, is the Jenkins Lane & Son Boot and Shoe factory. Not visible in this photograph is Lane's house, where the carriage is stopped. The Federal-style house in the photograph is the Simeon Reed house, built *c.* 1829, which later became a boardinghouse. In 1877, the house was moved to 123 Market Street. It was eventually taken down for business development. Simeon G. Reed Jr., who was born in the house, moved to Oregon and made enough money to establish Reed College in Portland upon his death.

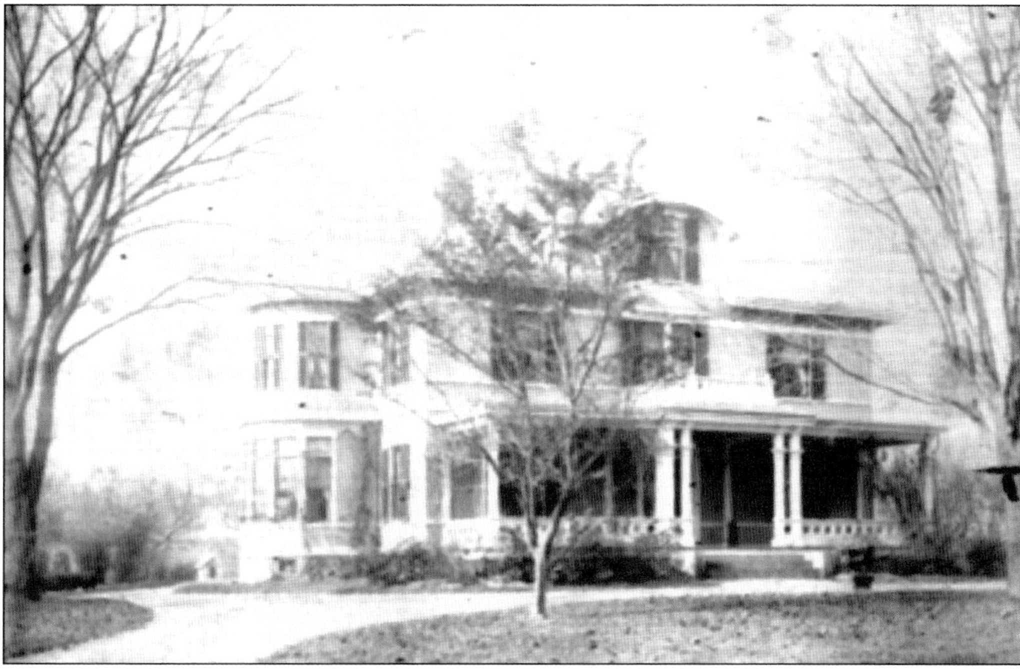

Alonzo Lane built this house at 24 Union Street in 1877, after moving his original smaller house off the property. James W. Spence bought this house after the turn of the 20th century. He moved the Simeon G. Reed house to Market Street in order to have a larger lawn.

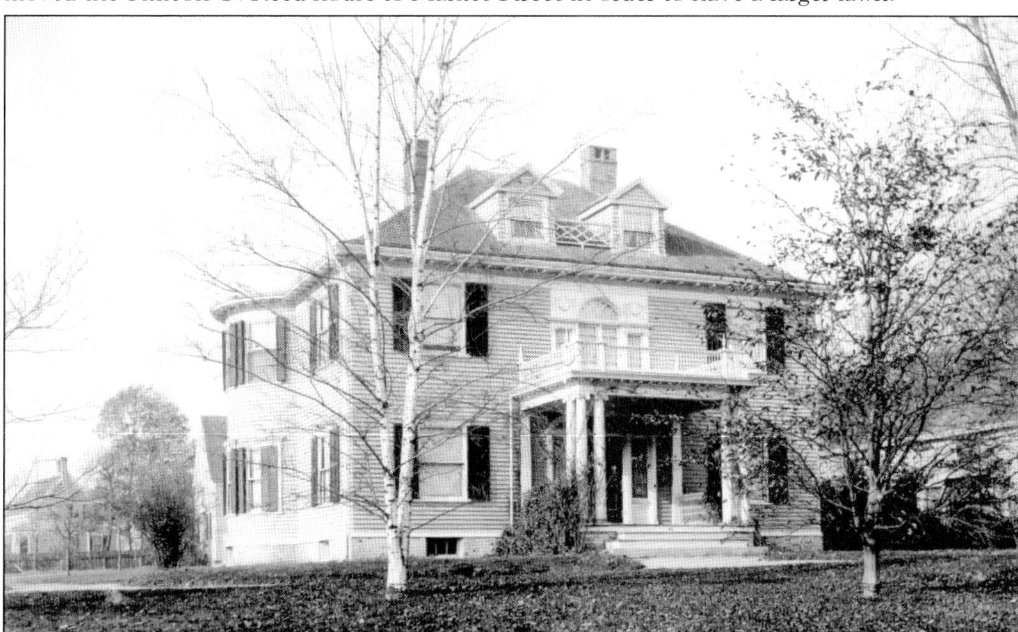

Stove manufacturer Stephen M. Howes built this house at 48 Union Street in 1893. A.W. Perry's second son, Herbert Garfield Perry, bought the house about the time of World War I. Herbert Perry dealt in real estate and was a civic leader. He was chairman of Rockland's school committee when the new high school was built in 1927. The school building is now Rogers Middle School.

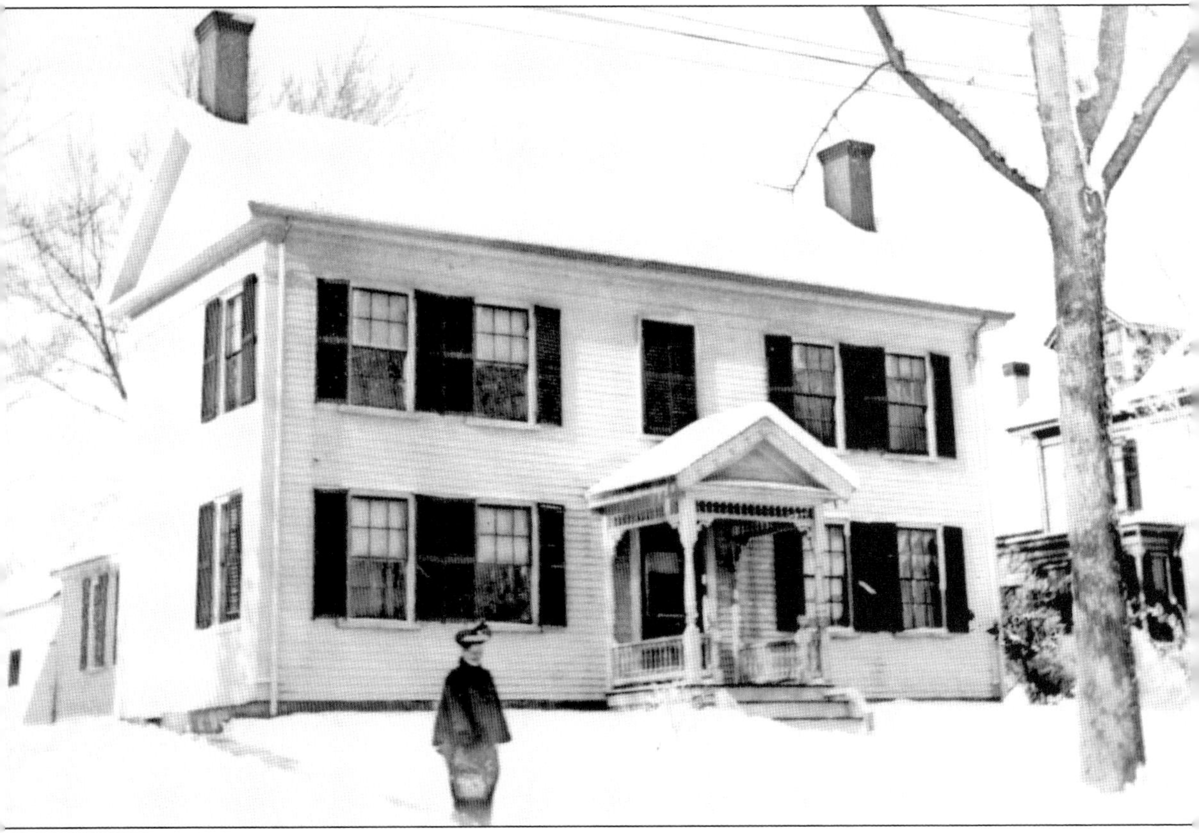

David Lane, son of Charles who lived at Lane's Corner, built this Federal-style house at 64 Union Street in 1816. The Federal-period front door is gone and was replaced with a Victorian front door and porch. The Federal-style represents the period from 1790 to 1839, when the nation was new. It is exemplified by the moving of the chimney from the center of a building to its sides. Central entrances began to sport sidelights and fan windows at the top. The style was generally a simplification of the classical designs used in the Georgian period, which preceded it. Victorian architecture refers to buildings built during the reign of England's Queen Victoria (1837–1901). The style reflected a search for the picturesque and led to such examples as the Gothic cottage, the Italian villa, and Queen Anne homes. This house is where the library association held its collection of books in a red box when it was organized in 1833. The red box is currently in the Rockland Memorial Library.

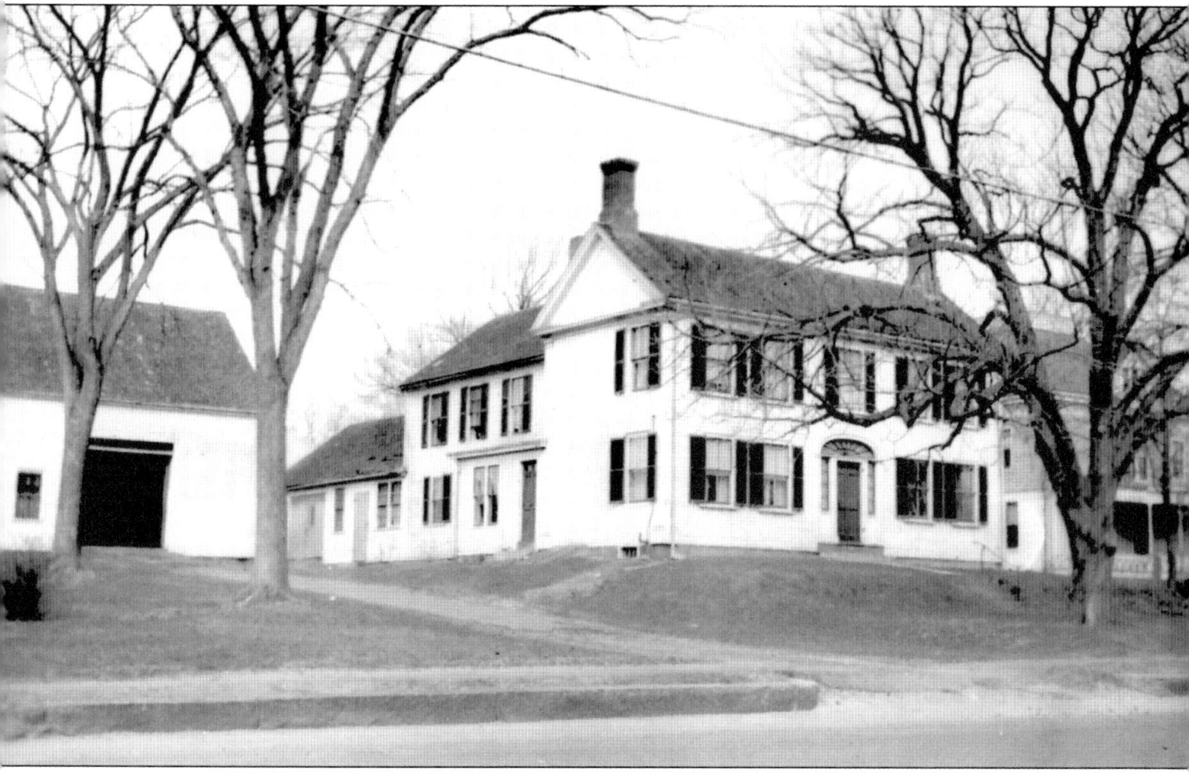

Deacon Ebenezer Reed, son of Capt. Thomas Reed, built this Federal-style house at 132 Union Street in 1818. Deacon Elijah Shaw also lived here when he wrote the *History of the Rockland Congregational Church*. The house is almost a twin of 64 Union Street, but this house still has its original front door. The house to the right was razed. The twin chimneys represent a move away from early American structures, which were built around a single chimney that anchored the center of a home.

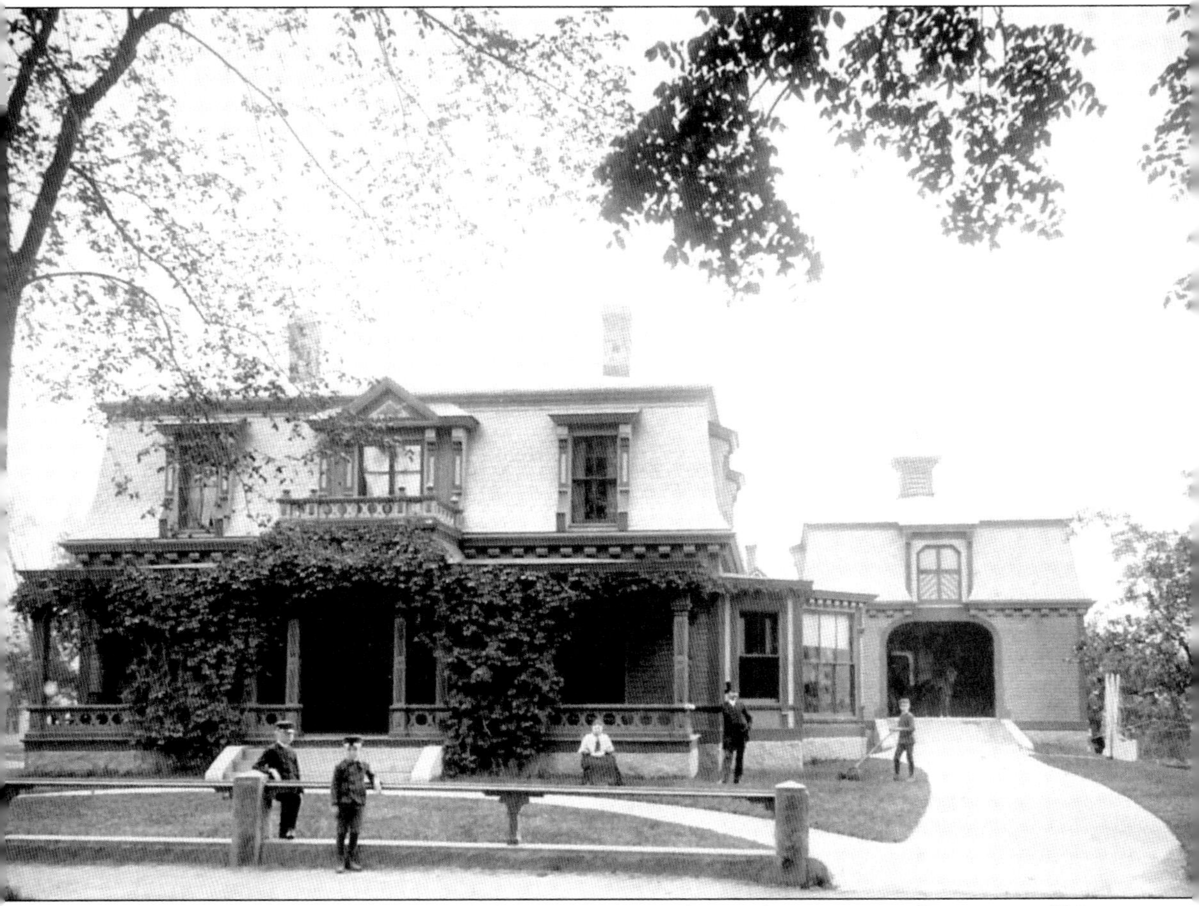

A.W. Perry built this mansard-style house *c.* 1878 at the southeast corner of Vernon and Union Streets. Pictured in this 1880s photograph is Alonzo Perry with his wife and sons. Seen here are, from left to right, Herbert G., Butler F., Isadora (French), Alonzo W., and Winthrop I. Perry. The Perry family played a big part in Rockland's history and economics during the late 19th century and 20th century, and now in the 21st century as well.

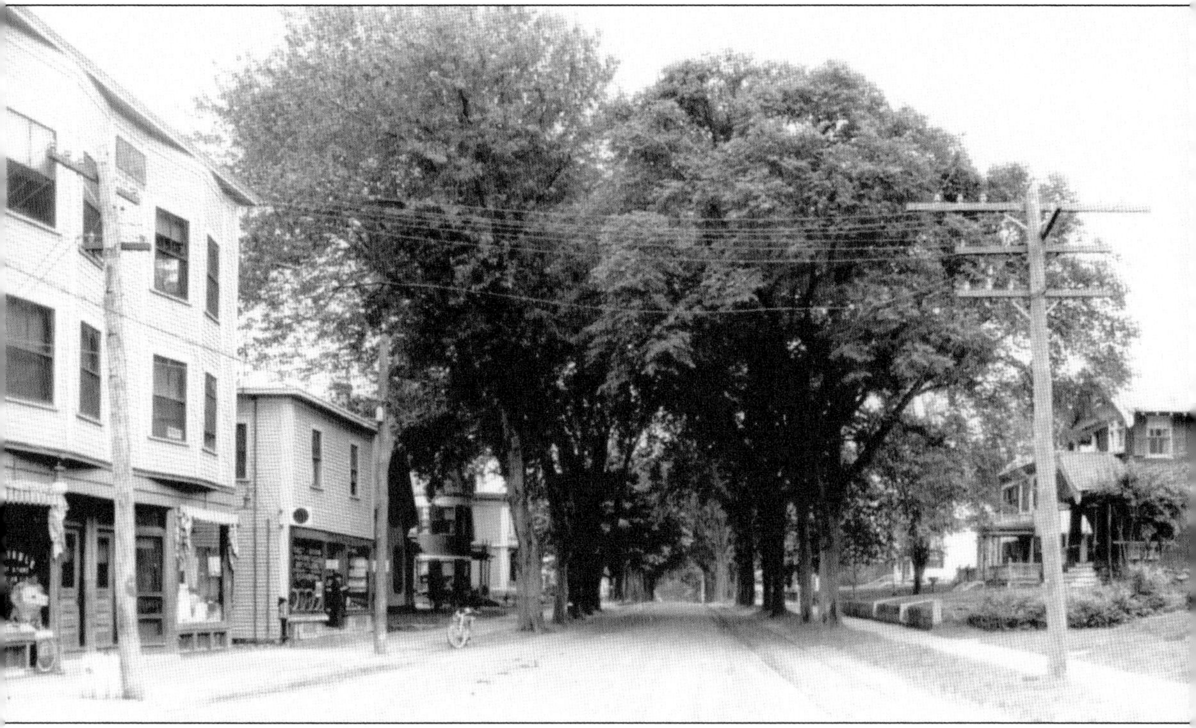

Looking south down Union Street, the house on the left side behind the bicycle is 141 Union Street, built in 1860. This house was moved across the street and is now behind 132 Union Street. The first house on the other side of the street is 154 Union Street, built in 1903 by A.W. Perry for his son Herbert on the occasion of his wedding. The next house, 148 Union Street, is that of Joseph French and was built in 1837. Alonzo W. Perry married French's daughter Isadora in 1870. After inheriting French's home, Perry donated this house as the French Home for Aged Women.

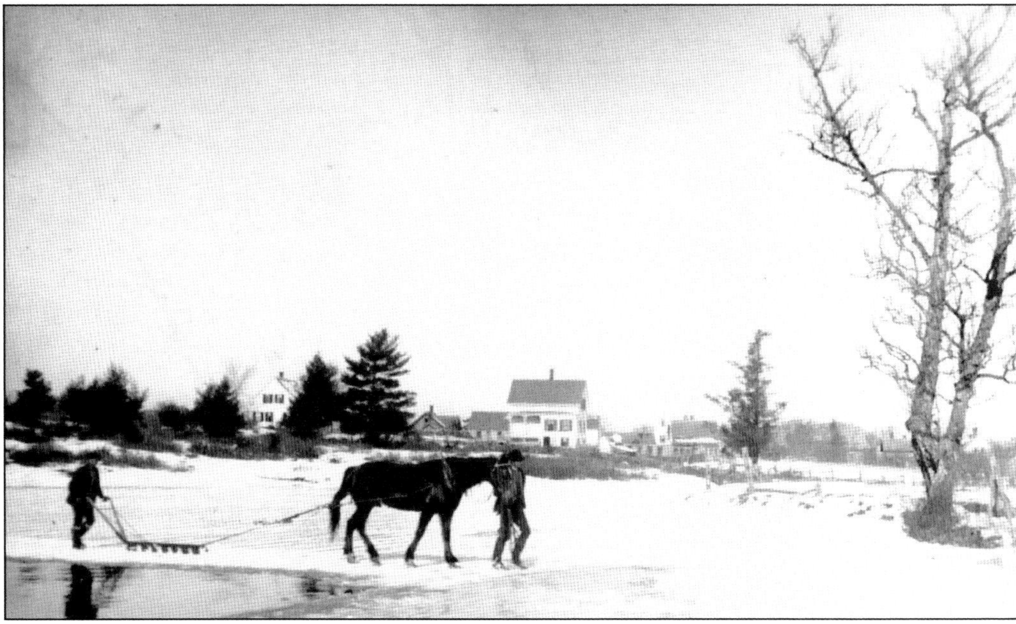

Cushing Brook was made into a pond at East Water Street by damming the stream. Ice harvesting was an important industry in New England before refrigeration. It offered work to farmers in the winter. Ice from ponds around Boston was exported as far away as India, a trail blazed by the famous "Ice King," Frederic Tudor.

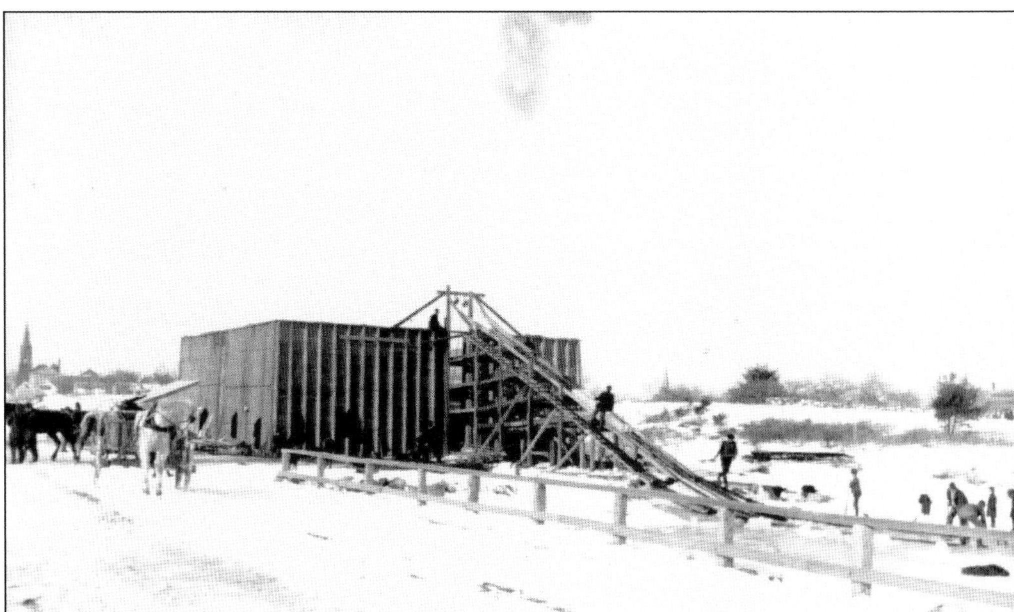

This is another view of Cushing Pond. After the ice was cut, it was floated to the conveyor that put it into the icehouse. Icehouses were insulated so ice would keep all summer. The Holy Family Church can be seen in the distance.

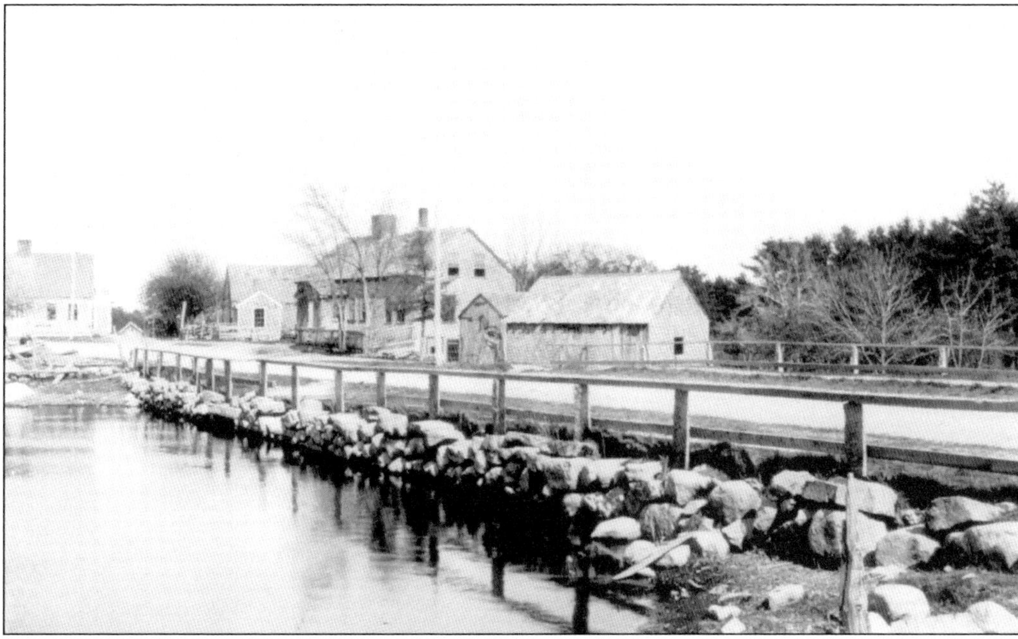

This photograph of the Cushing Pond dam dates to the last part of the 19th century. The pond that provided ice and power for a mill is gone, but not all of the old houses have vanished. The house with the two chimneys is 313 East Water Street, and the house on the far left of the photograph is 323 East Water Street.

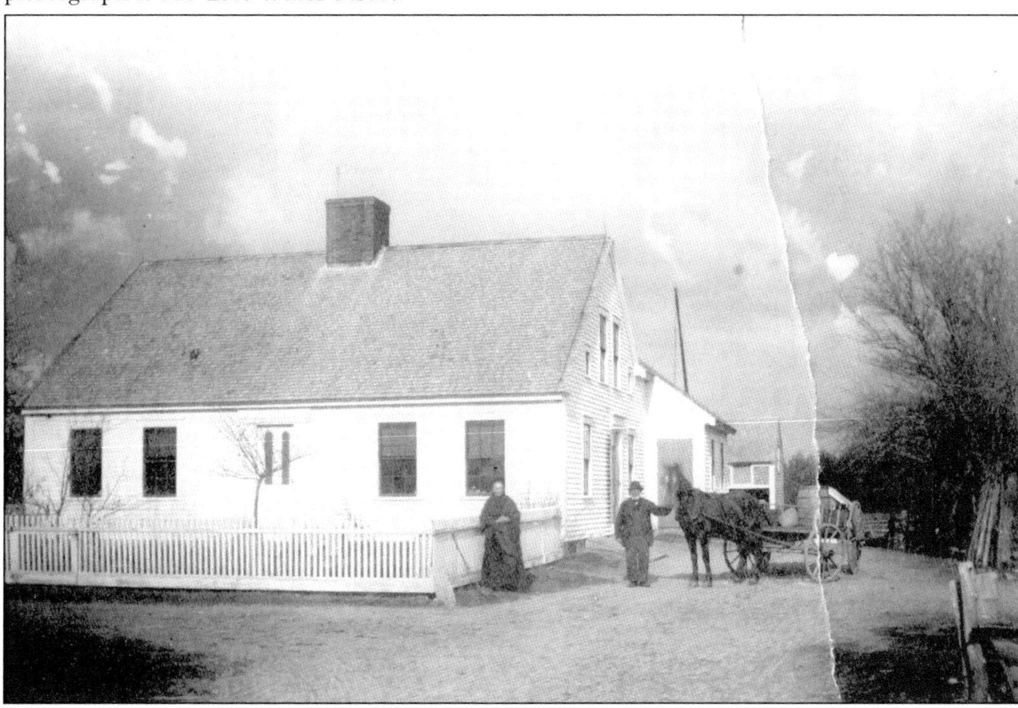

This Cape at 323 East Water Street was built c. 1807. The people in this picture look like they are ready to go and sell a barrel of meal produced at the gristmill, which was on the pond until 1897. A sweep of an old well looms behind the ell and the horse-drawn carriage.

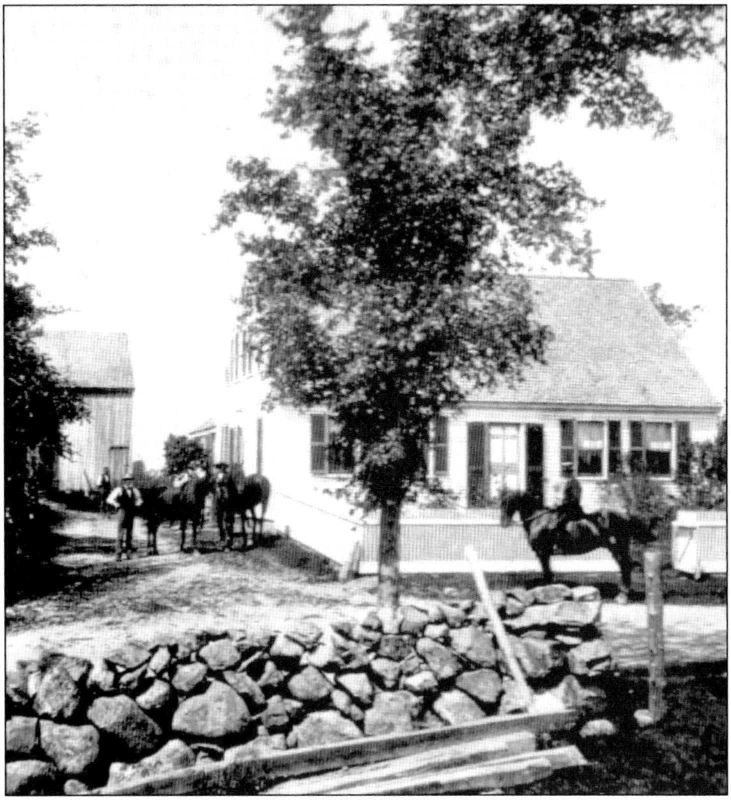

Nathan Beal built this house at 422 East Water Street *c.* 1818. The stonewall in front of the house is a reminder of the clearing of farmland in New England. Early farmers worked for days and weeks to remove the rocks that covered the New England soil. Rather than just toss them aside, they used them to build the walls that bounded their estates. One South Shore historian has joked that if America had been settled in reverse, west to east, the pioneers would have reached New England, looked at all the rocks, thrown up a fence, and called it a national park.

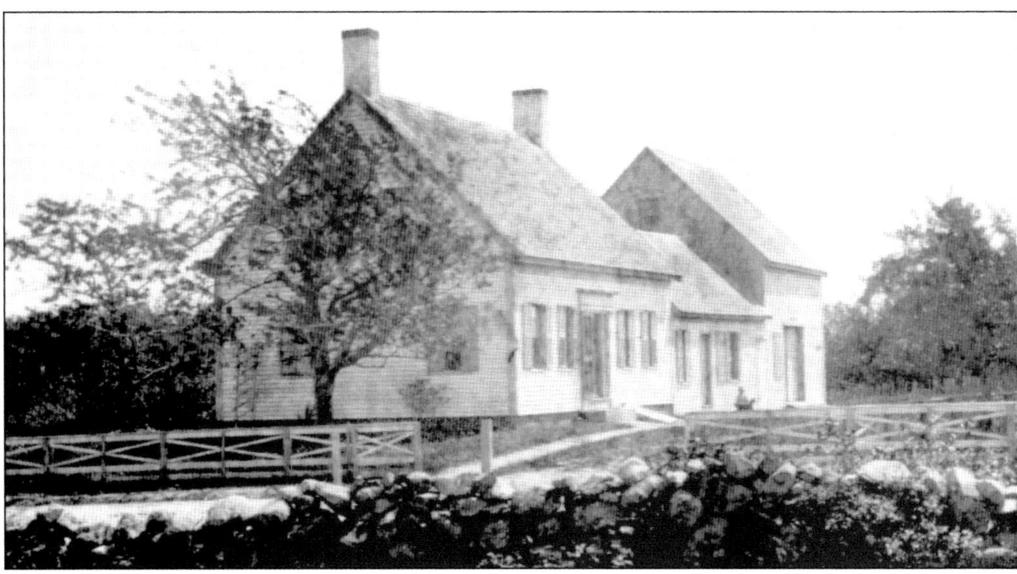

This Cape at 269 East Water Street was probably built later than the others on the street. Rather than the central chimney of the early Capes, this one has its chimneys on the sides, typical of the Federal period. Its barn is attached, while barns in previous photographs were not. The fence, known as Kentucky-style fencing, is more elaborate than the simple picket or stonewall fences of the other homes.

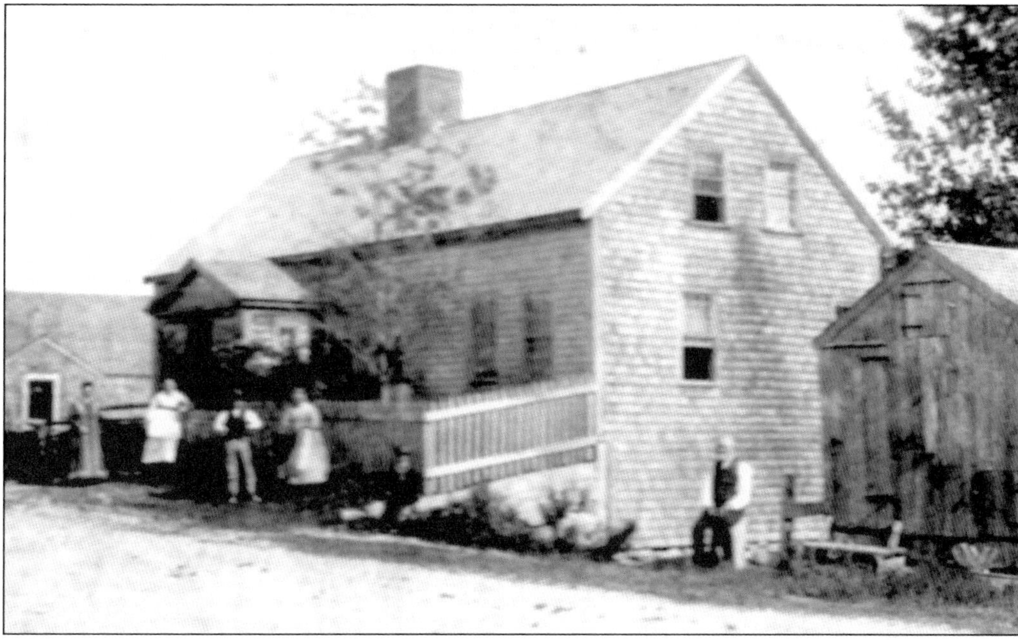

This house can be seen clearly in the photograph on the top of page 53. It was most likely built as a typical Cape with a central chimney, then remodeled and extended on one side. The residents may have derived some of their livelihood from the commercial activities on the pond.

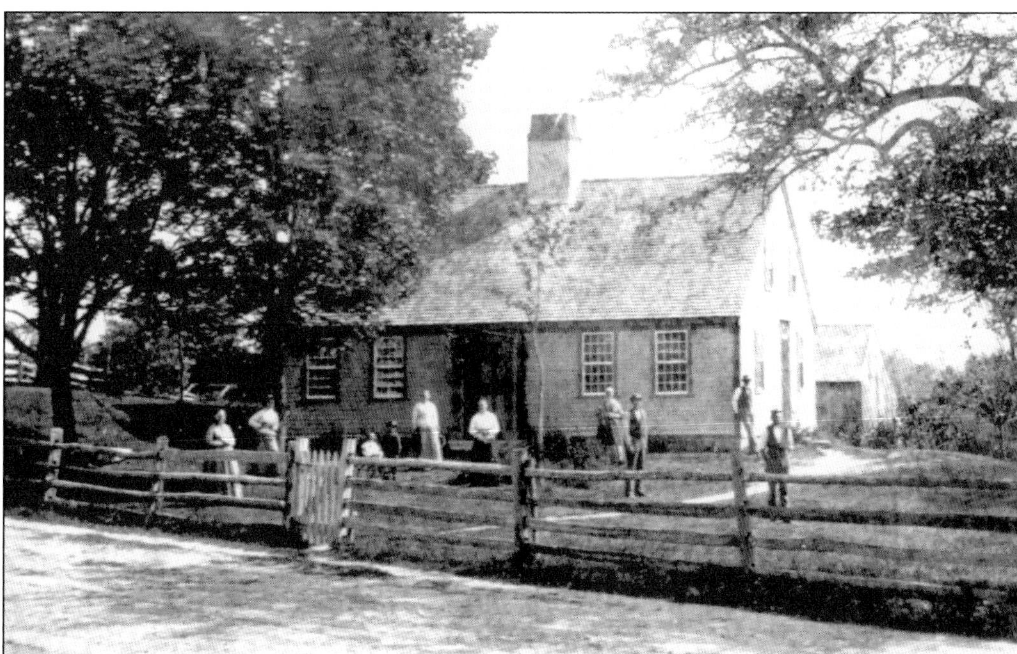

Noah Beal Sr. built a house at what is now 437 East Water Street in 1748. His son Noah Beal Jr. built this house in front of it *c*. 1780. The Beals were not the first to build along East Water Street. The Thaxter family from Hingham had built there as early as 1721. The Thaxter house was taken apart and removed in the 1760s.

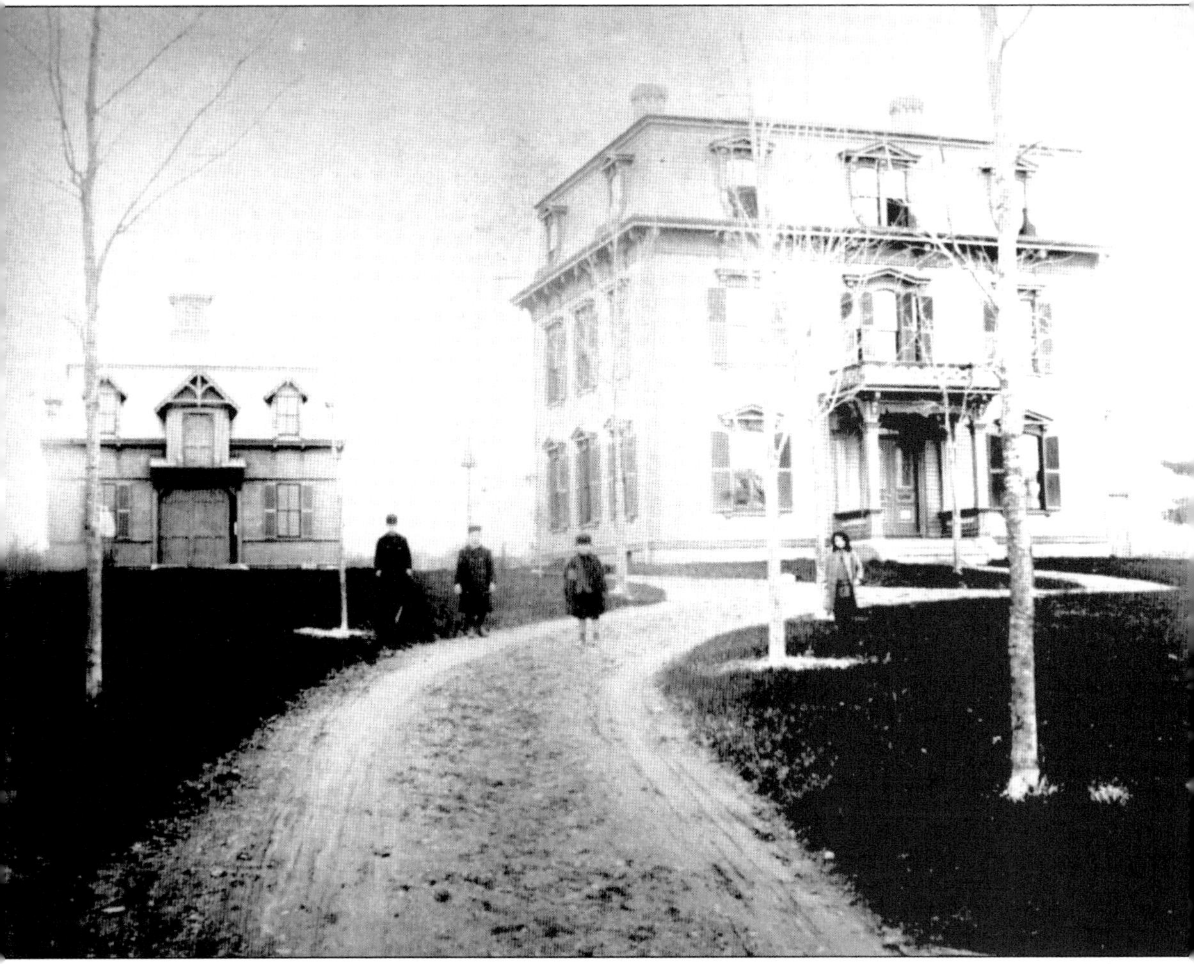

Joseph Stanley Turner built this Second Empire (mansard) house in 1872. Turner owned the J.S. Turner & Company shoe factory on Howard Street. Turner—whose children, Edward Granville, Joseph Chester, Bessy Abigail, and Annie Payne appear in this photograph from left to right—died in 1897. After Turner's wife died, the children of her brother-in-law inherited the house. One of his daughters, Bessy A. Turner, married Dr. Joseph Frame and lived in the house. Frame died in 1941, and Bessy lived there until 1962. Symbolic of the time the house was built, the house dwarfs the carriage house (left). The house's builder only needed such a building as a utilitarian structure to store his carriages and house his horses, and not as a tool of business. Even with just that simple purpose, however, the owner had enough money to architecturally liven up the structure a bit, to make it much more than just a typical outbuilding. Mansard-style, or General Grant–style, roofs were known for the French architect who designed them and for the president in office at the time of their highest popularity. The style represented the American search for trendsetters and tastemakers in architecture. In the late 1860s and early 1870s, France was regarded as one of the centers of culture in the Western world.

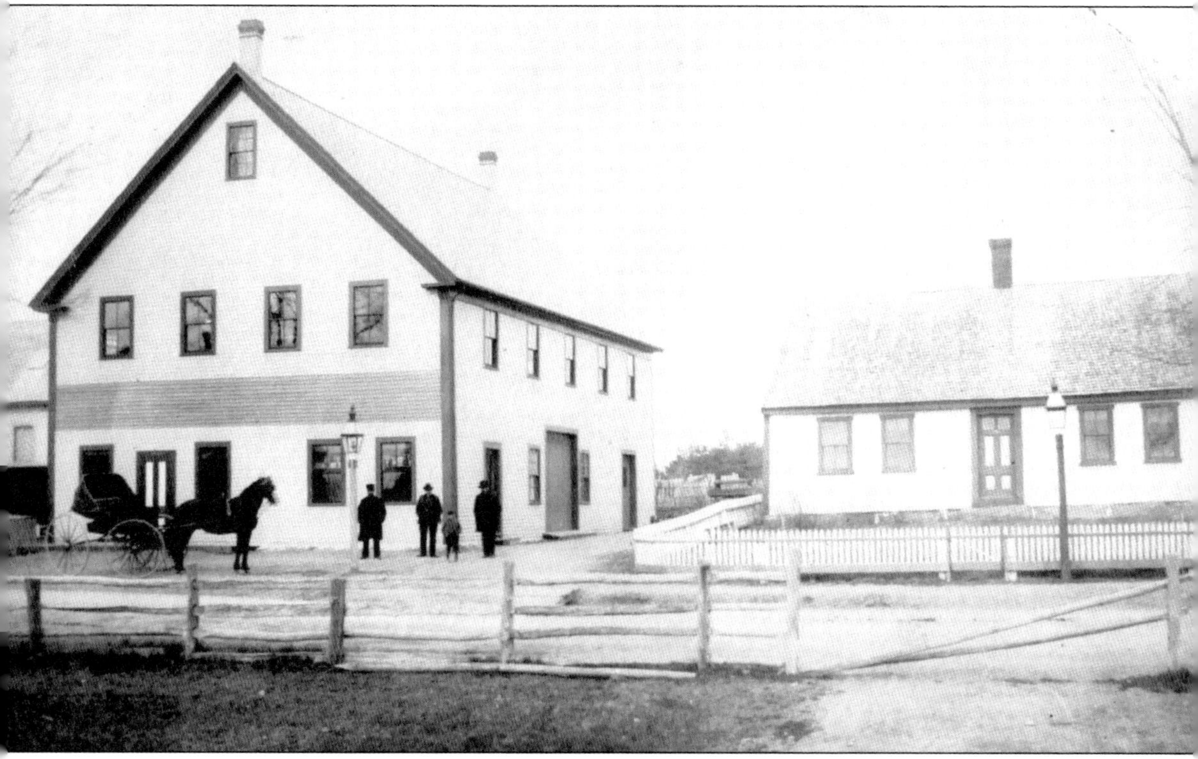

Conversely, this home on Liberty Street, one of Rockland's oldest streets, showed the harsher realities of life in old East Abington before the Industrial Revolution. The barn dwarfs the house; both were built in a time when most Americans were tied to the soil and farming life. Liberty Street, built before Union Street was constructed in 1815, was one of the first main streets in Rockland. This is the house of Capt. Joshua Curtis, built *c.* 1761. He was a mariner and settled here with his English wife. The house was first built near Forest and Pleasant Streets and was moved to 649 Liberty Street in 1825. It was taken down in 1962.

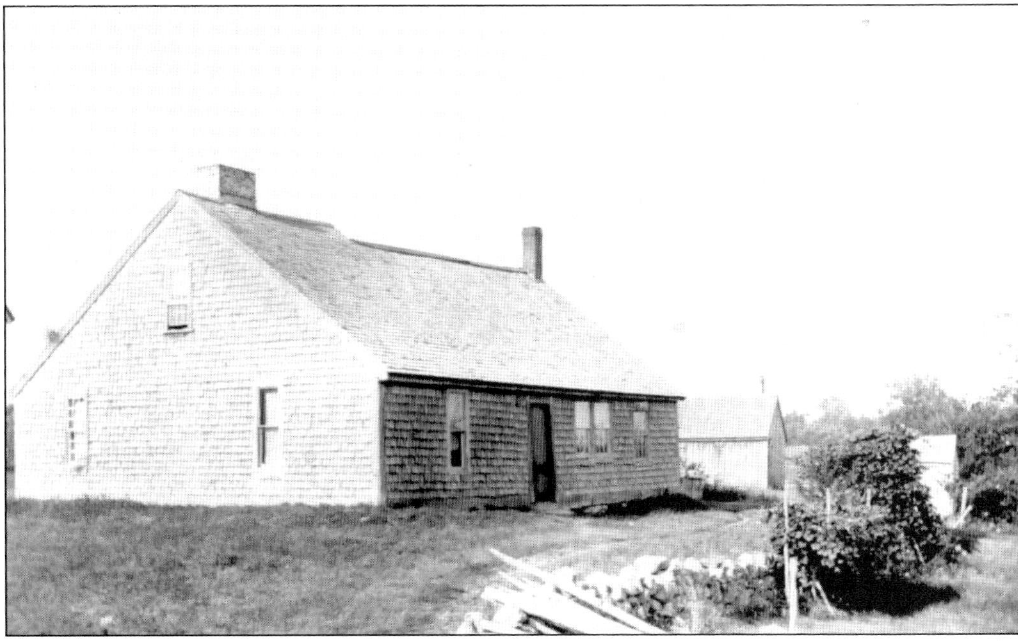

This is the John Smith house on Liberty Street, built in 1753 and taken down in 1896. This simple home was one of the oldest houses on the street when it was razed. It appears that the house could have been built in two stages, as indicated by the change in the roofline.

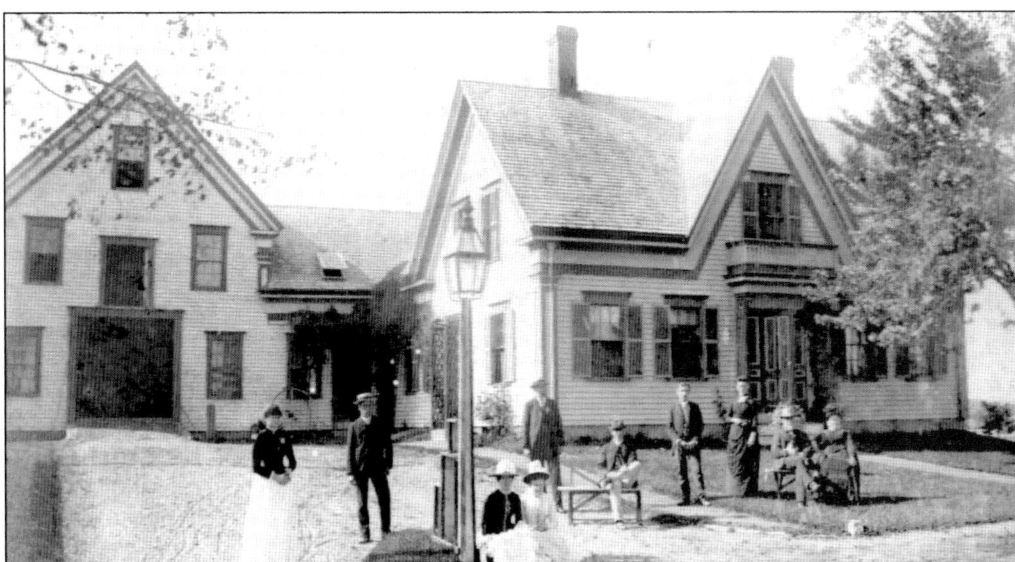

On this summer's day, the members of the Torrey family are all in their Sunday best to have their picture taken in front of their home. The house is a Cape with a very steep dormer. This type of house was seen c. the mid-1800s, when there was a revival of the Gothic style of architecture in America. Note the Penny Farthing bicycle, with the big wheel, leaning against the house.

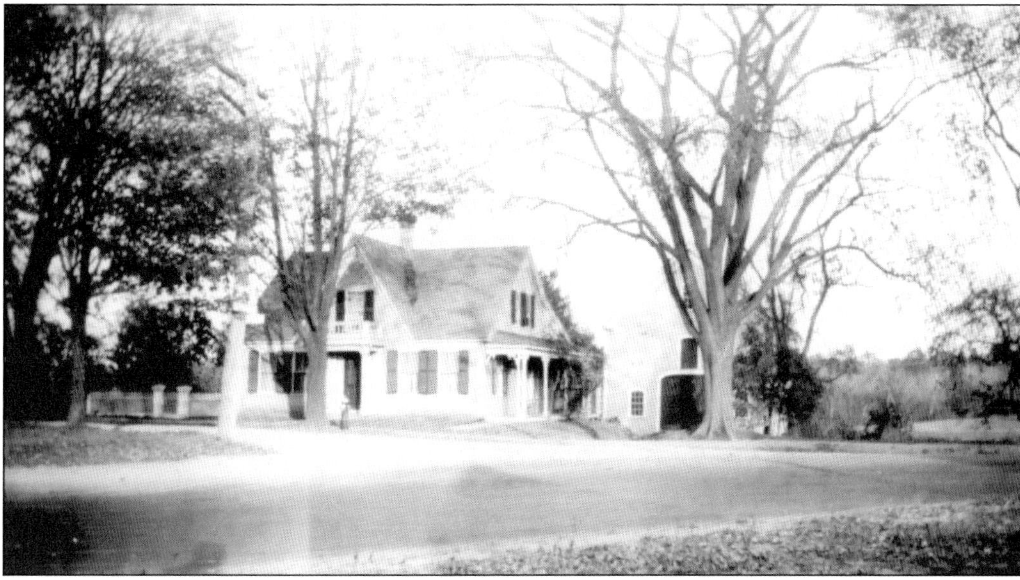

The setting seen here is 3 Pleasant Street. It exemplifies a comfortable home with Victorian standards. One of the major indicators of changes in American life is the inclusion of a porch in the building's design. The concept of relaxation never occurred to America's first settlers, so their homes were simple and functional. As life changed with the Industrial Revolution and the concepts of weekends and holidays evolved, many Americans realized that sitting in a rocking chair on a porch on a sunny Saturday afternoon was not a bad idea after all.

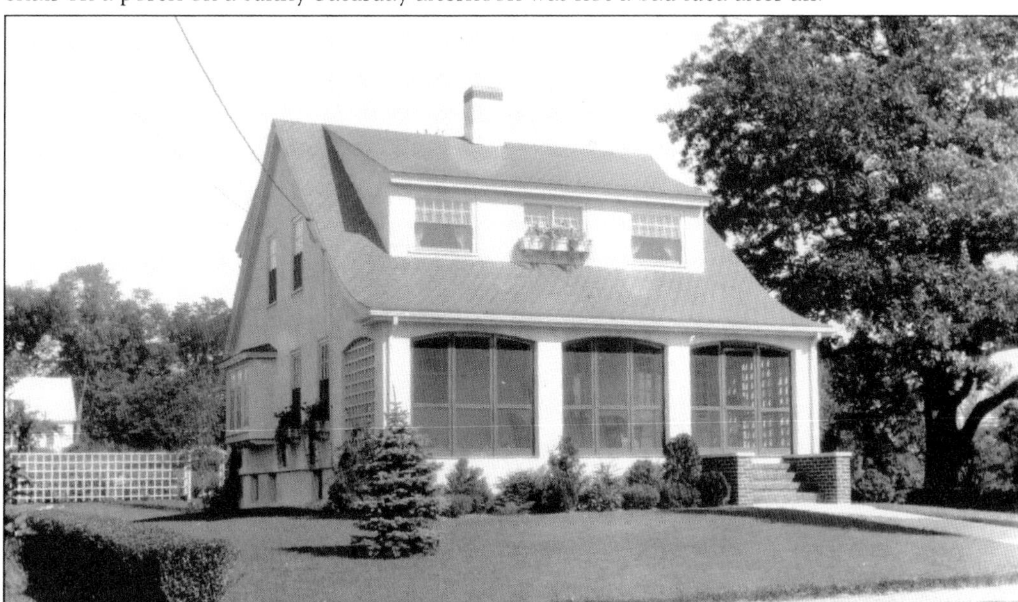

Crescent Street was not connected to Union Street until *c.* 1906. This house was built soon after the new street was opened. Notice how the roof comes down right over the front porch, a feature found in the craftsmen and bungalow houses of the early 20th century. Another feature of the house is the foundation plantings. This type of landscaping came with central heating. Foundations were constructed higher to allow for the furnace, and people hid the foundations with the plants.

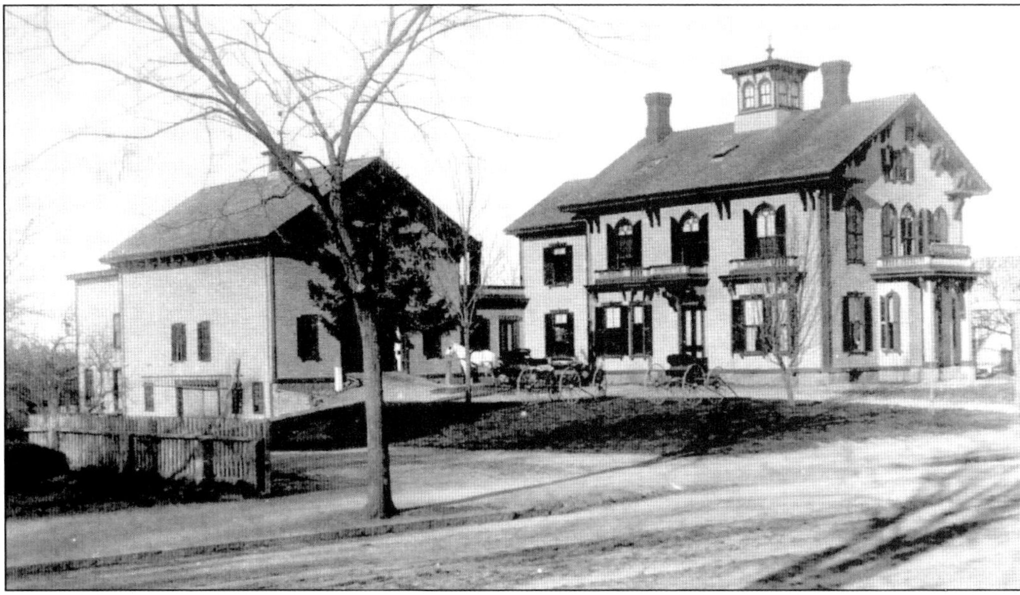

This house, originally the Sumner Shaw house and then the Sherman House, was located at the corner of Belmont and Union Streets. As business grew in Rockland, salesmen came to town by train and rented rooms and rigs to see their customers. This bracketed Victorian building served such clientele. When Alfred W. Donovan, the general manger of E.T. Wright Shoe Company, built his home on this lot in 1908, this house was moved down Belmont Street.

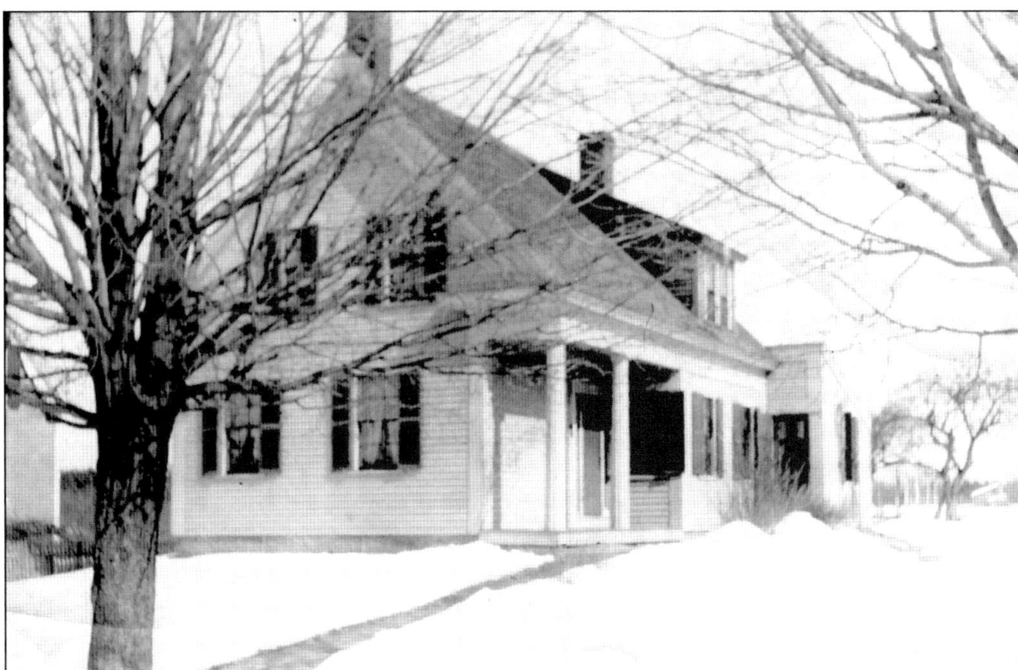

This Cape on Liberty Street is typical of the modifications made in the Greek Revival style in Rockland. The gable end is turned toward the street. An interesting feature is the small side porch with columns. The dormer was added later.

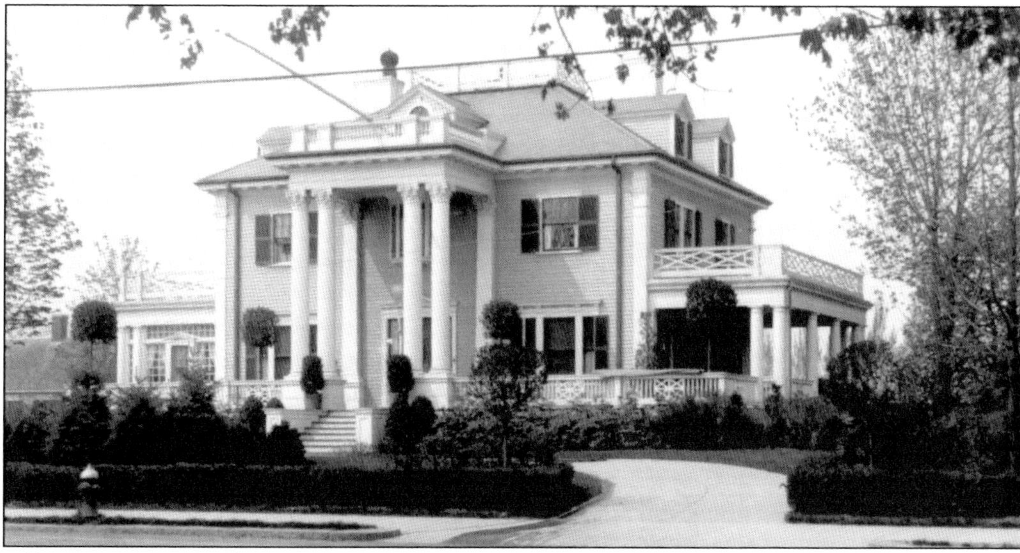

Alfred E. Donovan, the aforementioned general manger of E.T. Wright Shoe Company, built this house in 1908, displacing the Sherman House on the corner of Belmont and Union Streets. The house is typical of the big Colonial Revival–style homes built in the early 20th century.

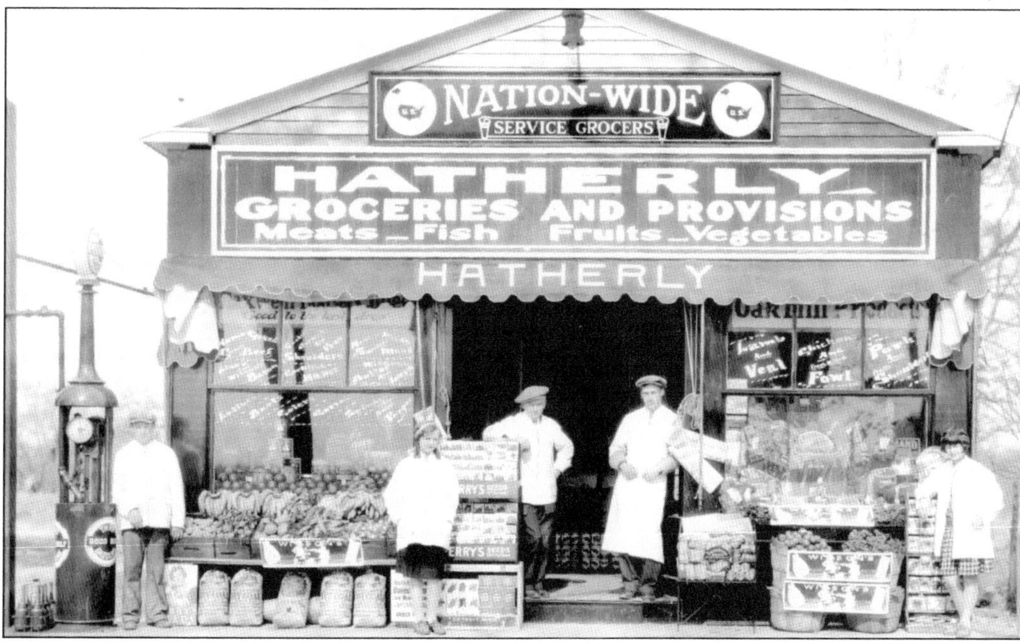

Frank McCaw, known as "Mac," had this store at 937 Union Street in the 1930s. Frank is to the left of the door, and an employee, Bertie Webb, is on the other side. Frank and his wife Mary Louise Stetson had six daughters—Irene M., Alta I., Anne Mea, Marie S., Elizabeth, and Nancy—two of whom are possibly pictured here. The name of the store reflects the section of Rockland, north of Salem Street, where the store was located. There was once a post office that canceled stamps with a Hatherly cancellation. The title comes from the original Hatherly grant, the land owned by Scituate's Timothy Hatherly. Hatherly was a merchant adventurer who helped finance early settlement of the South Shore. The Rockland town seal is the Hatherly family coat of arms.

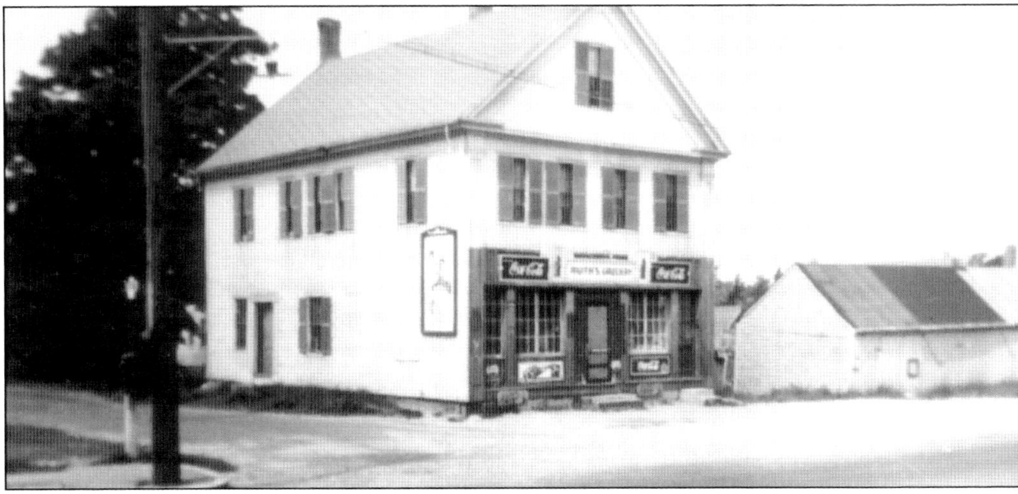

This Greek Revival–style building constructed *c.* 1845 is on the corner of Oregon Avenue and Union Street. There was a store in the North Union, or Boxberry Street, section since the time that Benjamin Vining operated one in the late 18th century. The sheds on the right are gone, and the store has been converted into a house.

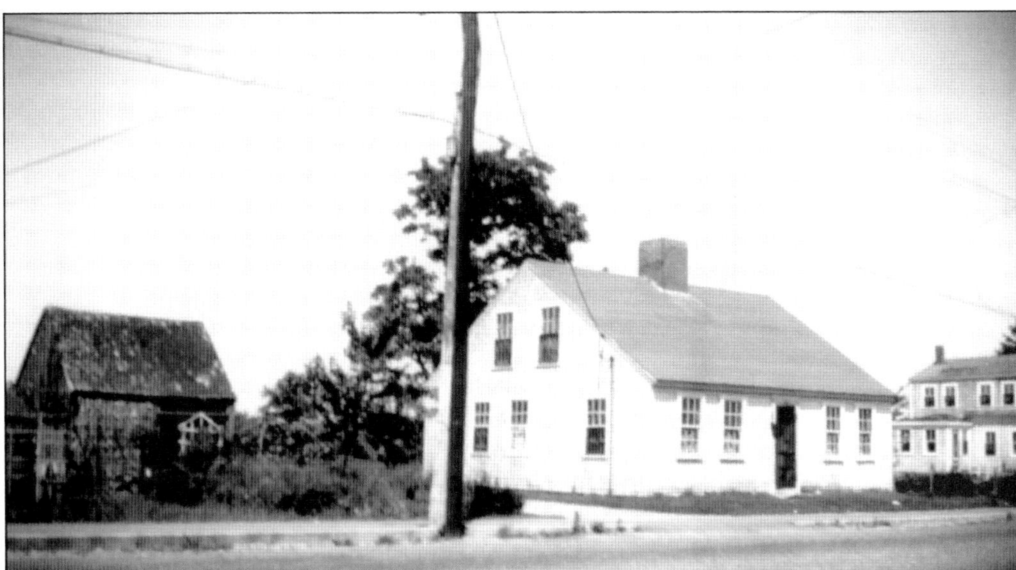

Abijah Beal moved from Weymouth as a boy, as did most of the settlers in this part of Rockland, North Union Street, in the 1730s. Beal built this house *c.* 1750 at 1126 Union Street. At this time, the Hatherly grant was being divided, and land was available. The house became the last house on the north end of Union Street when the South Weymouth Naval Air Station expanded in 1958.

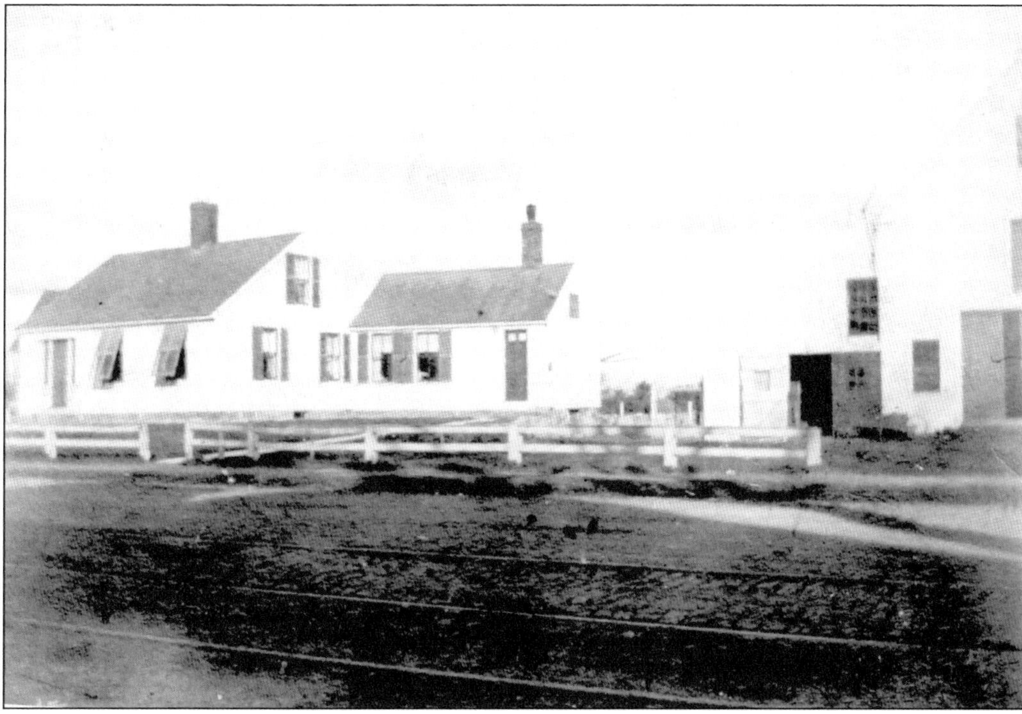

This house at 821 Union Street, on the corner of Union Street and V.F.W. Drive, was built *c.* 1824 and started life as a school at 844. It was moved to its current location in 1845. This house is known as a half-Cape, with two windows on one side of the door but no windows on the other. The storm windows are opened, as it was probably springtime when this photograph was taken. The house and barn still exist.

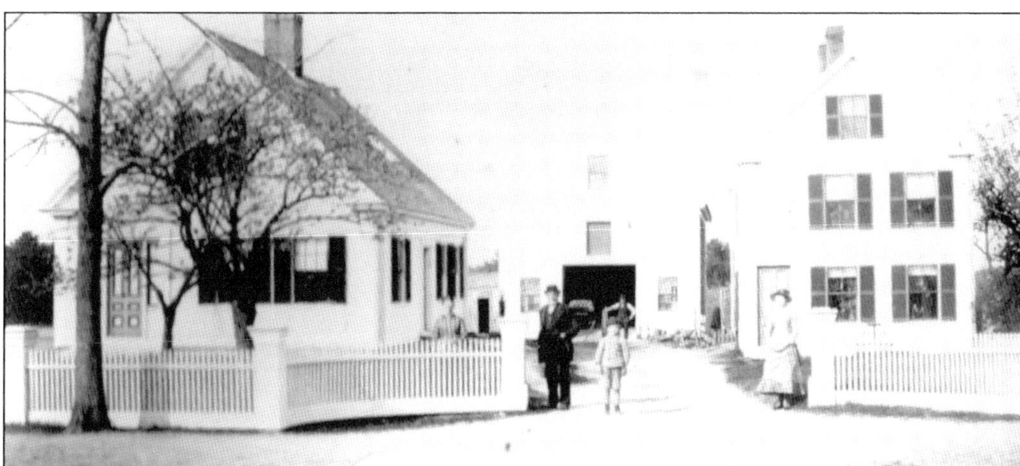

The Hunt house, on the left, is at 959 Union Street, the southeast corner of Forest Street. On March 9, 1874, Rockland became a town. On March 10, 1874, Samuel A. and Mary Emma Hunt had a son. The joy of having the first baby born in the new town prompted the parents to name him George Rockland Hunt. It is likely the boy in the photograph is Rockland's first citizen.

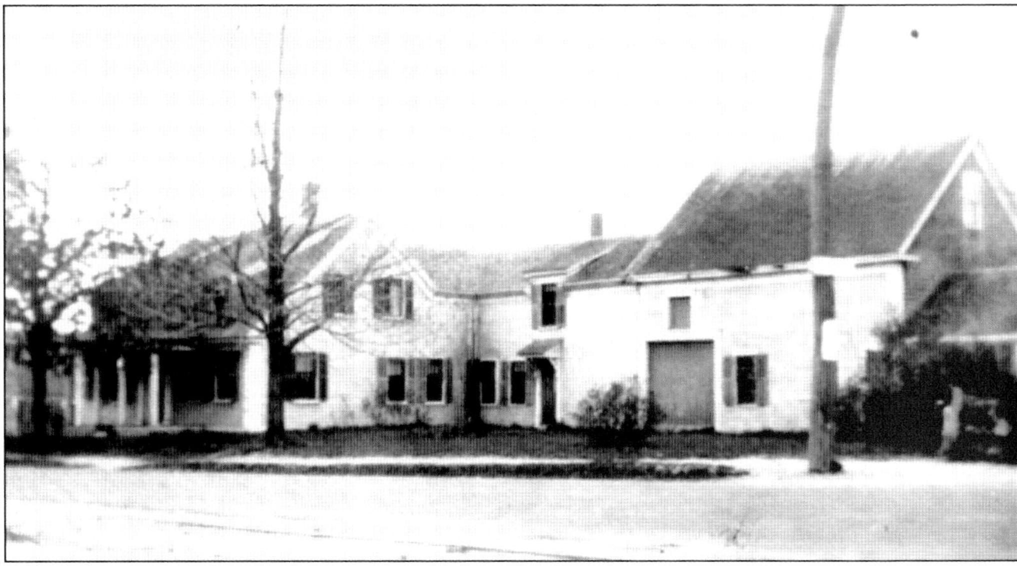

Timothy Thayer moved his family from South Weymouth and built a home at 979 Union Street, the corner of Forest and Union Streets, *c.* 1740. In 1800, Thomas Hunt lived in the house. That first house disappeared, and Warren Hunt, who was town clerk of Abington from 1861 to 1870, built the house in this photograph in 1825. Off of the barn is a shoe shop from the days of the ten-footers. The name comes from the 10-by-10-foot shops in backyards where shoes were made.

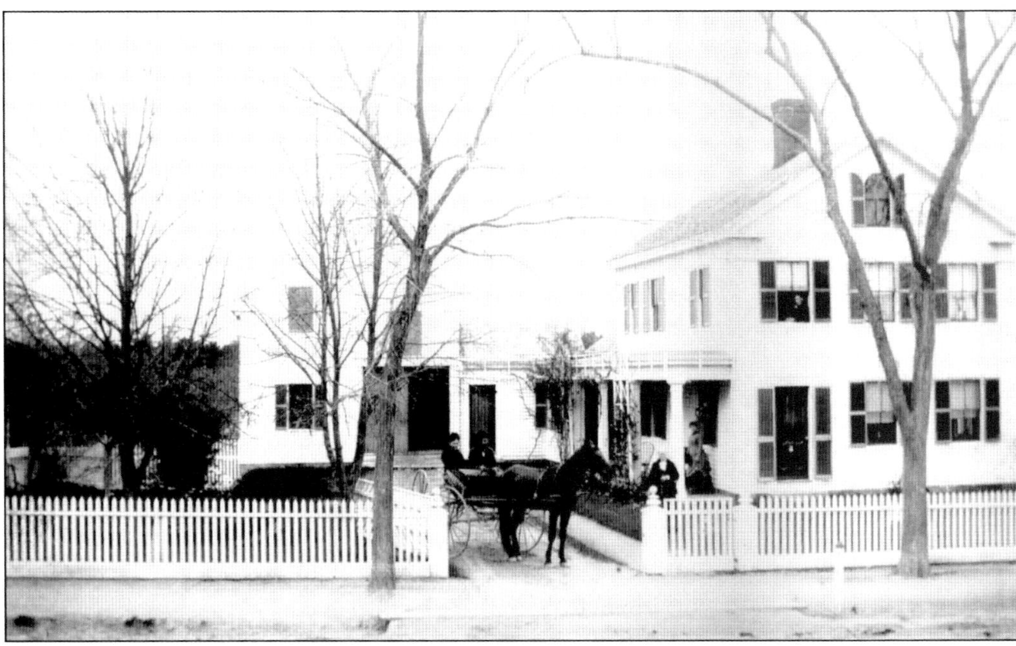

This Greek Revival–style home, built *c.* 1835, currently stands at 978 Union Street. The style is simplified, as it does not have columns. It does have its gable end to the street and a side hall entrance, and the corner boards are pilasters. The overall appearance is of a Greek temple. Insurance man Amos Phelps was born in this house. The authors do not know who the people in the photograph are, but perhaps the man in the second-floor window is Amos.

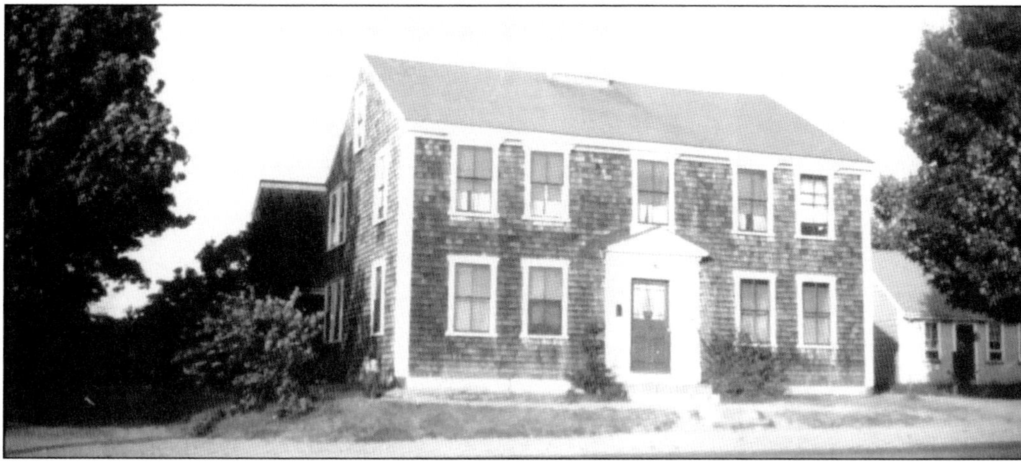

Jonathan Torrey, the first to settle in this northern section of town, built the first house on this site sometime in the 1720s. In 1785, Benjamin Vining bought the house and later, in 1797, replaced it with the house in the photograph that currently stands at 1007 Union Street. Vining farmed and had livestock and a store. Abner Curtis worked for Vining, and in 1827, he bought the house and business. Curtis kept the farm and store and branched out into the shoe business. He bought Hunt and Loud, the first commercial shoe manufacturer, after they went bankrupt. Obtaining a pattern for Spanish-type shoes, he was able to manufacture and export shoes to Cuba. He had a near monopoly in this trade. A major setback from which he never recovered was the loss of his warehouse and stock due to the Boston fire of 1872. By 1880, he liquidated his holdings, and in 1882, he died at the age of 81.

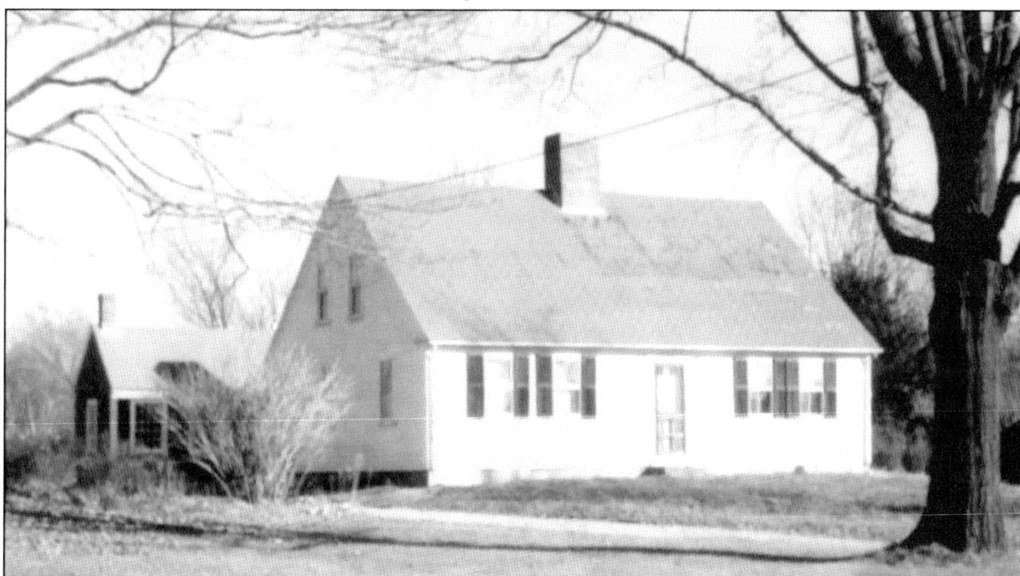

The Abram Shaw house was built in 1765. This was moved from the woods near Forest Street to the road. The building to the rear of this house is possibly one of the ten-footers where shoes were made in the early 19th century. At the time this house was built, North Union Street was known as Boxberry Street. This street originated in South Weymouth. The homesteaders in this section moved south from Weymouth to take advantage of the land that opened up in the 1720s.

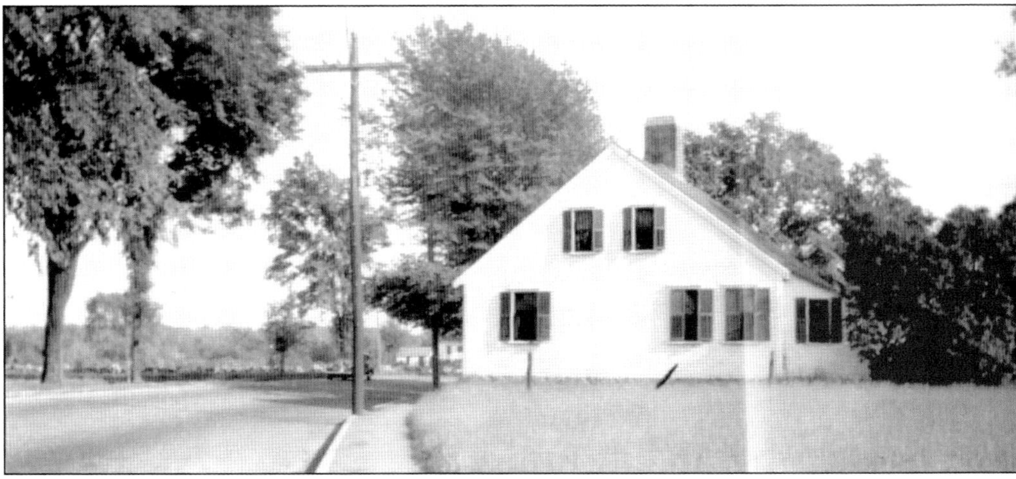

David Whitman Jr. (1780–1832) probably built 1300 Union Street, the last house in a very interesting part of Rockland. It was moved to Circuit Street in Hanover c. 1960. This section of Rockland has some of the oldest historical associations in the town. The early settlers and Native Americans named the line that separates Rockland from Weymouth and Plymouth County from Norfolk County the Accord in 1664. The line is also the northern boundary of the Hatherly grant of 1656. Boxberry was one of the earliest settlements established. Thomas Hunt started the commercial shoe business in this section in 1793. All the houses from number 1138 to 1300 were either moved or razed for the expansion of the South Weymouth Naval Air Station in 1957.

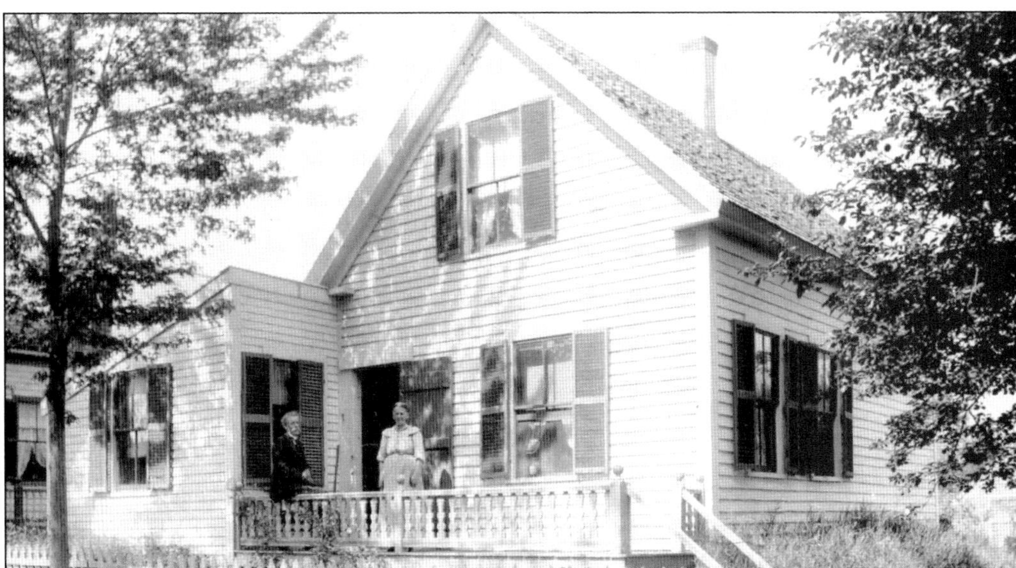

In the 1840s, the Irish suffered the Great Potato Famine, and many immigrated to America. During this time, the Old Colony Railroad was being built, starting in 1845, and the shoe industry was expanding. There were jobs for the immigrants in what became Rockland. The Irish section was on and around North Avenue. This house is at 15 Dublin Row. Patrick O'Hearn and Elizabeth (Lizzie Flanagan) O' Hearn are on the porch in this photograph. He made shoes in a backyard shop. The couple bought this house from the estate of John Flanagan, Lizzie's brother, who was killed by a train on the Hanover Branch in 1873.

Four

A Place to Pray
Rockland Churches

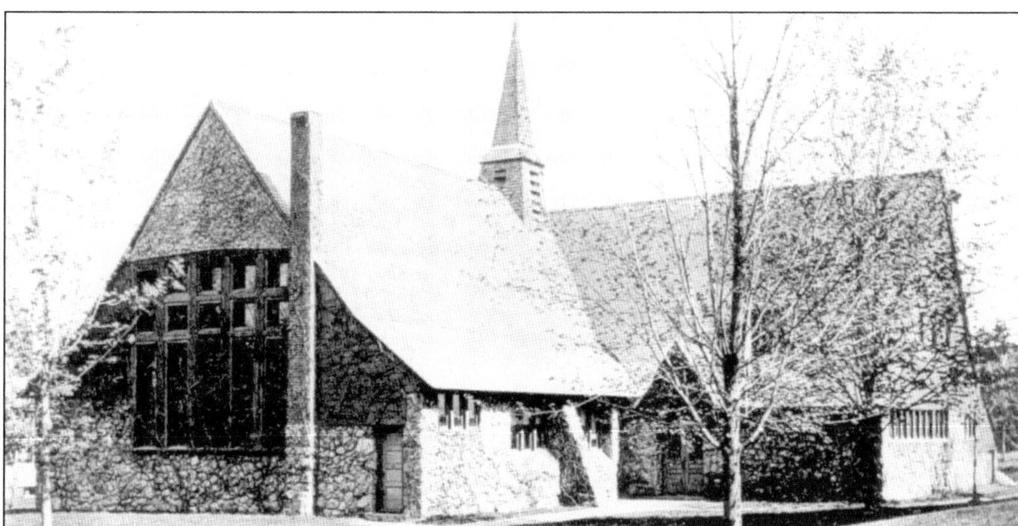

Early New Englanders drew much strength from their religious affiliations. Many of the churches they built were impressive in appearance and symbolic of the faith and commitment that brought parishioners together. In Rockland, as in most communities that had the geographic freedom to do so, many of the churches were built on hills, affording all the chance to see their chapel of choice from a distance. In 1883, Judge George W. Kelley and a list of petitioners requested the formation of a Unitarian religious society in Rockland. This Unitarian church on Webster Street, one of the few churches in town not located on Union Street, was built in 1889 after consultations with architect T.M. Clark. The roof tiles came from Wales, United Kingdom. In 1961, the Unitarian church merged with the Universalist church.

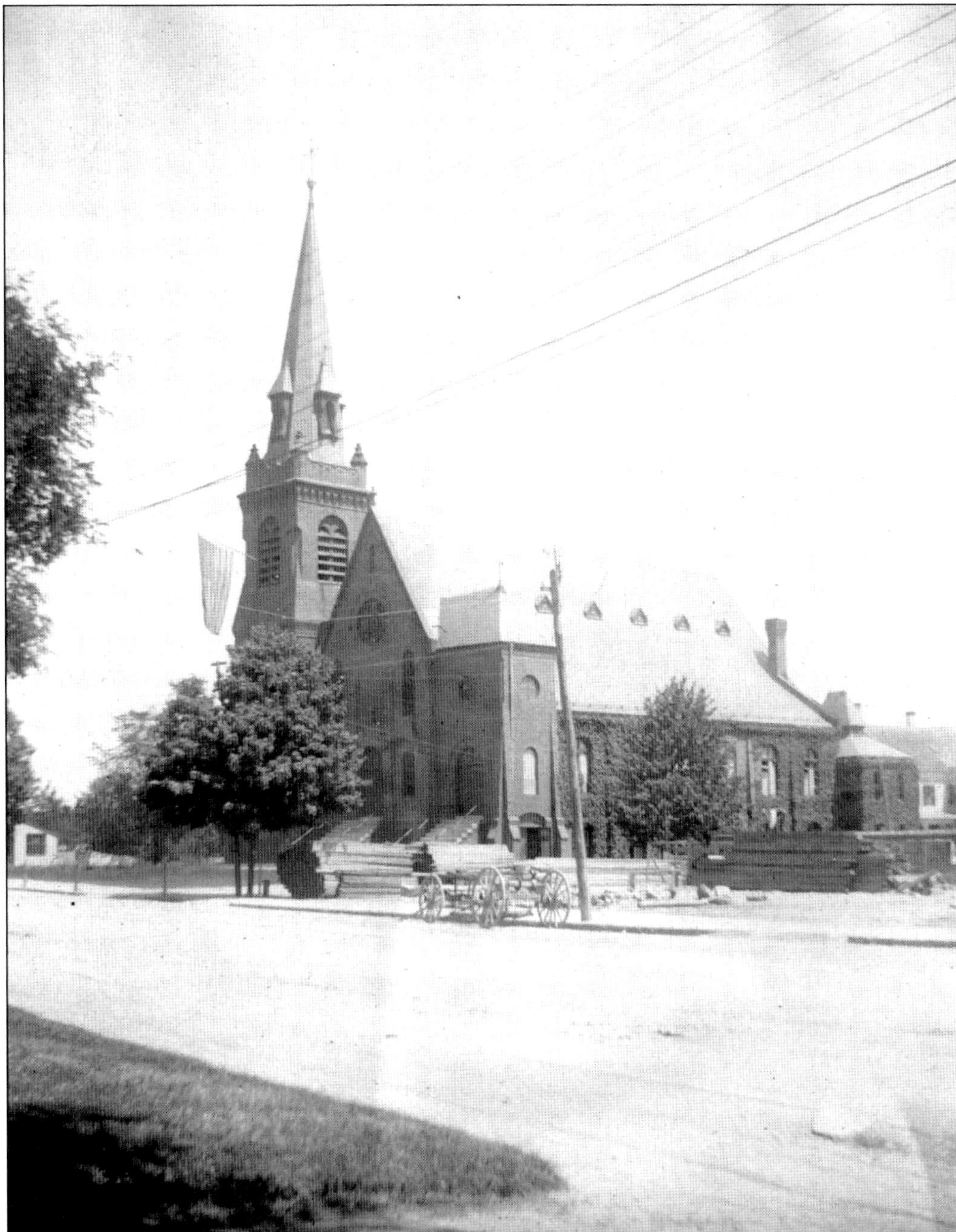

The Holy Family parish became a separate parish from St. Bridget's parish in 1883, about the same time the church building was completed. This photograph was put in the Congregational church's century box in 1901. The wagon and the building material are probably intended for the construction of the rectory next door.

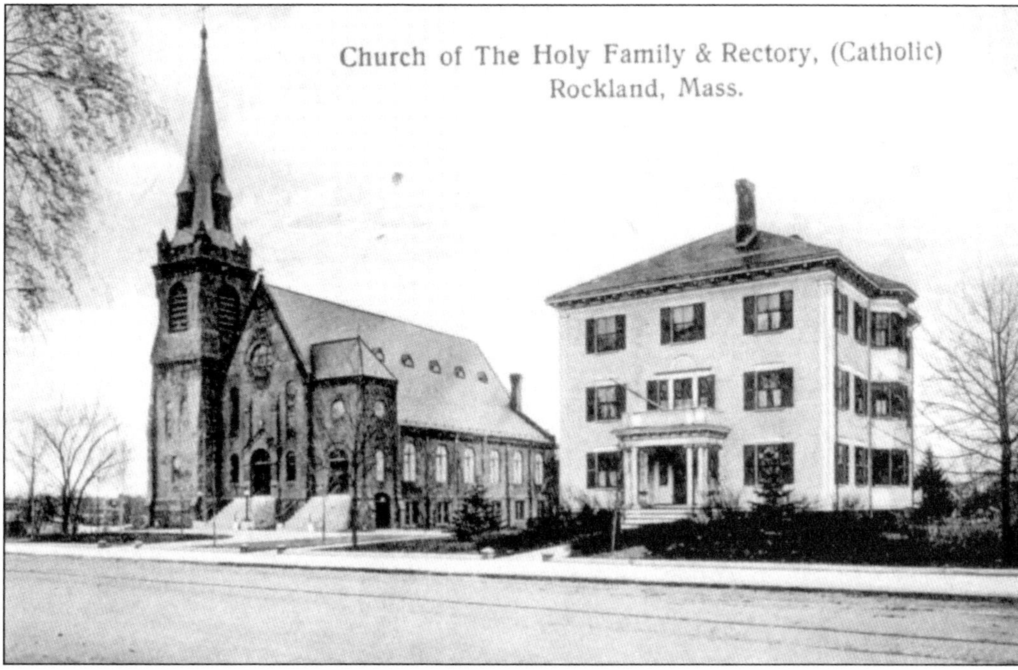

This early 20th century postcard view shows the Holy Family Church and the completed rectory. With the exception of an elevator and some landscaping, the scene is not much different than it is today. The rectory was built in 1902.

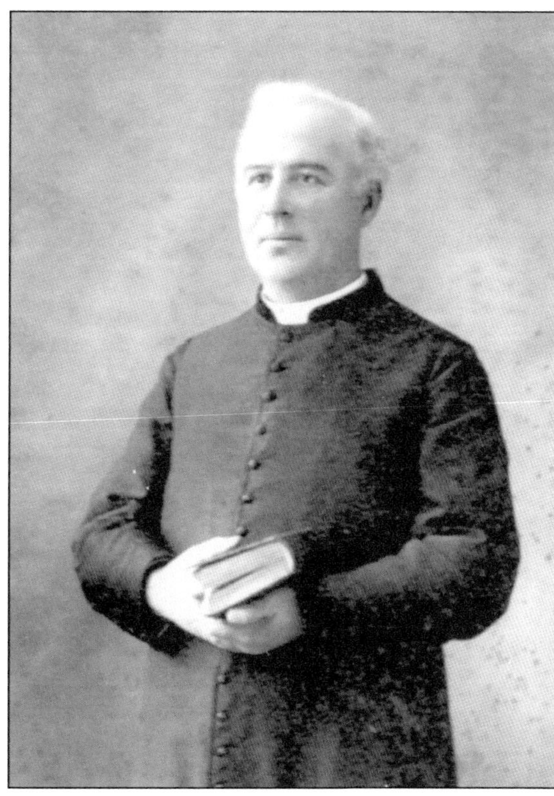

In many cases, a church's parish is only as strong as the conviction of the man or woman at its helm. For the Holy Family Church, that strength was drawn for many years from the Reverend J.H. O'Neil.

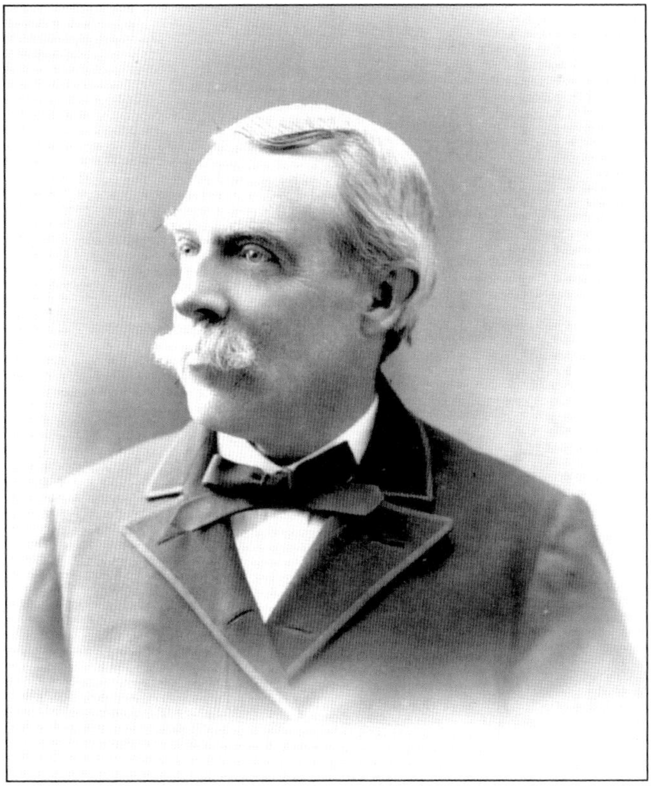

Joshua Snow Smith, a dedicated member of the First Congregational Church community, was born in Edgartown, Martha's Vineyard, in 1845, "of American parentage." He served as editor of the *Rockland Standard* for 34 years, was the first postmaster of the Rockland post office, and was elected clerk of his church in 1882. In his own words, scrawled on the back of this photograph, "The active part of my life has been spent in this community."

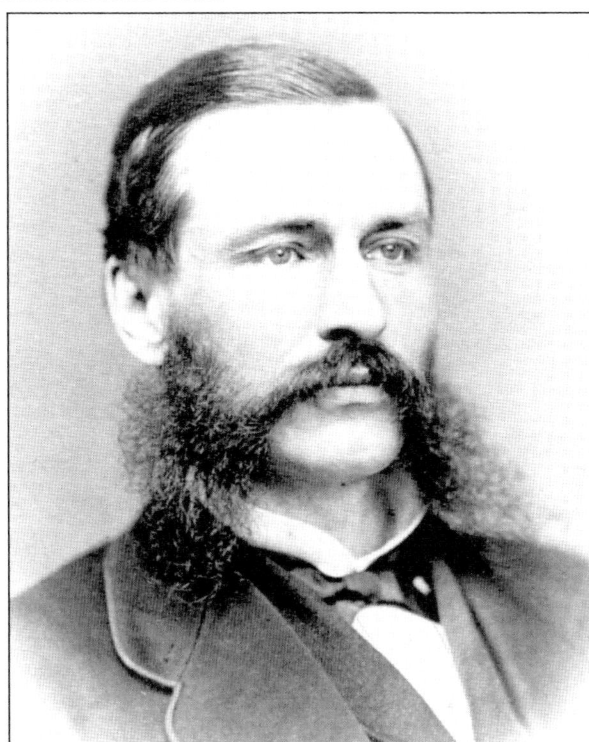

The accomplishments of Rev. Jesse Jones, especially his exploits in the Civil War (his bullet-dented breastplate is on display at the Dyer Memorial Library), could fill a book unto itself. After taking the pulpit in Rockland in front of 94 other candidates, Jones advocated the general use of cereals in the daily diet and published *The Bible Plan for the Abolition of Poverty*. After a short stay in Rockland, he moved on to even greater things in Abington.

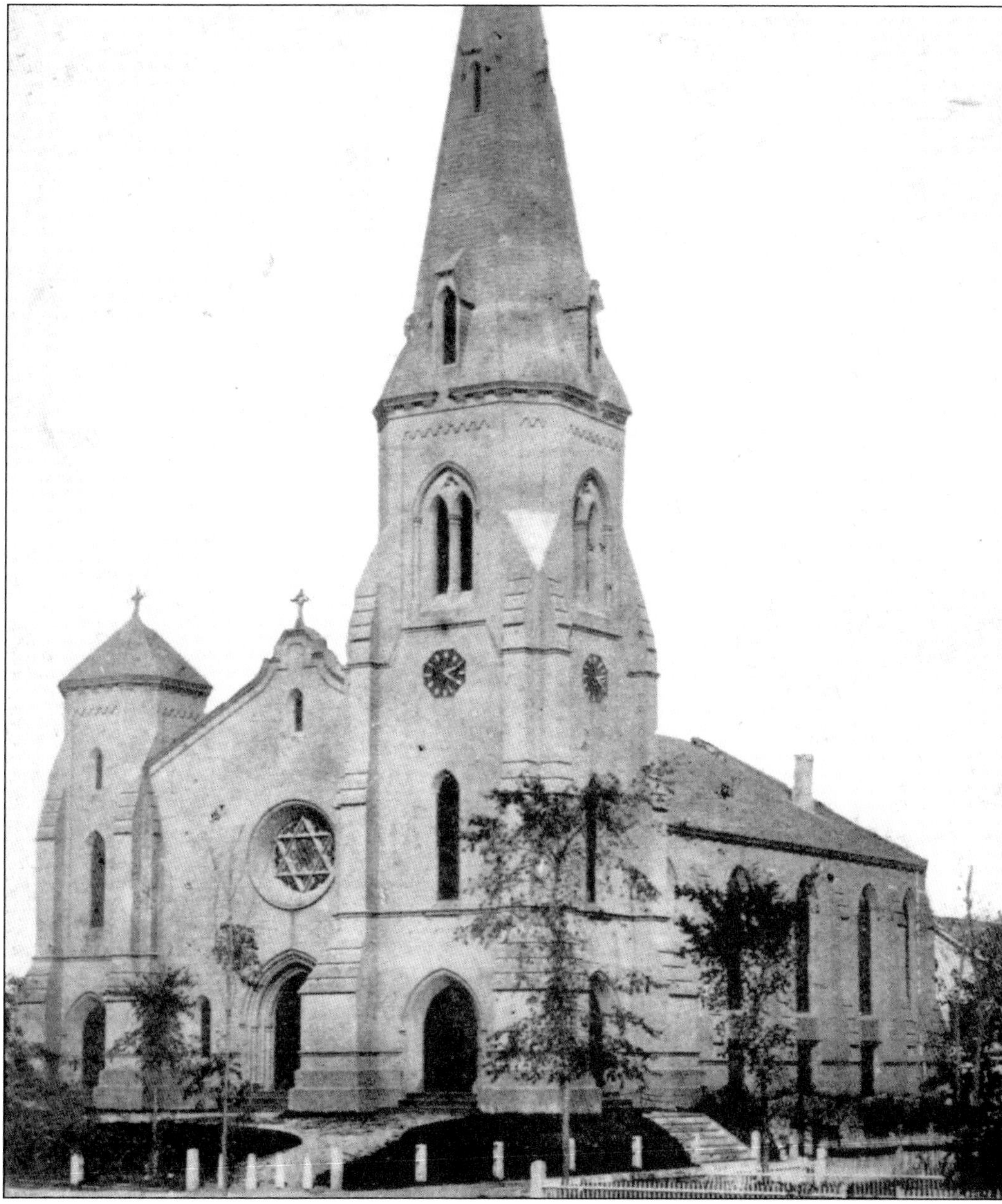

It was 1812, a pivotal year in American history, when the people of East Abington organized the third parish of the Congregational church. David Hersey gave land, and a church was built in 1813. At this time, there was not yet a road leading to the church. After some negotiation with the town and the county, Union Street was built in 1815, connecting communities in the north of town to those in the south of town. As membership grew, a larger church was needed. In 1857, the first church was moved back along Church Street and became a shoe factory, where Washington Reed made his fur-lined boots from buffalo hides. The church in this photograph was designed by Ambrose Bancroft and is known as the Brown Church because of its color. The Congregational church was a leader in the abolitionist movement before the Civil War. When Ephraim Stetson's grandson wanted to give a pulpit Bible to the new church, he was refused because of his business in the South and his feeling about slaveholders.

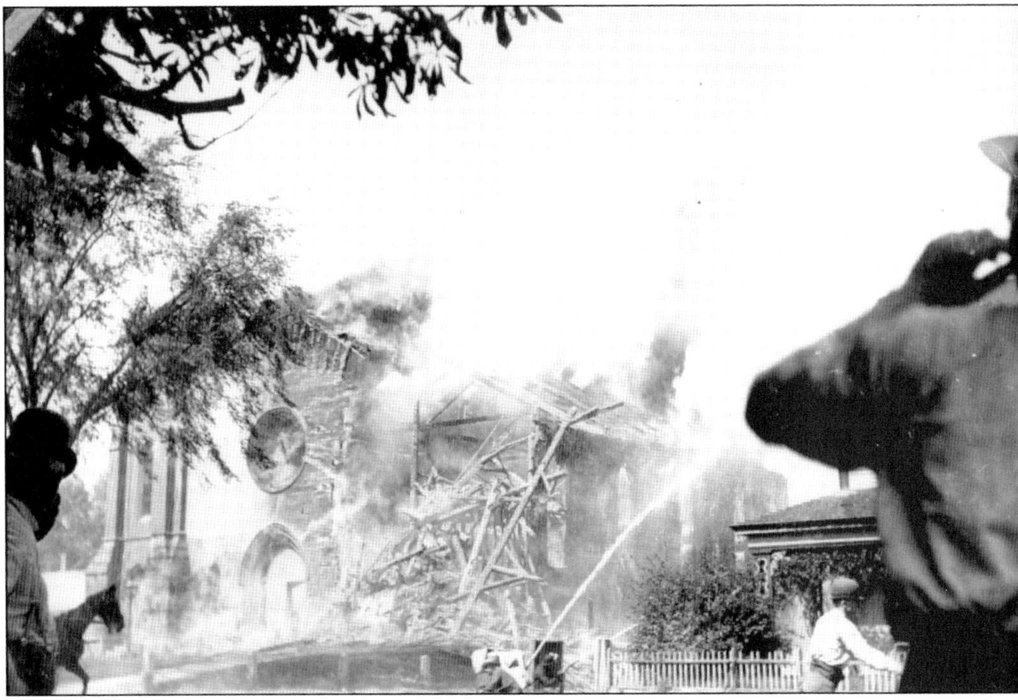

The church caught fire on July 16, 1890, when workmen were removing paint with a torch. In this photograph, the steeple is down, and the rest of the church will soon follow. The one hose on the church seems a feeble attempt to stop the fire.

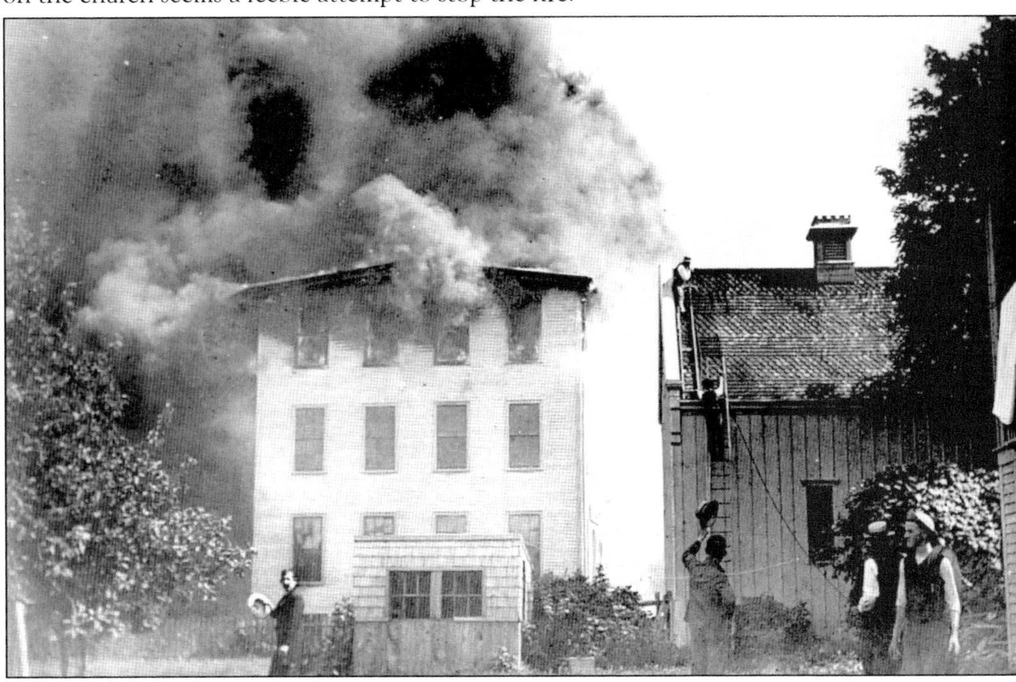

Many brave attempts were made to protect and save property during the church fire. It appears that these men do not know what to do. It is likely that the fire was bigger than the community's ability to fight it.

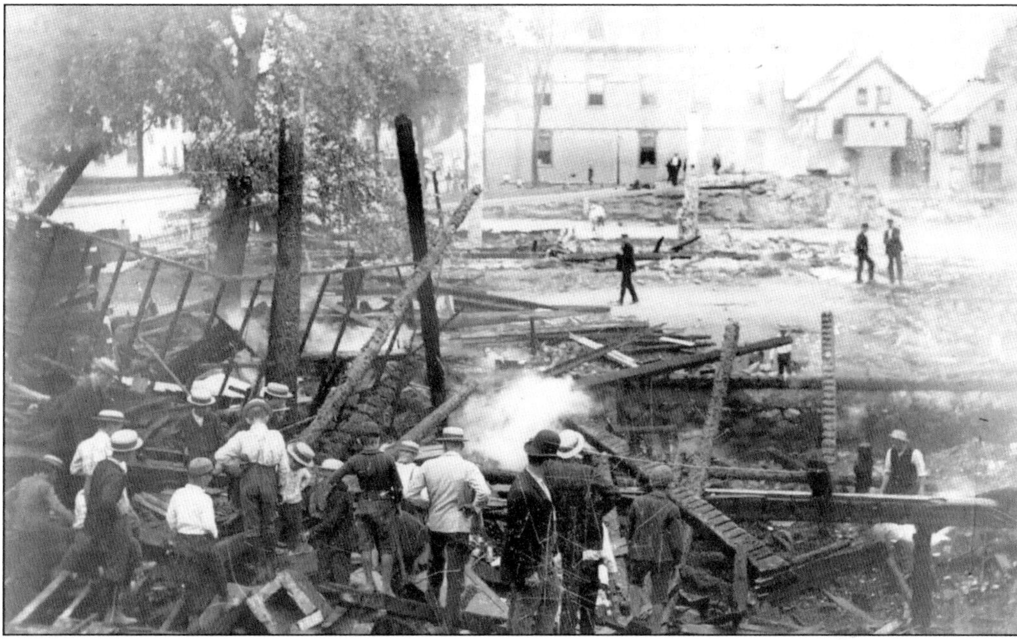

This is the day after the fire. In the background is the Webster Block, just north of the church on Union Street. This fire is the most noted of all Rockland fires. It destroyed 14 buildings in the center of town, including the original church, the Underwood Building (where the town offices were located), a school, the police lockup, factories, and homes.

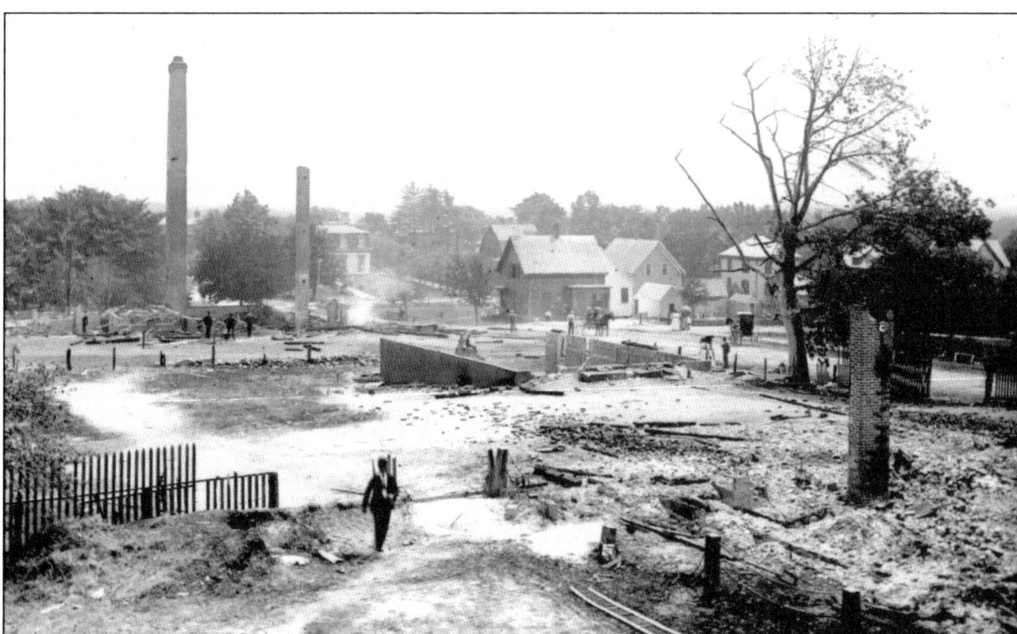

Only the smokestacks of factories that were lost and a tree that was half burned are left. The man in the foreground is coming up from the ruined factories along Church Street. After the fire, both the water system and fire department were improved to be among the finest in the area.

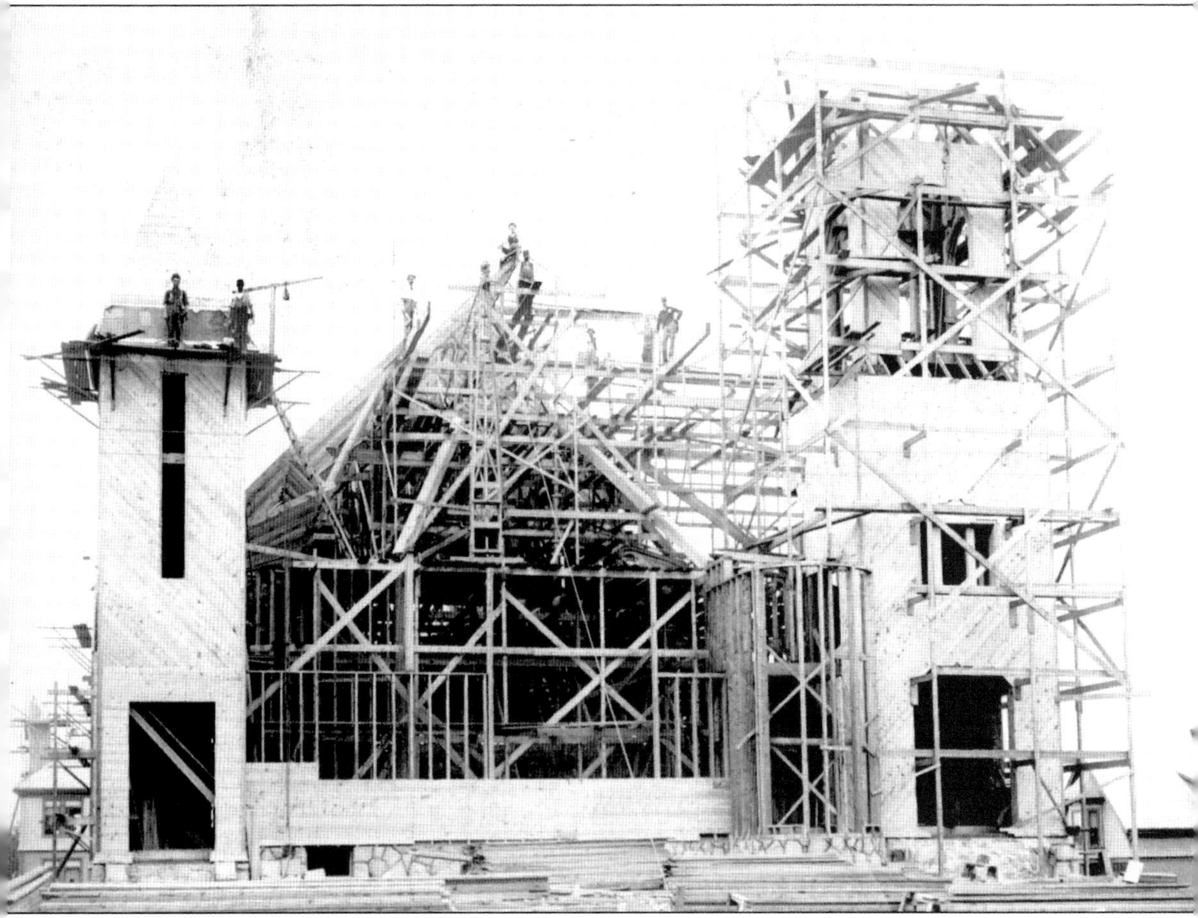

Architect Warren H. Hayes designed the third Congregational church, built in 1892 on the same site as the Brown Church. The resolves of 1842 were hung on a marble plaque in the new church. The resolves, still there today, state the congregation's continued opposition to slavery. They are: "Resolved, 1st: That the enslaving of human beings, and holding them subject to the privations necessarily involved in the chattel system is, under all circumstances, a sin against God; and against we, as a church, do bear our most decided and solemn testimony. Resolved, 2nd: That to have respect for persons in our assemblies, on account of complexion or any other outward and divinely constituted peculiarity, is directly contrary to the letter and spirit of the Gospel-a sin in those who practice it themselves or countenance it in others; a dreadful cruelty towards those who are the subjects, and ought to receive the unqualified condemnation of every Christian church. Resolved, 3rd: That we will not give our support to a man for our minister who silently or openly gives his consent to the system of American slavery, and we do, therefore, request our pastor not to invite any who do thus sustain the system to the communion or pulpit."

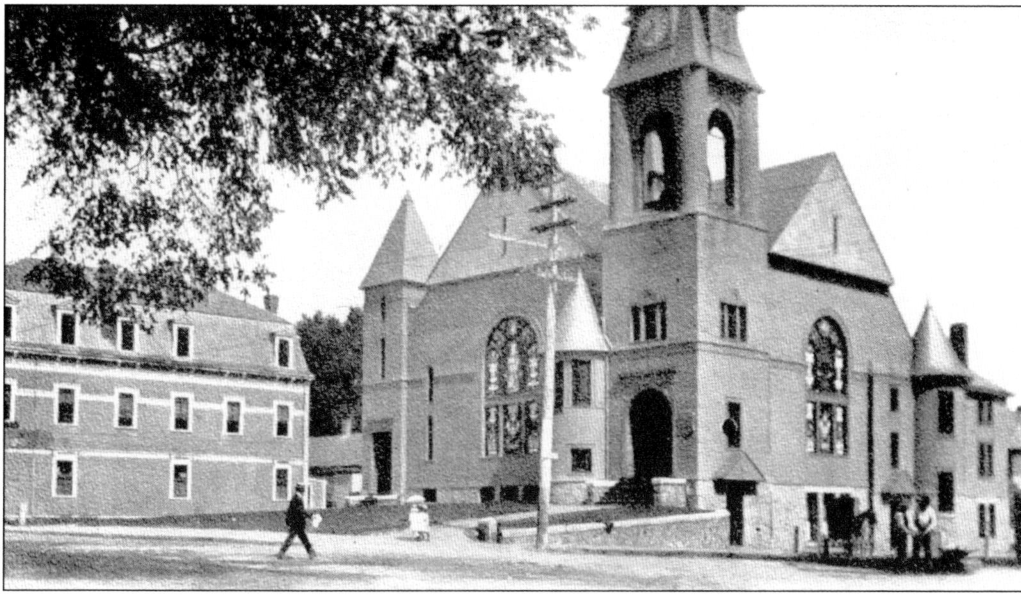

Seen here are the new church and two girls waiting to go home after a service. In 1863, a May breakfast was organized in order to supply bandages to Union soldiers in the Civil War. This May breakfast has taken place every year since. Church ladies made dresses for the church missions in Hawaii. The church also organized a time capsule in 1901 called the century box, which was kept in the Rockland Saving Bank for 100 years and opened in 2001. Some of the photographs from the box appear in this book

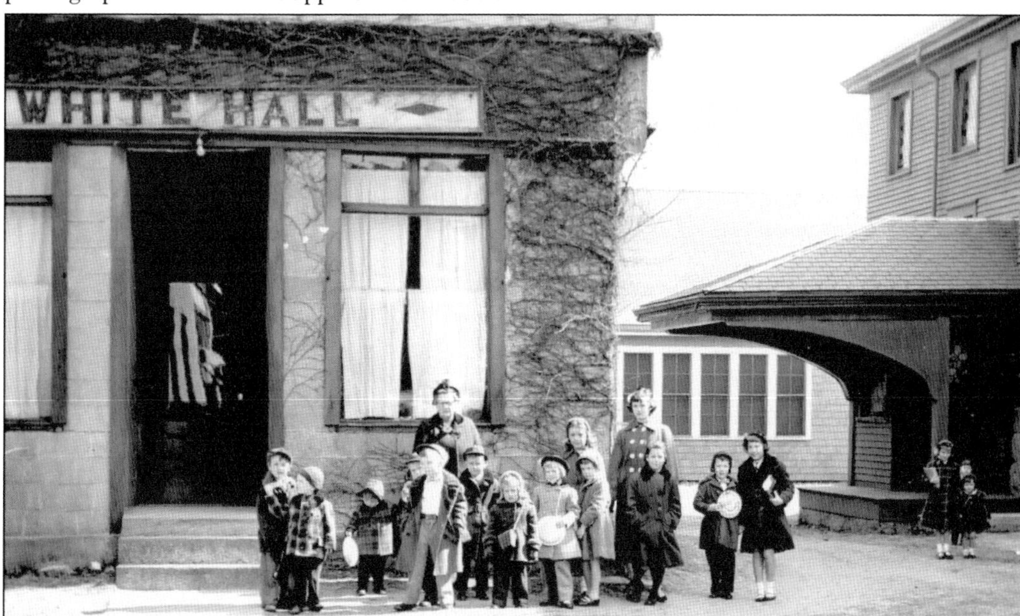

Henry M. White bought the *Rockland Standard* in 1917, and in 1922, he leased a small piece of land from the Congregational church. On the land, he built White Hall facing Union Street. The Veterans of Foreign Wars hall stands in the background. White had his office and print shop here until 1935, when he retired. The church used the building for meetings until it was razed in 1965. Here, Marjorie Barnes stops her Sunday school class for a quick photograph.

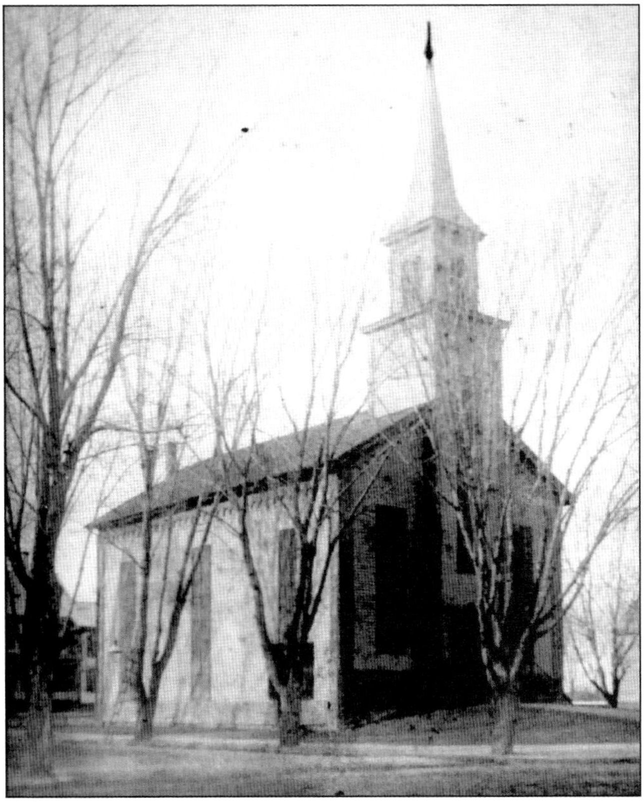

The Baptist church was built in 1856. This photograph was taken before 1892, when an addition was completed. Alonzo W. Perry's family attended the church. In 1922, Perry donated a tower clock to the church. The clock had a previous life; it came from the Bedford Building located at 99 Bedford Street in Boston, which Perry's company owned until 1982.

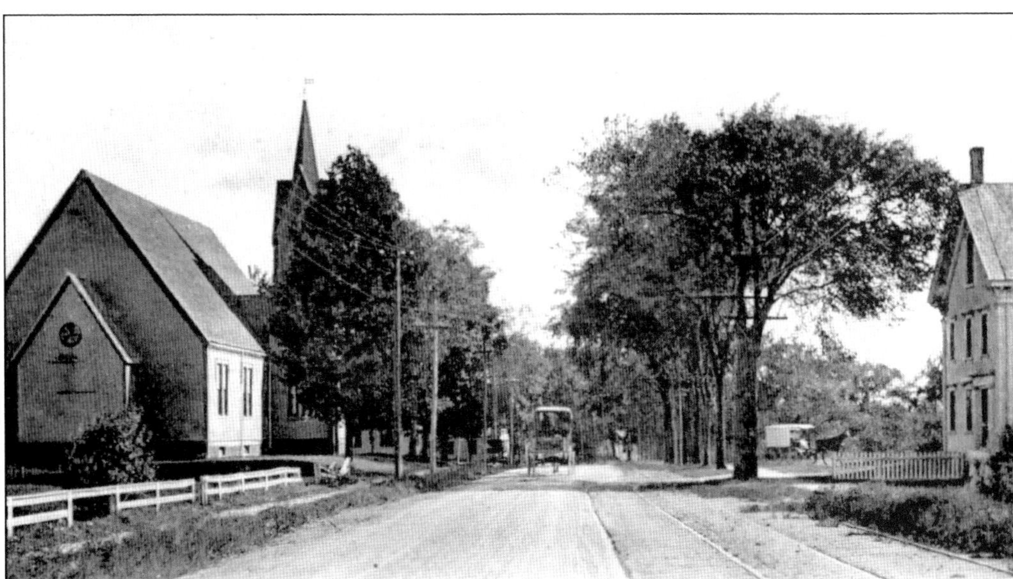

The Hatherly Methodist Episcopal Church (United Methodist) was built on Union Street in 1871. This view from a *c.* 1900 postcard shows a country scene in spite of the trolley tracks.

Five

A Community's Pride
Rockland's Municipal Buildings

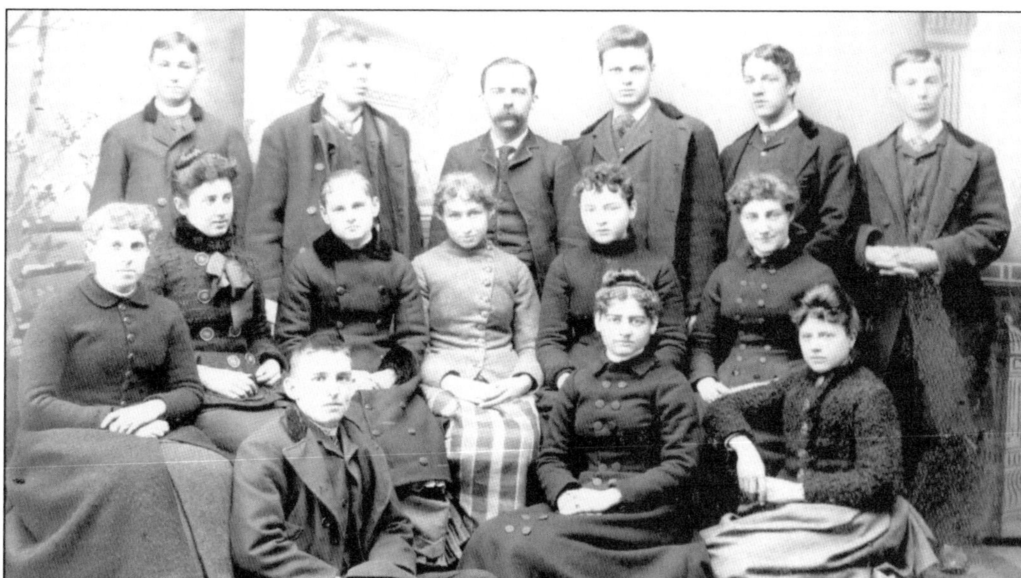

A person's true colors can be determined by how he or she treats the elderly and children. The soul of a community is similarly reflected in its design, maintenance, and treatment of its commonly owned buildings, from schools to town office buildings and more. Theodore H. Farr, longtime principal of Rockland High School, standing third from the left in this picture of the high school class of 1887, spent much of his career with the local school system, pushing for larger schools with better accommodations for his students, whom he regarded as the future of Rockland.

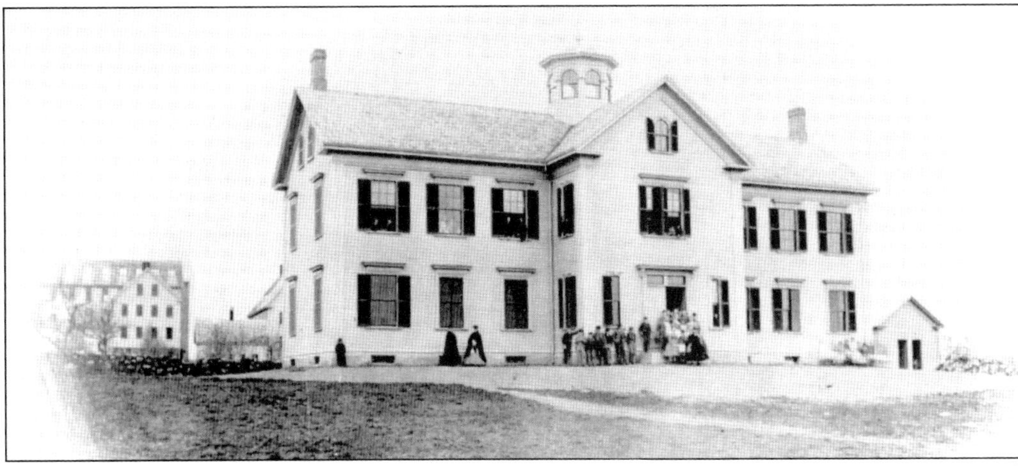

This school was unnamed when the town purchased the private road, Stetson Court, on which it sat. When the town renamed the road School Street, the school adopted the name School Street School. The school was built in 1867 and cost less than the Dunbar School that was being built in Center Abington, a fact that finally caused the break up of the old town in 1874. It served as both an elementary and high school for many years and burned in 1927, leaving a lot that remains empty today next to the Grand Army Hall.

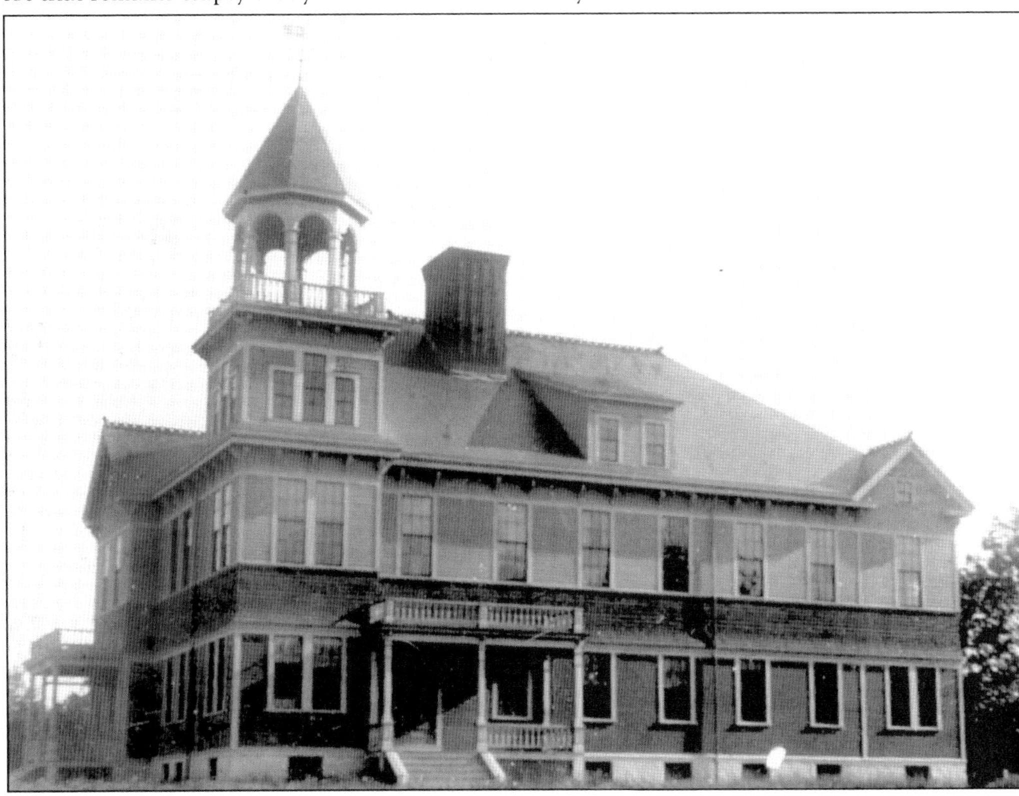

The Lincoln School, built as the town's first dedicated high school and later used as an elementary school building, featured a beautiful fourth-story tower capped by a weathervane. The building, minus the tower, stands today on the corner of Church and Howard Streets and is used by the North River Collaborative.

The Gleason School has lived many lives. It was originally located on Church Street next to the Hurley Brothers shoe factory, on the site currently occupied by the Veterans of Foreign Wars hall, behind the Congregational church. It was later moved to North Union Street. It has served as not only a school, but also a Knights of Columbus hall, Assembly of God church, and even a bra factory. It remains today as a two-unit condominium.

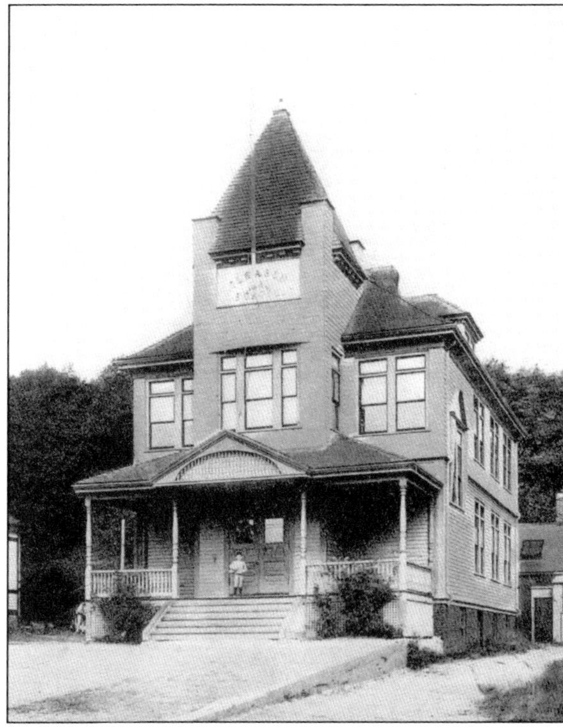

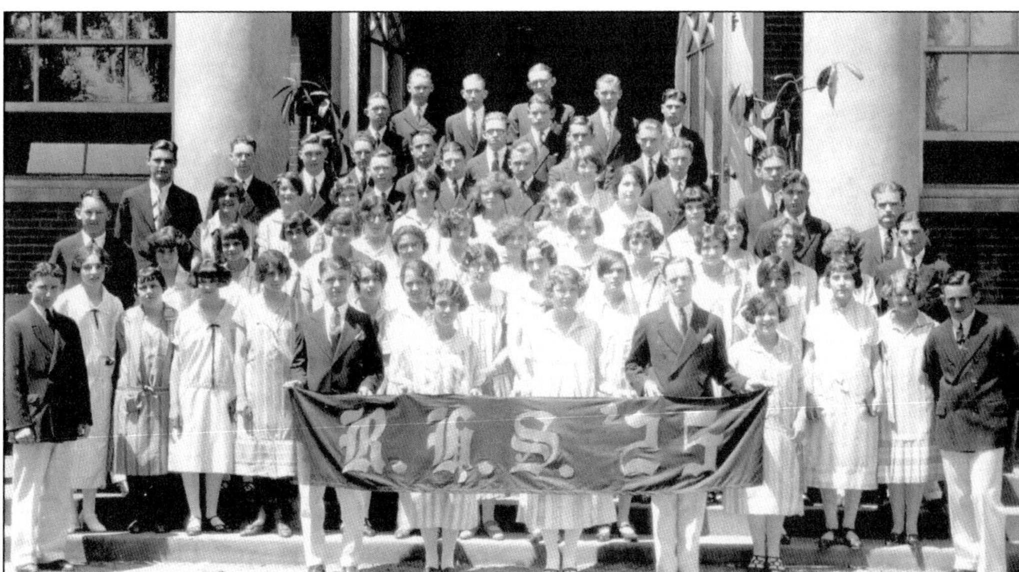

As Rockland grew in the late 19th and early 20th centuries, so too did its class sizes and the need for bigger school buildings. The class of 1887 graduated with a total of 14 students. Less than half a century later, the class of 1925 held three times as many young scholars. They matriculated at the town's second dedicated high school building, now known as the McKinley School, built in 1908. A third high school building was built in 1928, and a fourth was built in 1960.

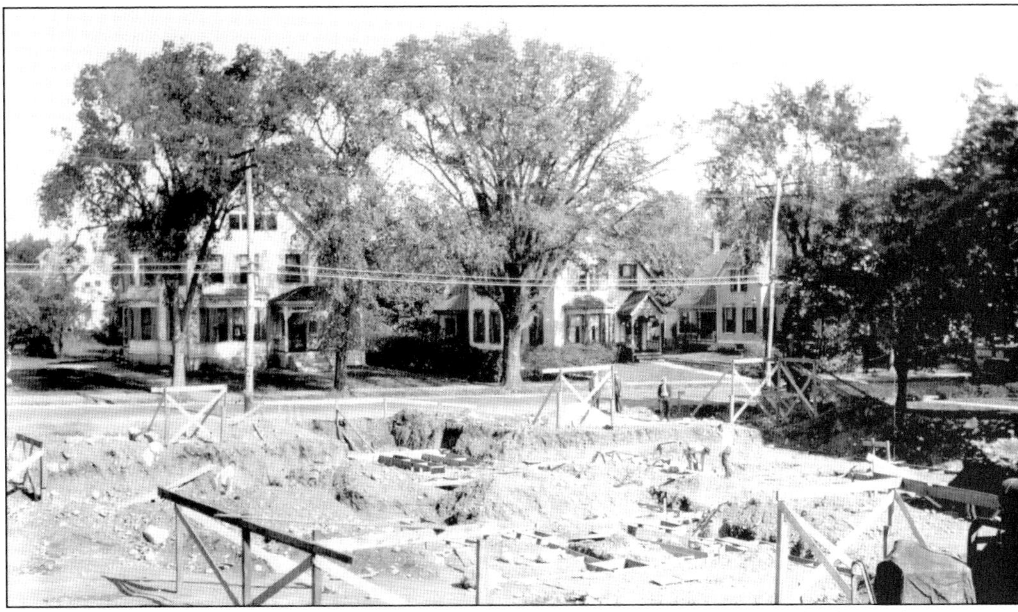

East Abington's first post office opened on June 15, 1831, with Goddard Reed serving as postmaster. The East Abington post office closed on March 13, 1874, after the town was incorporated. It reopened the same day as the Rockland post office under postmaster Joshua Snow Smith. A second post office, in the Hatherly section, operated from February 16, 1887, to April 30, 1906, opening under original postmaster Thomas H. Burke.

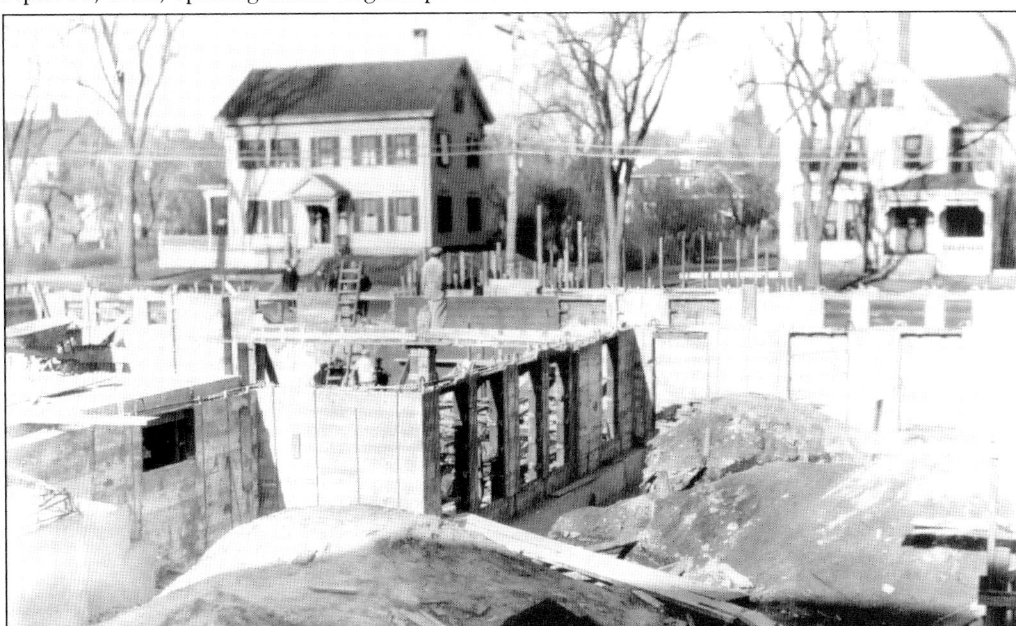

The current post office building was the first structure built by the federal government in the town of Rockland. It was designed by J. William Beals, the same architect that drew up plans for the Dyer Memorial Library in Abington and the Abington Savings Bank. Here, as the foundation for the new building on Webster Street cures, "sidewalk superintendents" have started to gather to critique the finer architectural points.

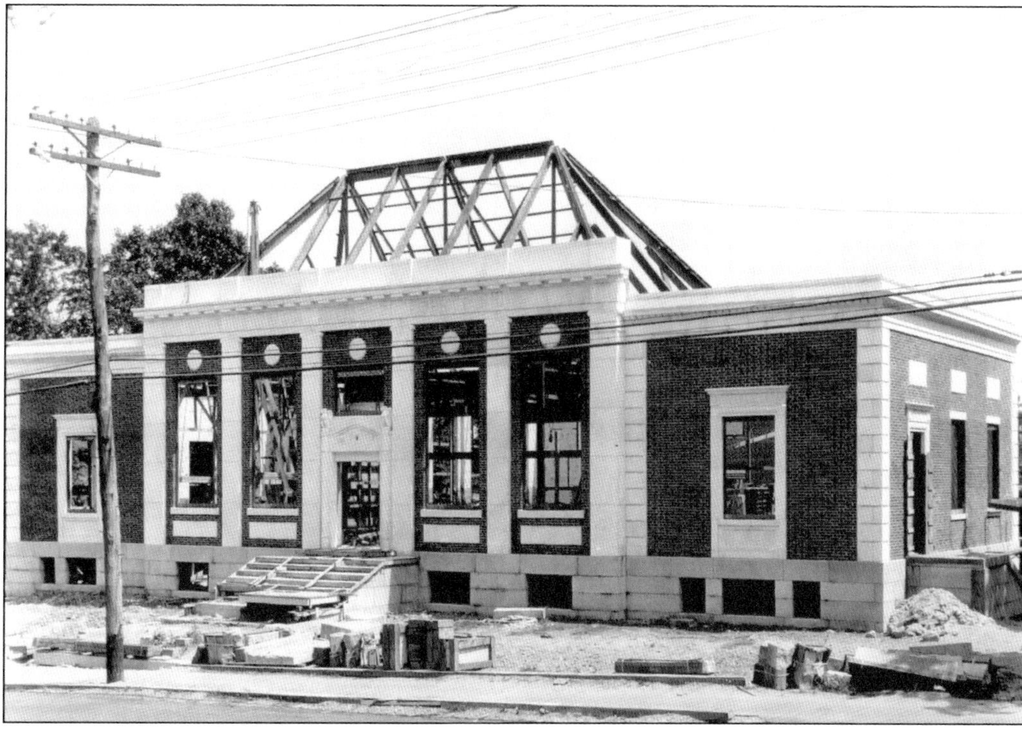

The post office building sits on a site formerly occupied by a doctor's office. Dr. Joseph Frame, who later moved into the big Second Empire home at 144 Webster Street, worked first on that spot. In this picture, taken on July 1, 1933, contractors J.G. Roy and Sons have nearly completed the granite, marble, and brick structure.

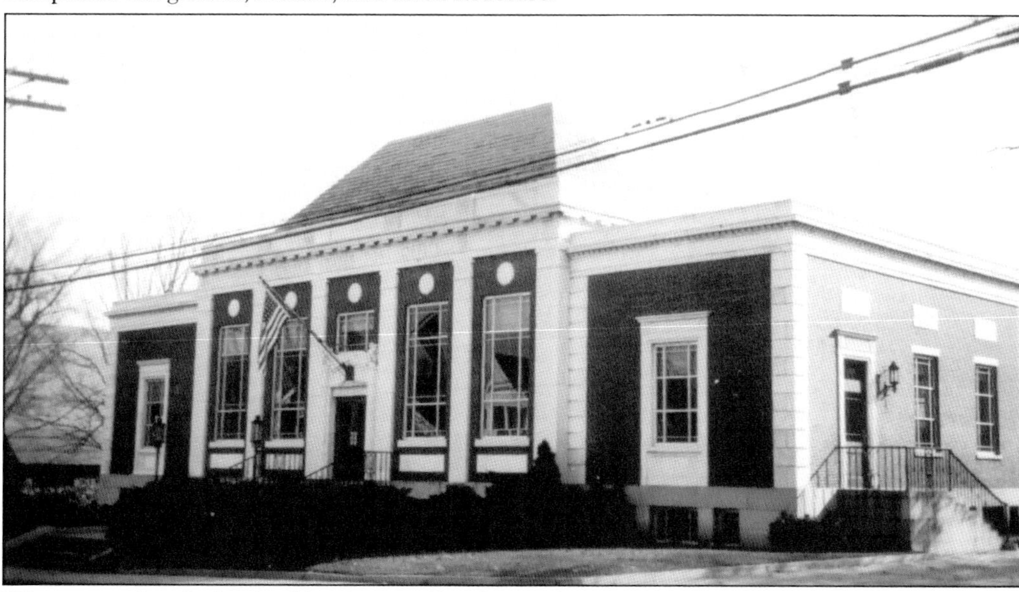

When completed, the Rockland post office fit neatly into a quaint neighborhood featuring the C.L. Rice Funeral Home, the Unitarian church, and two small cottages, one noticeable for its Gothic-style windows. Although now nearly seven decades old, the building still serves the community well.

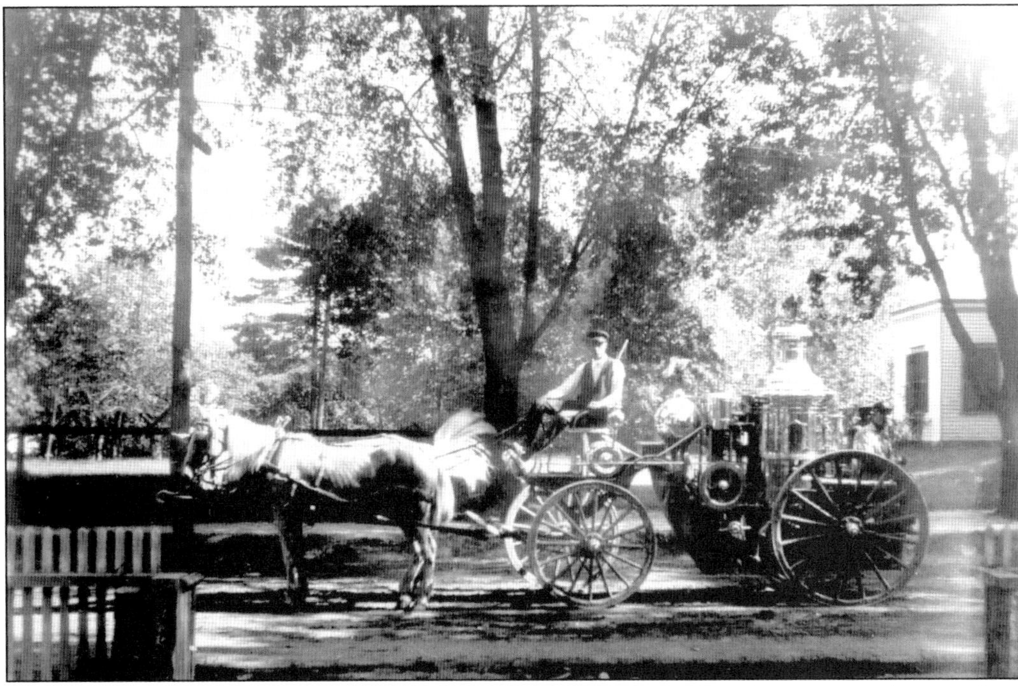

Rockland learned its lesson after the 1890 Brown Church fire. Already blessed with many local men who vowed to respond whenever a conflagration threatened life and property, the town purchased a state-of-the-art La France steam fire engine at a cost of $3400 in 1894. Delivered on Friday, March 9, 1894, one day before the 20th anniversary of the town's incorporation, it was immediately put to use fighting Rockland's many fires.

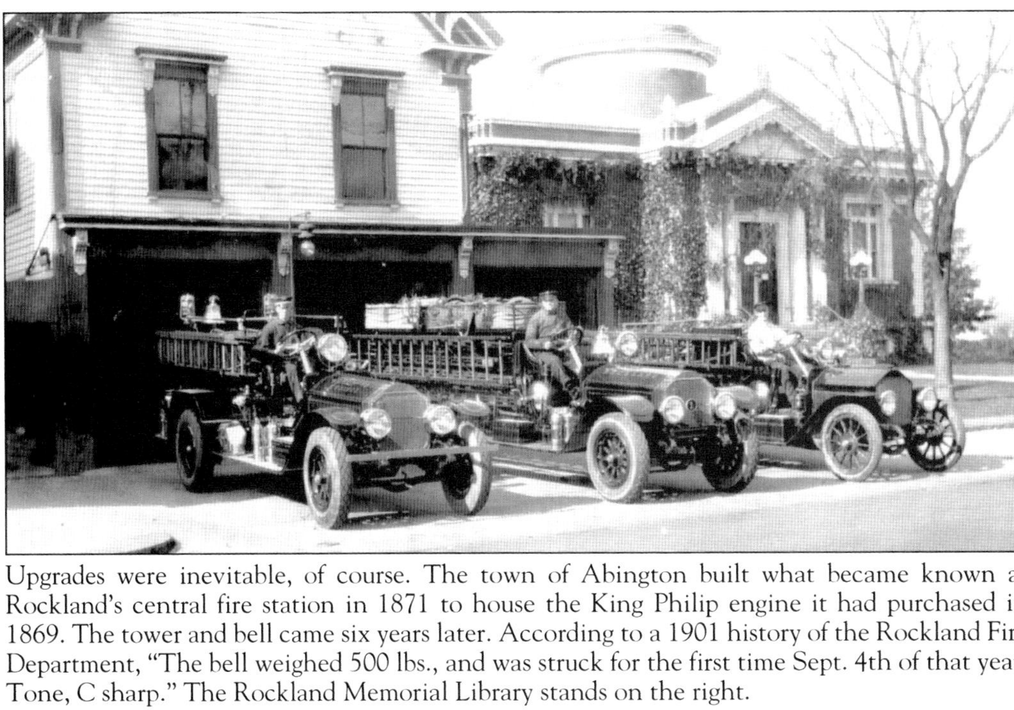

Upgrades were inevitable, of course. The town of Abington built what became known as Rockland's central fire station in 1871 to house the King Philip engine it had purchased in 1869. The tower and bell came six years later. According to a 1901 history of the Rockland Fire Department, "The bell weighed 500 lbs., and was struck for the first time Sept. 4th of that year. Tone, C sharp." The Rockland Memorial Library stands on the right.

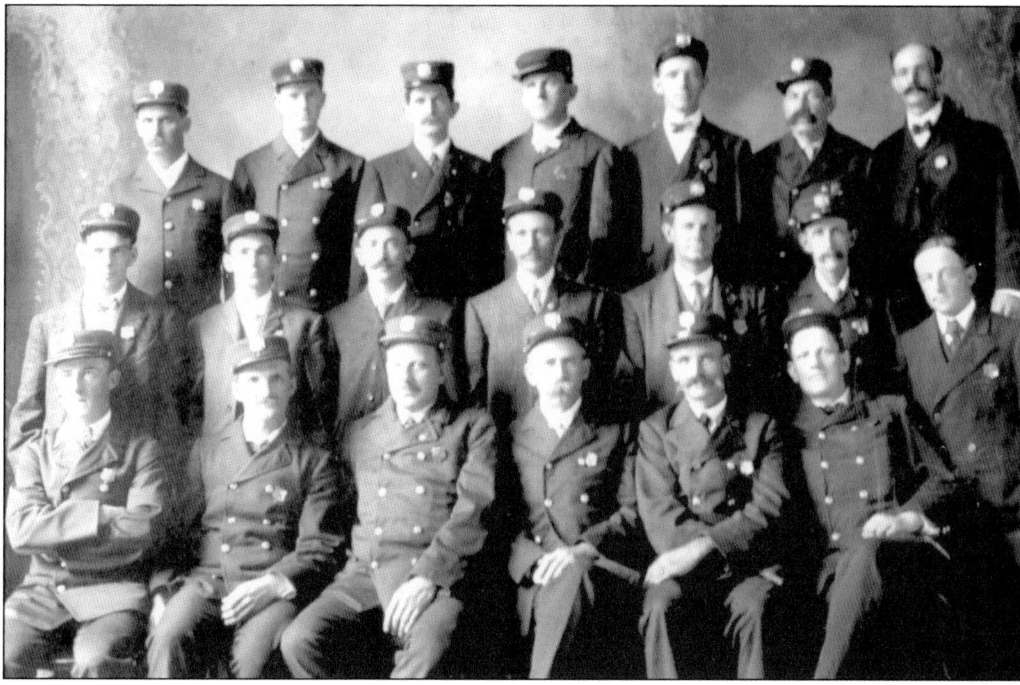

Rockland's bravest are seen here. They are, from left to right, as follows: (front row) Lorenzo Gilson, Hiram Babcock, Fayette Briggs, Frank Shaw, Abram Wright, and Charles W. Briggs; (middle row) ? Gurney, Frank Hammond, Tony Miller, Andy Locke, George Fish, G. Stetson, and unidentified; (back row) Robert Norris, Seth Chandler, Fred Chandler, Bert Chandler, George Sheldon, Ethan Simmons, and Chester Valedge.

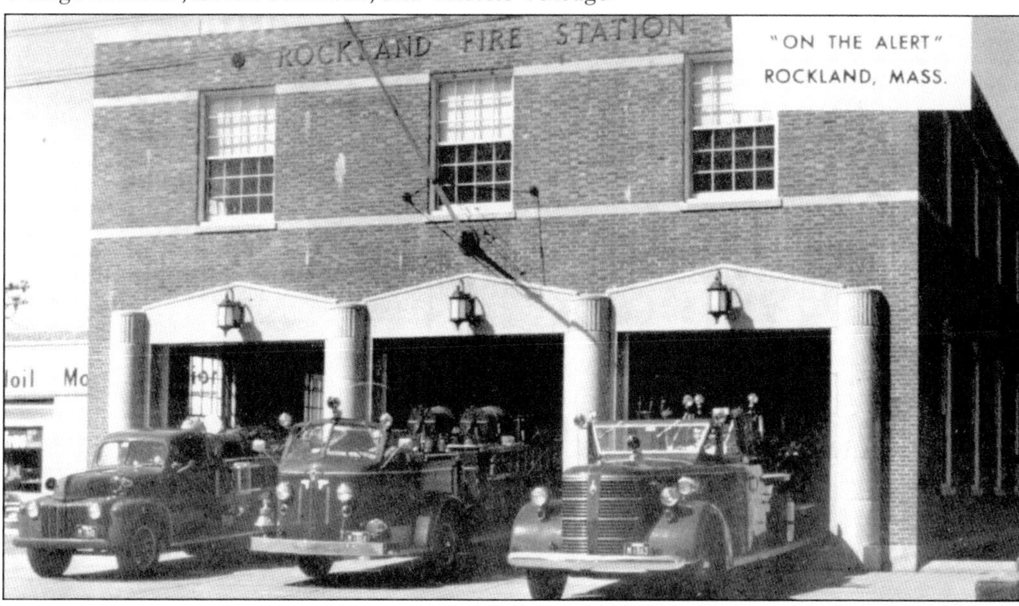

As the King Philip and La France steamers gave way to newer engines, the older central fire station gave way to a new building, as shown in this 1940s view. Local men employed by the Works Progress Administration, one of the relief effort programs of President Roosevelt's New Deal during the Depression, built the modern facility in 1939.

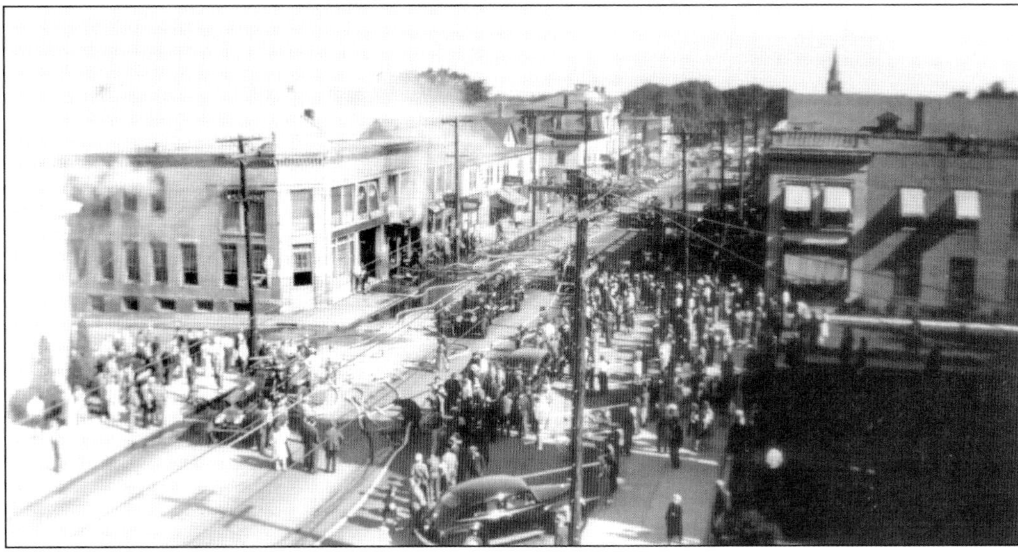

One of Union Street's biggest blazes took place in June 1941. Fruit-store owner Giacomo Figlioli opened the door to his establishment in the Gladstone Building, at that time also the home of the Rockland town offices. The space was formerly occupied by C.L. Rice's furniture company. He noticed smoke coming from the rear of the building, and when he opened his store's back door, "flames burst forth in his face," according to the *Rockland Standard* of June 12. Joseph Feeney, passing by the building, pulled the alarm on box 14, calling the Rockland Fire Department to the scene.

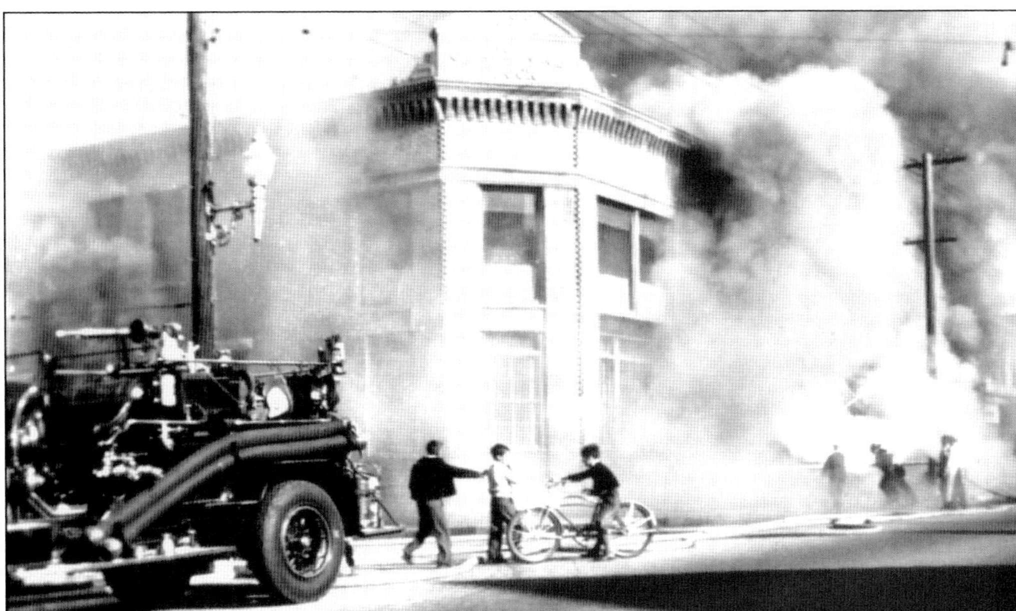

Chief Clyson Inkley immediately called for backup help from the Abington and Brockton fire departments. Fearing that the fire would jump to the Lincoln Block to the north, he placed men on top of the building, but the brick wall of the Gladstone Building held the fire in place. Spectators young and old crowded the scene, but stayed back far enough to allow the men of the department to do their work.

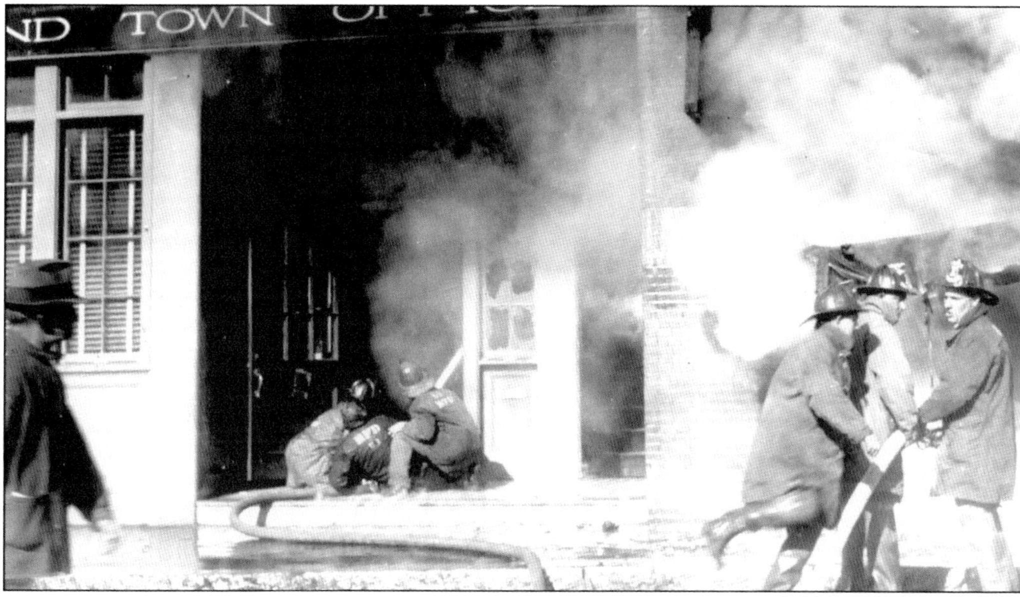

According to the *Standard*, "Much concern was felt over the town records, but they were locked in the safes and also the big vault at the rear of the building. While the ceiling was burned away and the heat was intense there was very little of the woodwork burned in the town offices. The falling embers ignited papers on the desks in the offices of the town clerk, the town treasurer, the assessors department and the water department and also in the selectmen's offices in the front of the building. The typewriters and counting machines were ruined by the heat, the keys curling up like paper. None of the filing cases were hurt."

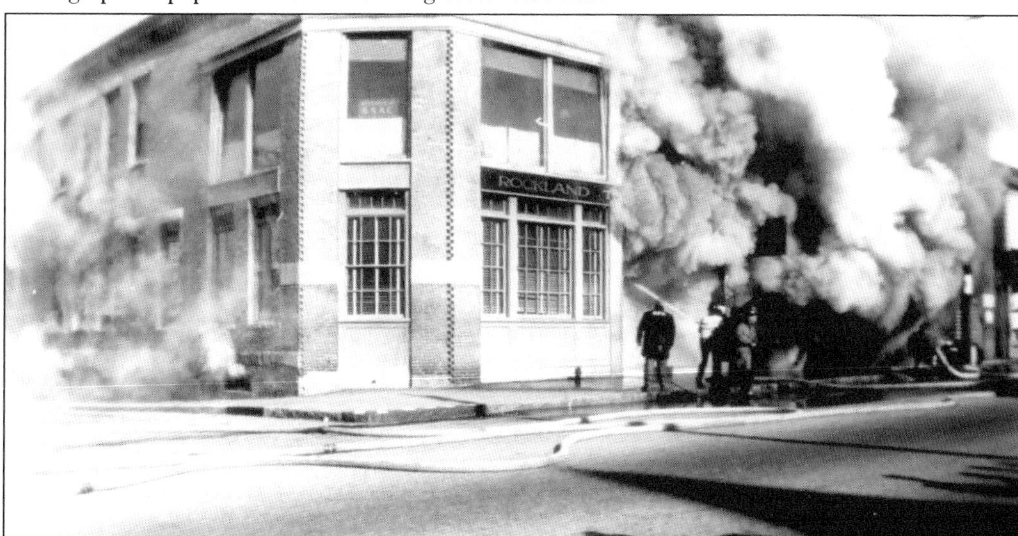

In all, the town offices and other users of the space in the Gladstone Block suffered about $50,000 damage. The fronts of Figlioli's fruit store and the waiting room were scorched. The Works Progress Administration's office in the basement received some water damage, while the quarters of the Rockland Aerie of Eagles, John Fucillo's barbershop, the Philip Collins insurance agency, and Charles D. Burke's law office were mostly affected by smoke. The town temporarily moved its offices into the Lincoln Block after the fire.

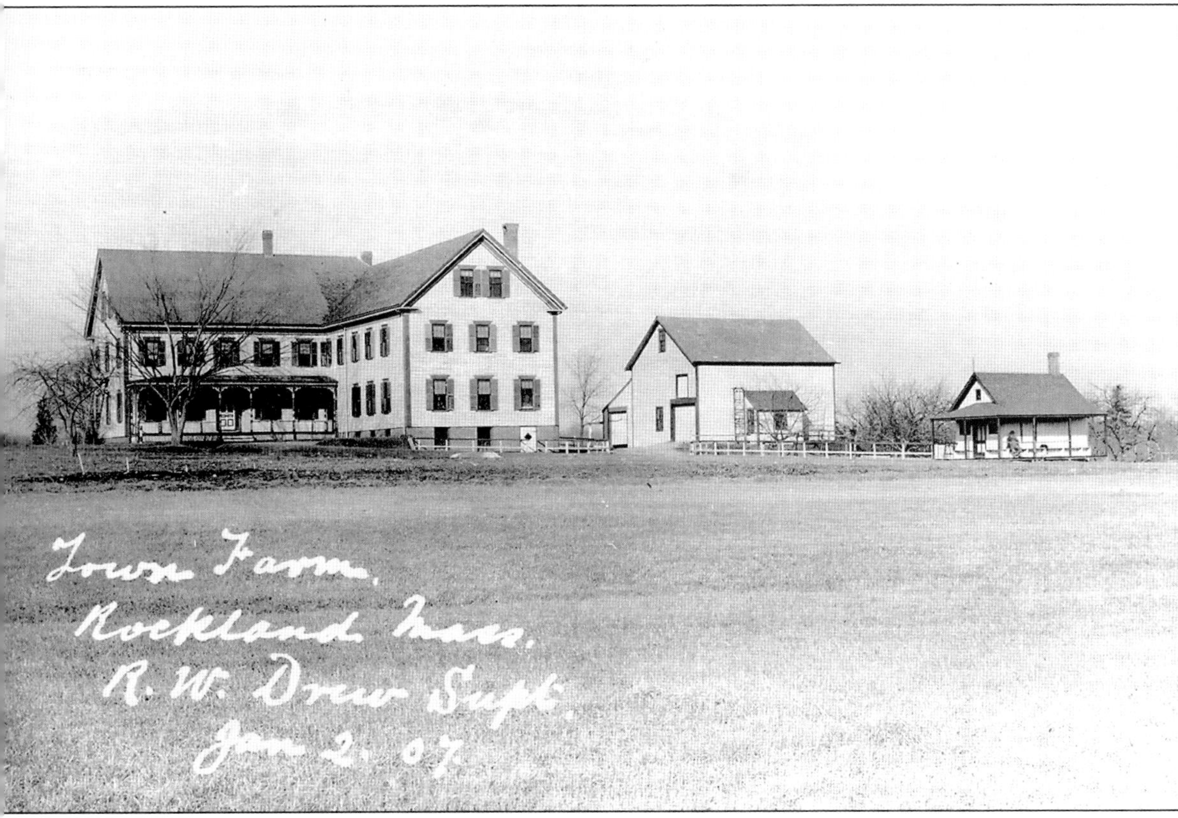

Although the village of East Abington had grown economically strong enough by 1874 to break away from its sister villages and form its own town, some residents remained destitute. Nine years after the Civil War, every community in America was caring for its wounded sons, some of which had given arms, legs, or more to the Union or Confederate causes. It was up to each community to best deal with its transients and those men and women who were unable to support themselves. One of the first acts taken by the people of the new town of Rockland was to maintain an almshouse, or poorhouse, to take care of its less fortunate citizens. The site selected was a farm on the corner of Beech Hill and Spring Street. Still standing today as the headquarters of the North River Educational Collaborative, the structure is listed on the National Register of Historic Places.

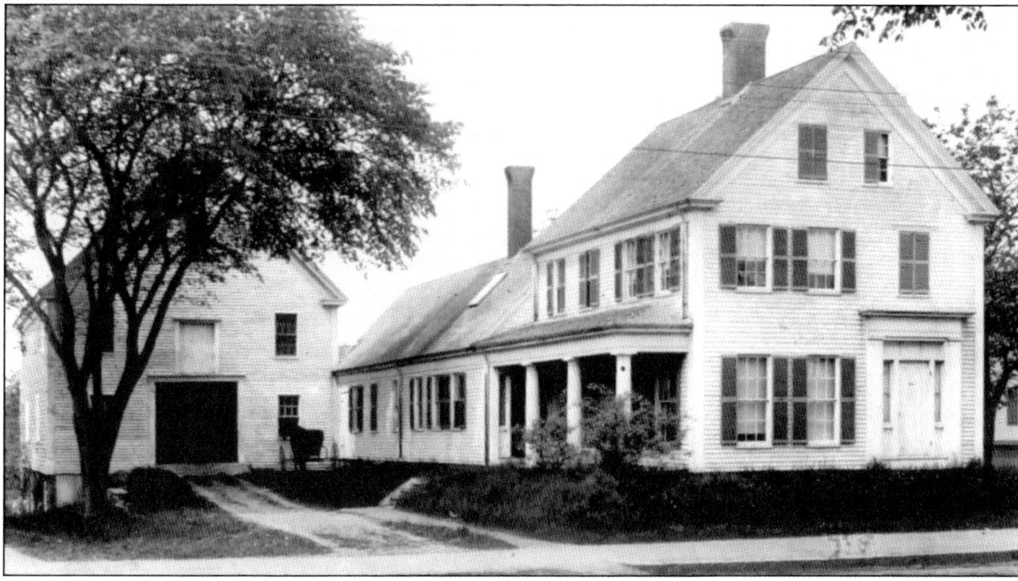

Rockland also found a way to memorialize its Civil War soldiers for all time through the construction and dedication of the Rockland Memorial Library. First, the town purchased and moved this house, owned by the Studley family, to Belmont Street to make room on the corner of Union and Belmont Streets. Previous to this time, the Rockland Memorial Library existed in a number of temporary locations, having purchased the 2,433 volumes of the private Rockland Library Association in 1878.

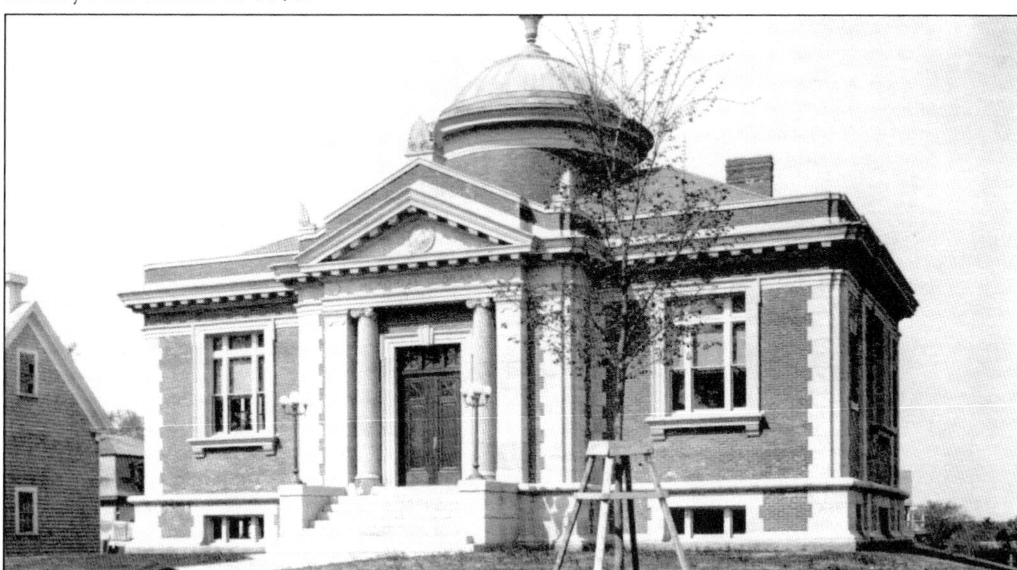

In 1902, steel magnate and philanthropist Andrew Carnegie donated $12,500 to the town to build a library building. Socialist protesters, angry at Carnegie, tried to stop the plan from coming to fruition, but newspaperwoman Hulda Barker Loud soothed the situation with well-chosen words. A.W. Perry served as the chairman of the building committee. Completed in 1905, the library could truly be described as a temple of knowledge and a temple of the people. The front vestibule and rotunda served as memorial space to Rockland's Civil War veterans. A 1992 addition increased the library's usable space by 600 square feet.

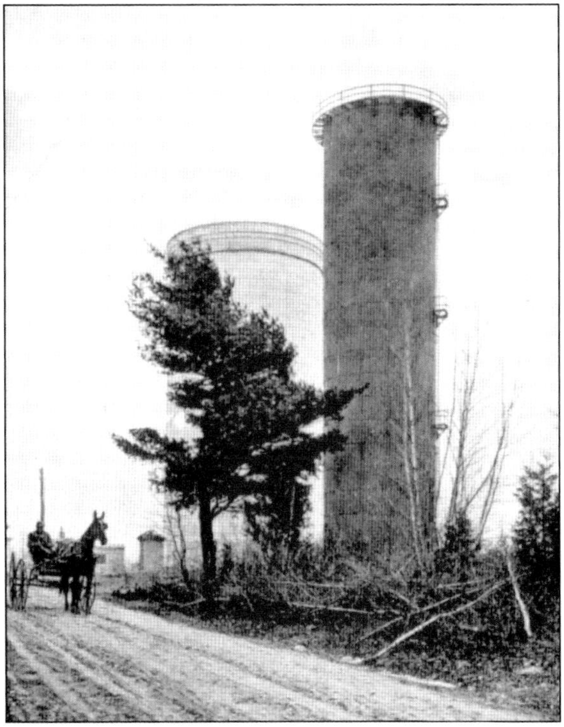

Five years before the Brown Church fire, Rockland and Abington formed a joint water works, providing for water needs for both communities with the construction of a steel standpipe on Beech Hill in 1885. Later, in 1912, a second concrete tower was constructed alongside the first. A third water tank, built in the Rice Park area, played a key role in the 1941 Gladstone Building fire, pumping 100,000 gallons of water onto the flames.

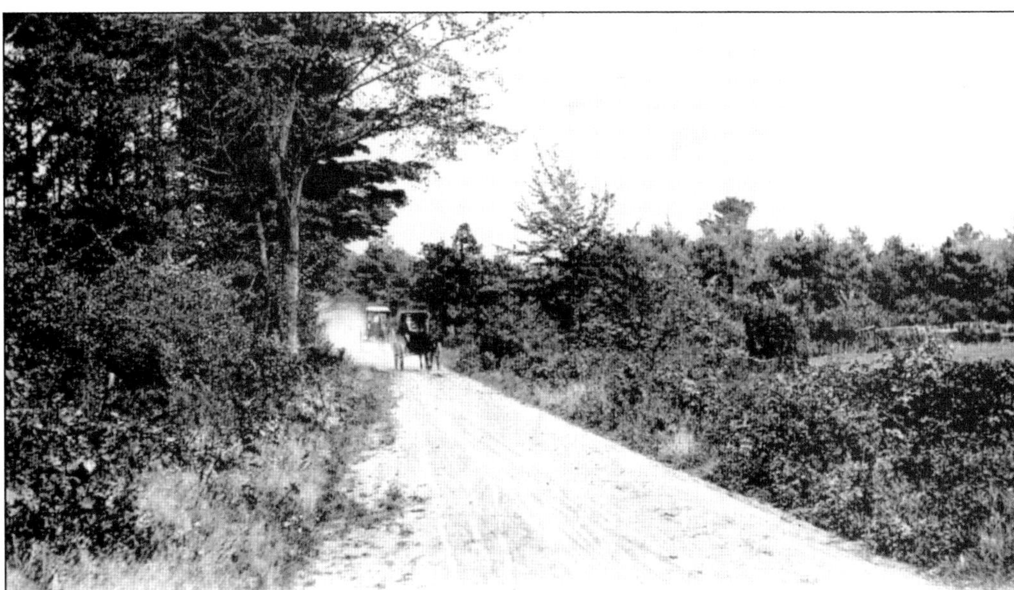

A ride down Summer Street, a connecting road running East to West between Hanover and Abington and crossing Beech Street, looks very different today. But at the time the first standpipe was built, dusty roads and horse-drawn carriages were the norm. Even with the ever-increasing activity on Union Street, some sections of Rockland remained rural, creating challenges for the town fathers in relation to their support through schooling, fire, and police protection, and other social services. Through hard work, Rockland persevered.

Six

GOOD TIMES, BAD TIMES

ROCKLAND EVENTS

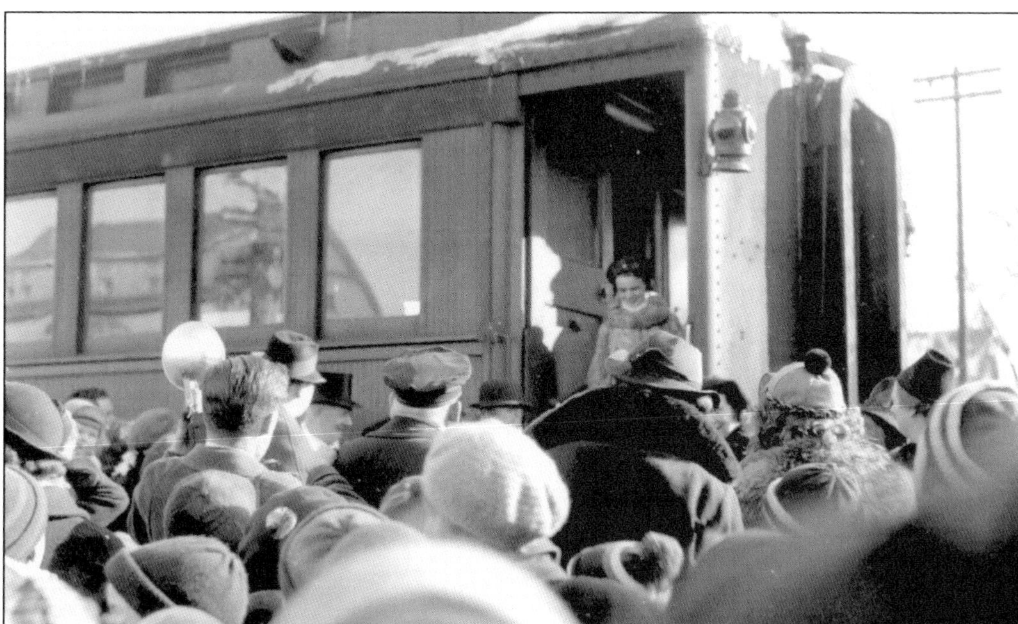

If there was not a fire burning somewhere in Rockland in the period between 1874 and 1956, there was probably a parade passing by. The citizenry in those days seemed to understand the value of stepping back from the workbench and blowing off some steam. Every gathering depicted in the following pages had a specific and appropriate purpose, like an anniversary celebration, a charity event, or the time the "movie queen" came to town.

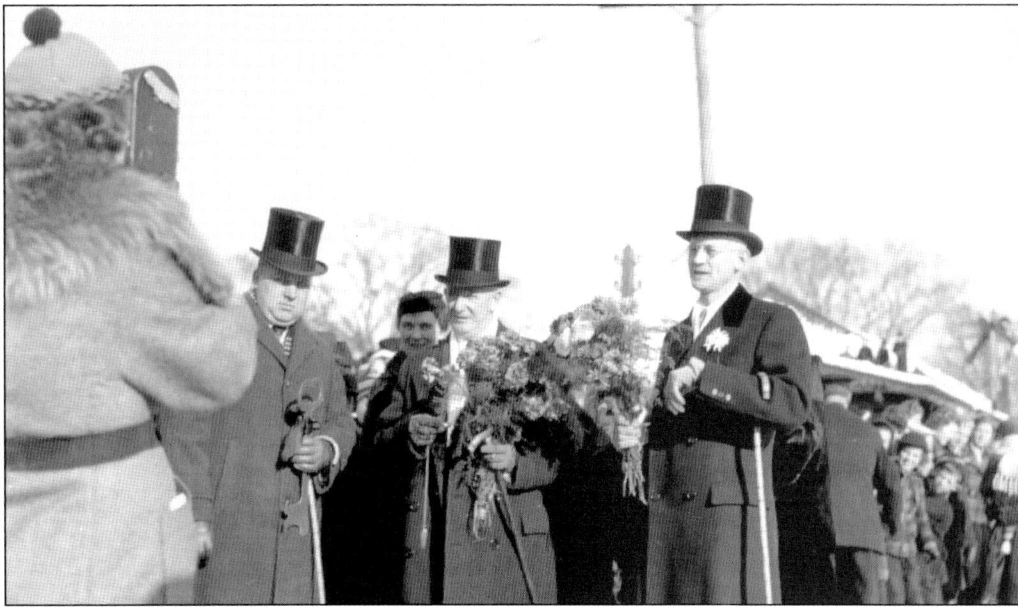

She was not a real Hollywood movie star, but for a short time in 1938, Rockland's Natalie Holbrook was able to pretend she was. Independent filmmaker Margaret Cram Showalter, shown on the left with her 16-millimeter camera, brought her well-tested script to town and put out a casting call for a "see-yourself-in-pictures" genre film, *The Movie Queen*. The selectmen, of course, were the first to heed the call.

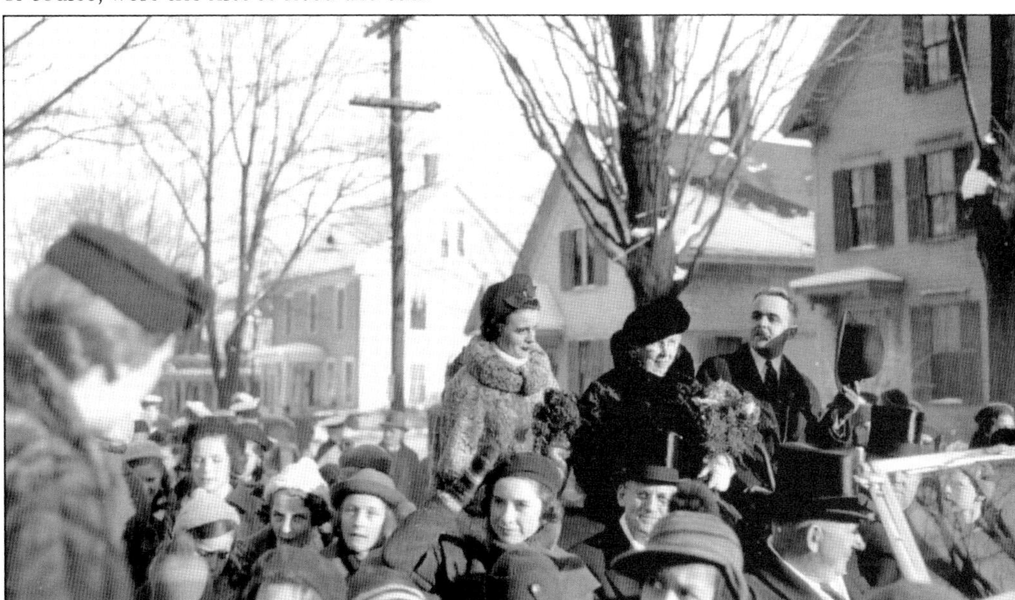

According to the script, Mary Brown, played by Holbrook, wins a contest by writing an essay about her petunia garden and is given a free trip to Hollywood. Upon arrival in Tinseltown, she is mistaken for the great Russian actress, Marlena Slarbo, and treated like royalty. When she returns to her home town she is greeted with a parade and carried through the streets with her mother, played by Mrs. George Hurley, and her high-powered Hollywood agent, played by Dana Collins.

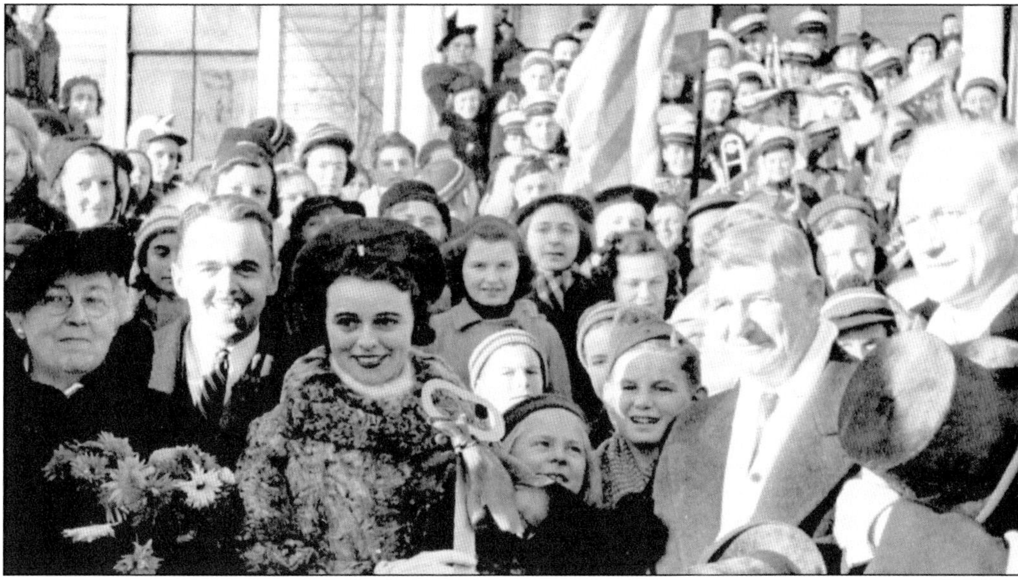

The cavalcade comes to a stop at the Grand Army Hall on School Street, where the town fathers present Mary Brown with the key to the town. After filming this scene, Holbrook suffered an attack of appendicitis and had to withdraw from the rest of the production. Dorothy Lee, her understudy, stepped in and filmed the balance of the movie, wearing sunglasses so as not to give the switch away. The film concludes with a kidnapping, and the local police force pulls off a rescue.

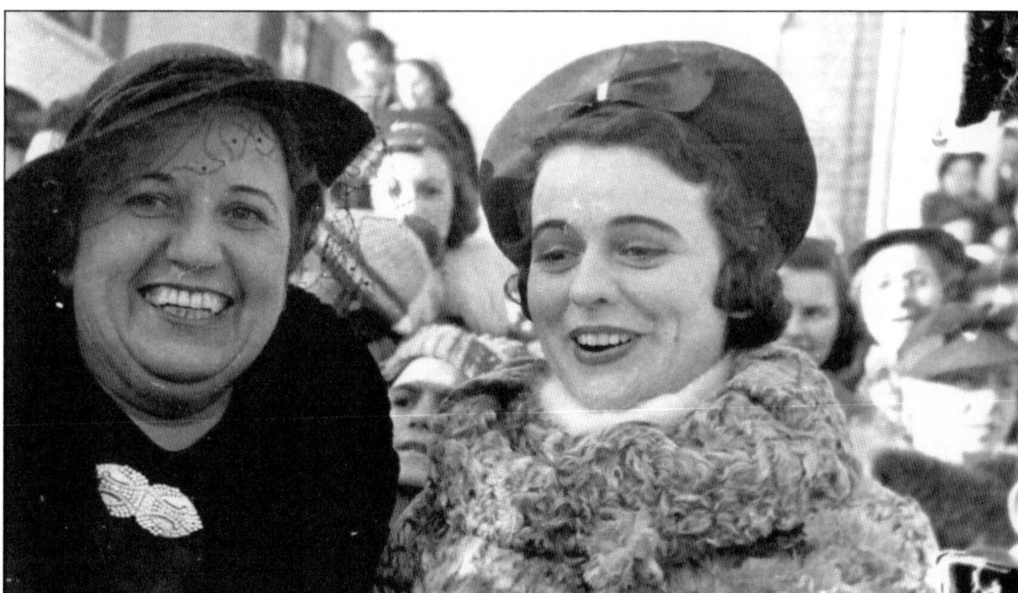

The Movie Queen served as a fundraiser for Rockland schoolchildren. When Judge Emil Fuchs's Boston Braves had to cancel their annual visit to town, school nurse Louise Considine, on the left, took control of the committee that brought filmmaker Showalter and her camera to town. The screening of the film took place on January 31, 1938, at Rockland High School, and the $600 in admission fees collected paid for milk for the students for the entire year. A videotape copy of the film still exists, and a search is underway for the original 16 millimeter film.

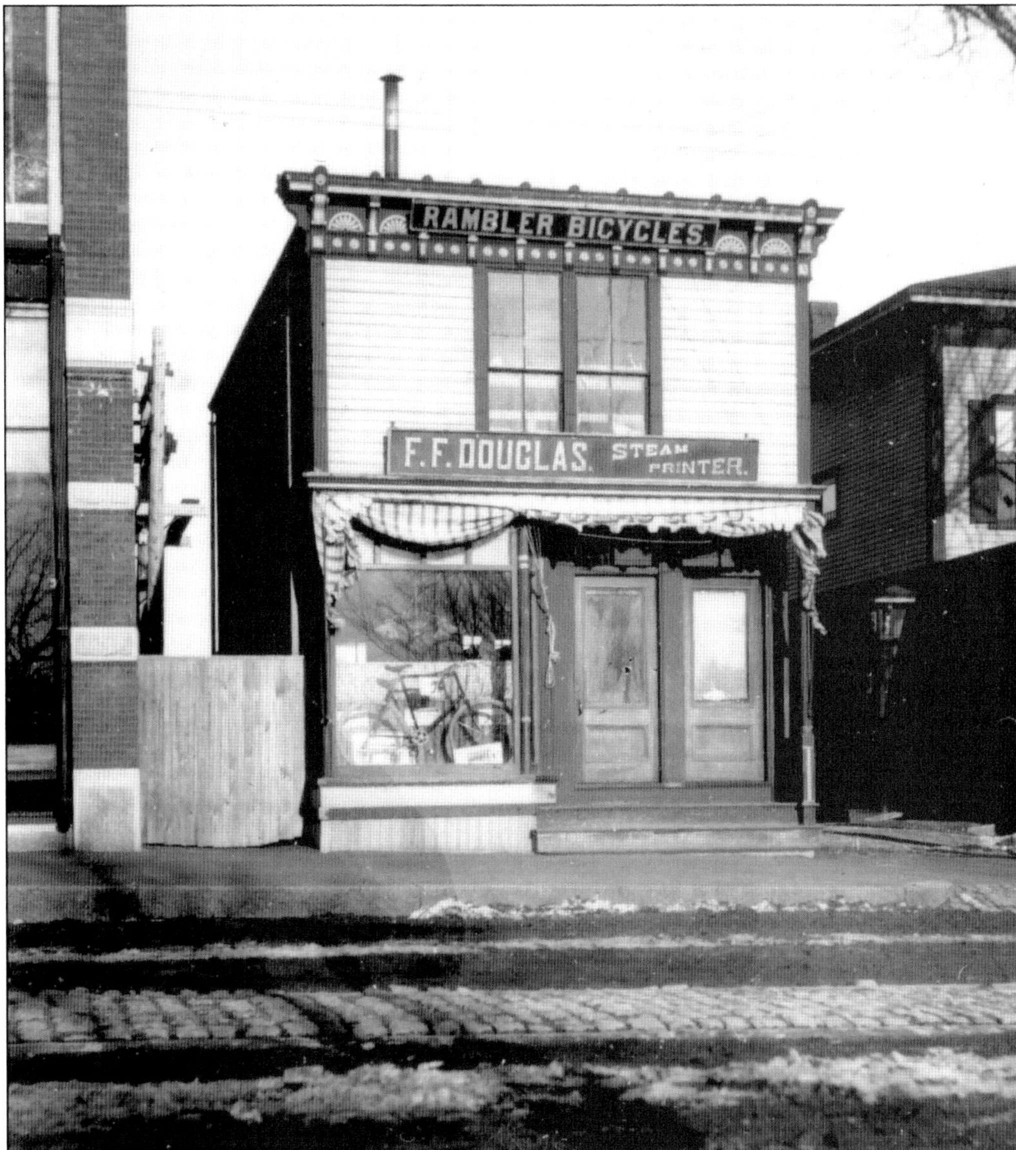

In 1876, Col. Albert A. Pope of Dorchester, a Civil War hero, visited Philadelphia to attend the Centennial Exposition, a look back at America's first century as a free nation and the amazing scientific and technological advances that had characterized the nation's growth to that point. Already a successful businessman manufacturing machinery parts for the production of shoes, Pope spied an item that would become the driving passion of his life: a Penny Farthing, a high-wheeled British bicycle. Pope imported it, formed the Columbia Bicycle Company, and began a national craze. If you wanted to purchase a bicycle in Rockland in 1898, at the apex of the "boneshaker" mania gripping the United States, you had your choice of salesmen. At 16 Webster Street was Horace M. Hunt, who could also repair any carriages that needed mending. On the corner of South Union and Linden Streets was C.W. Burgess. On the Hill were F.S. Chute in the Bigelow Building and the Douglass Cycle Company next to the Rockland Savings Bank block.

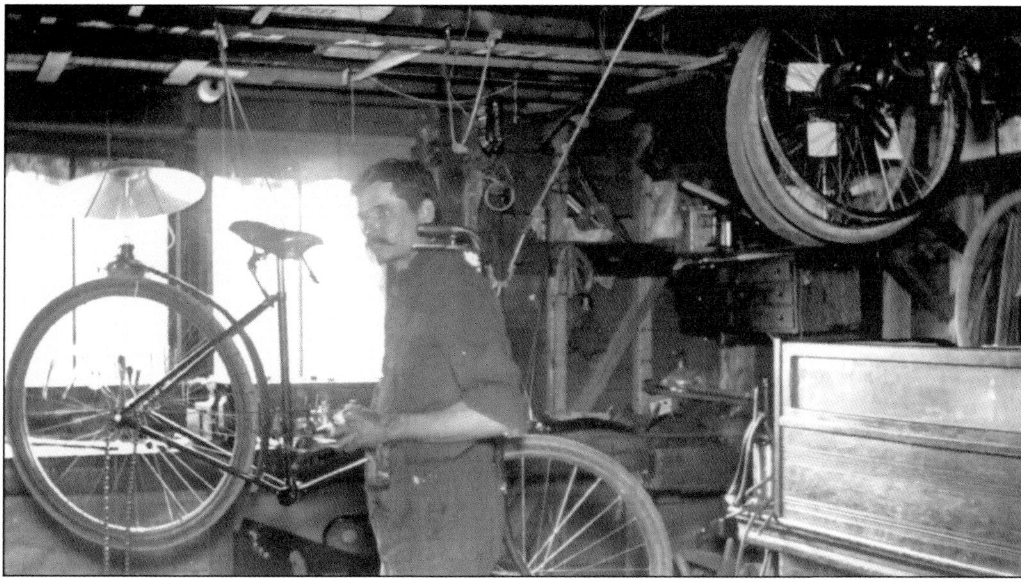

Bicycle repairmen like F.F. Douglass were the heroes of the late 1890s. Just before the widespread use of the automobile, rattletraps introduced a new dimension of speed to the American way of life. Never before, except maybe on runaway carriages, had Americans moved with such reckless abandon, and the notion of an implement of individual transportation that needed neither food nor sleep boggled the mind. Rockland's first car, a Stanley Steamer owned by Frank Nesmith, appeared on the streets in 1900.

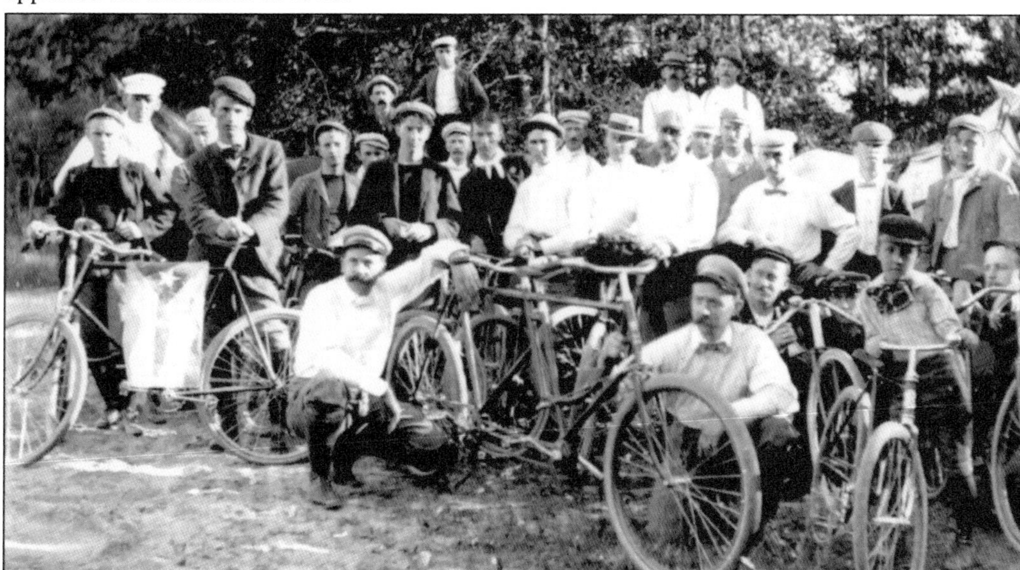

Bicycle clubs formed across America, and cyclists took to the streets. Bones broke everywhere, as the country's roadways had not improved from the time of the Pilgrims. Riders dealt with frozen ruts in the winter, mud pits each spring, and dust clouds in the summer. Before moving into automobile manufacturing with his Pope-Hartford and Pope-Toledo models, Pope paved the way for a better road system for America, lobbying for macadamized surfaces. Better roads meant more enjoyment for cyclists, and happier cyclists meant better sales for Columbia. The cycling bug bit Rocklanders as it did the rest of the nation.

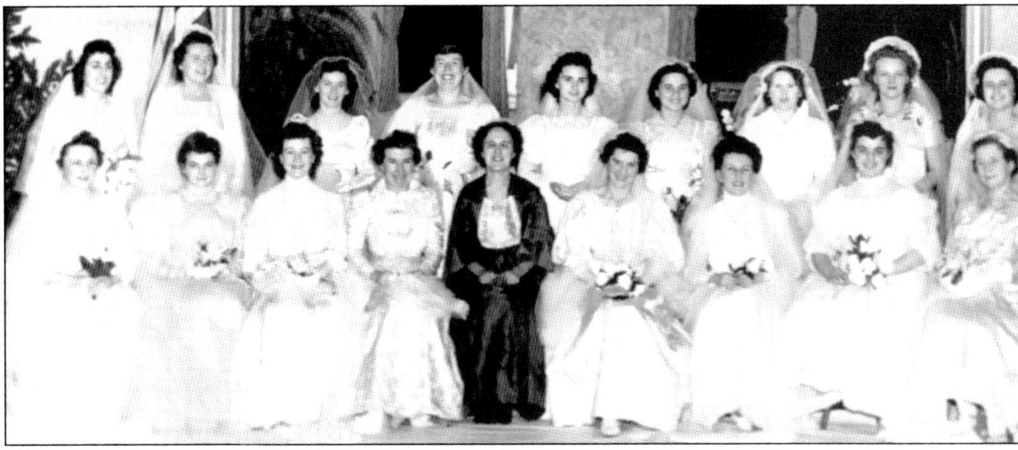

Before reality television, the internet, video games, DVDs, and other technological inventions, Americans joined common-interest societies, from book clubs to whist clubs to neighborhood-improvement organizations. To take their minds off the war in Europe, the Rockland Women's Club staged a bridal pageant, with gowns dating back to the Civil War. Seen modeling here, from left to right, last names only, are the following: (front row) Lamkey, Tedeschi, Lyon, Osgood, Ferguson, Fitzgibbons, Shoughrow, Robbins, and Lanigan; (back row) Cane, Spurr, Tedeschi, La Tarzi, Haggerty, Caplice, Senman, Bell, and Farrar. (The newspaper article from which this information was taken did not provide the women's first names.)

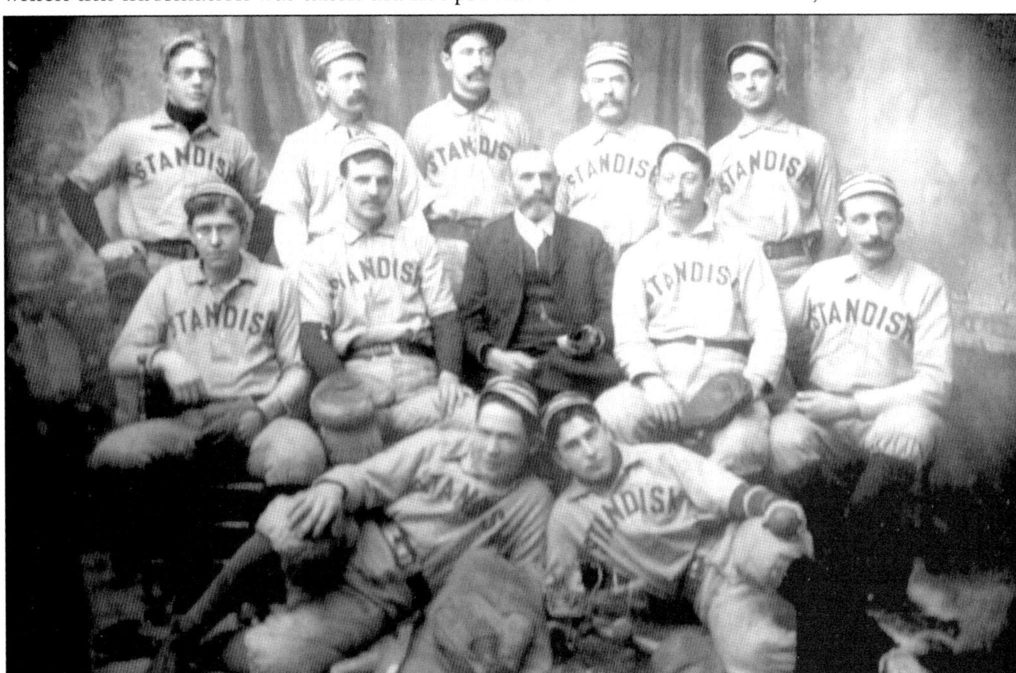

The Standish Lodge No. 177 Independent Order of Odd Fellows of Massachusetts met in the Phoenix Building on Union Street at its founding on October 6, 1876. It later moved to the hall over the Rockland Pharmacy and then the Grand Army Hall. The women's counterpart, the Rose Standish Rebekah Lodge No. 71, was instituted on October 22, 1888, and closed down in 1972. Almost a club within a club, the Standish Lodge had its own baseball team. Insurance man Amos A. Phelps is seated on the far right.

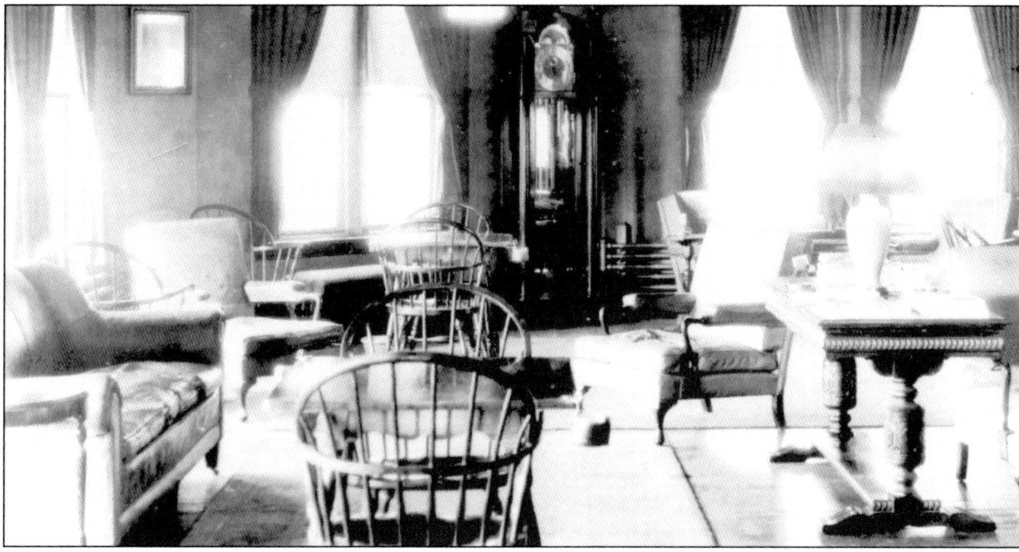

No one seems to have a picture of the members of the all-male Union Glee Club in action, but their final quarters in the Rockland Savings Bank building looked elaborate. From formal balls, masquerades, and lavish dinners to quiet evenings of cribbage and billiards, the club appealed to all men of stature in Rockland. Its baseball team rivaled any in town and was undefeated in 1903. Massachusetts governor James Michael Curley spoke before the group, as did Adm. Richard Byrd, describing his adventures in Antarctica.

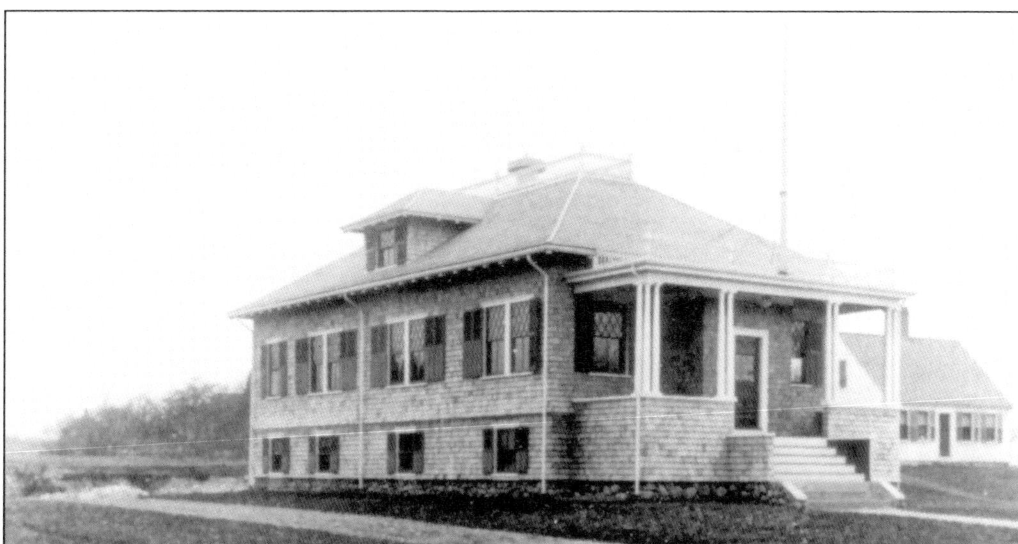

In 1895, five young men, A.B. Studley, James Gammon, G.A. Stoddard, Charles Poole, and Austin Baker decided they needed a place to congregate after work each night, so they rented a room above the L.A. Whiting Shoe factory on Webster Street. Three years later, with a ballooning membership, they voted to lease the factory's entire second floor. By 1909, they needed their own building and purchased the land at the corner of Webster and Hingham Streets to build the Webster Club House, dedicated on November 17, 1910. Today, the Webster Club House is the Rockland Knights of Columbus hall.

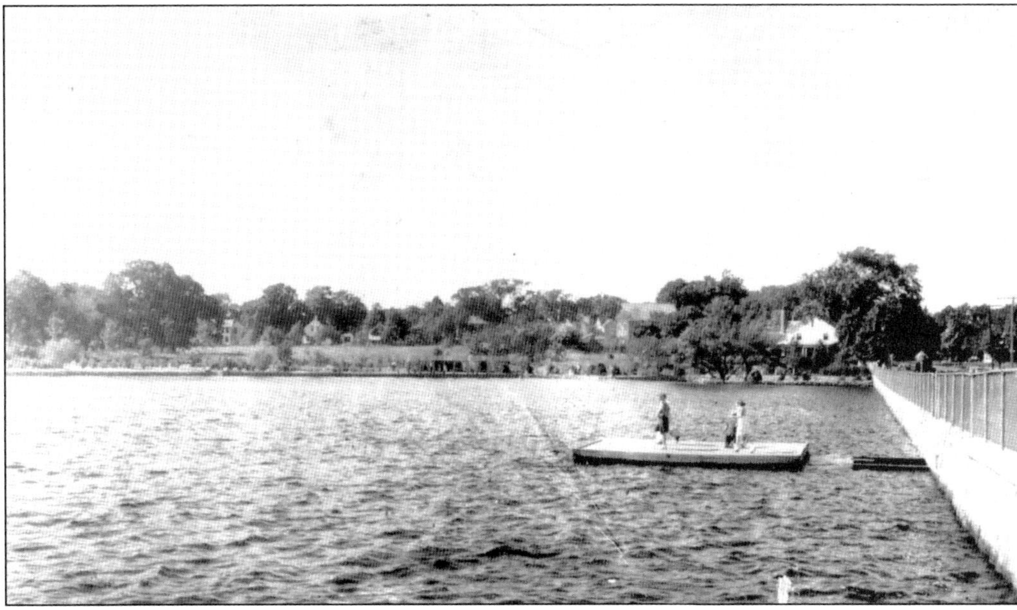

Who needed a clubhouse when good weather rolled around? Early settlers created many of New England's small ponds. By damming a tiny flow of water, a pond could be created. A sluiceway from a gate at the dam could run to a turbine or overshot wheel in order to power a sawmill, gristmill, or lumbermill. Such was the history of the man-made body of water known through the years as French, Reed's, or Studley Pond.

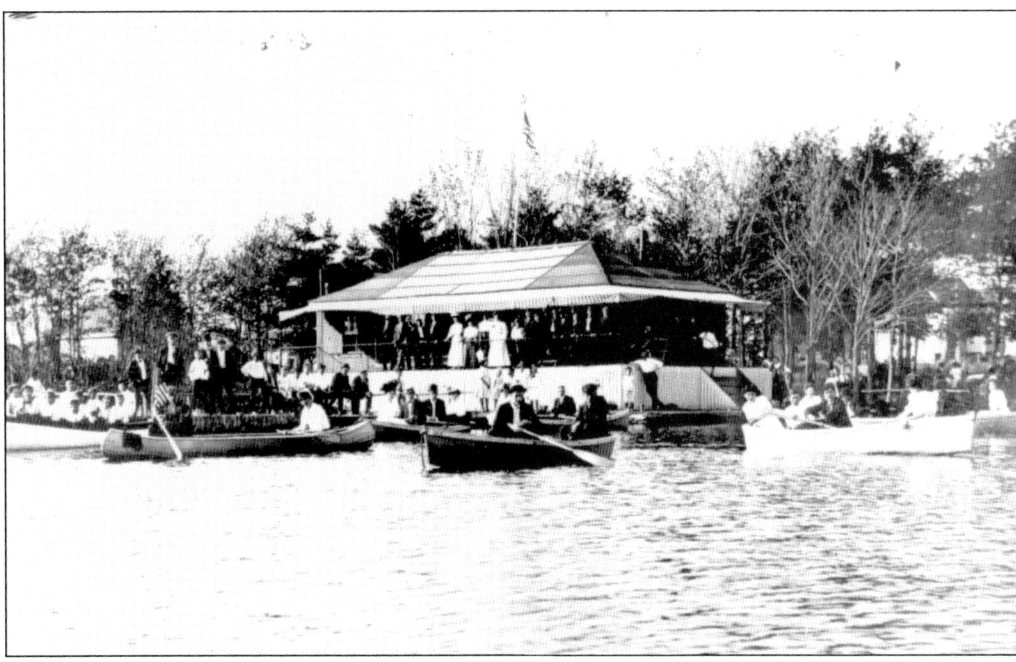

Over the years, ponds became more than just tools of industry. Reed's Pond became a favorite spot for Rockland youngsters interested either in beating the summer heat by taking a flying leap into its cool water or sitting in the shade and dropping a fishing line below its surface. More sophisticated types chose instead to play on its surface in canoes and other small boats.

If the weather did not cooperate, Rockland residents had the choice, at least from the 1920s onwards, of seeing the latest in Hollywood's dramatic creations at the Strand Theatre in the remodeled Temperance Hall on Union Street. On September 24, 1956, at 10:00 p.m., a fire broke out as 30 or so patrons sat through a double feature.

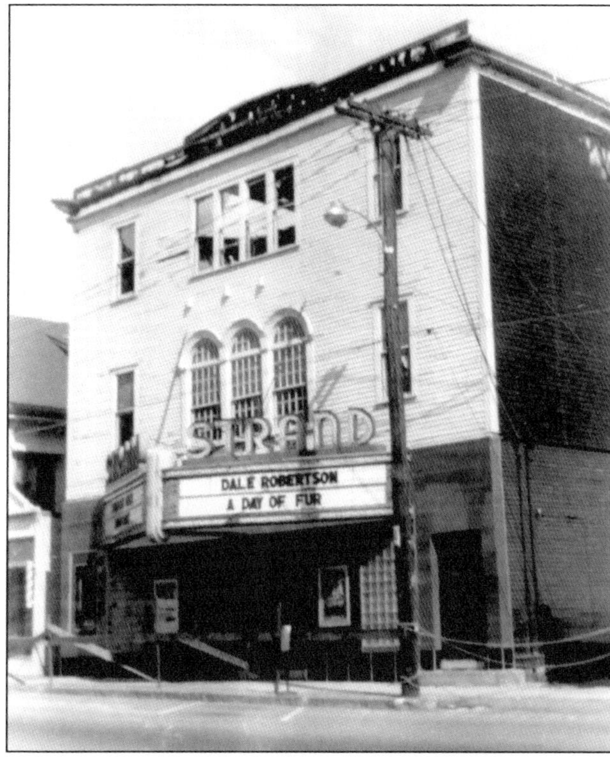

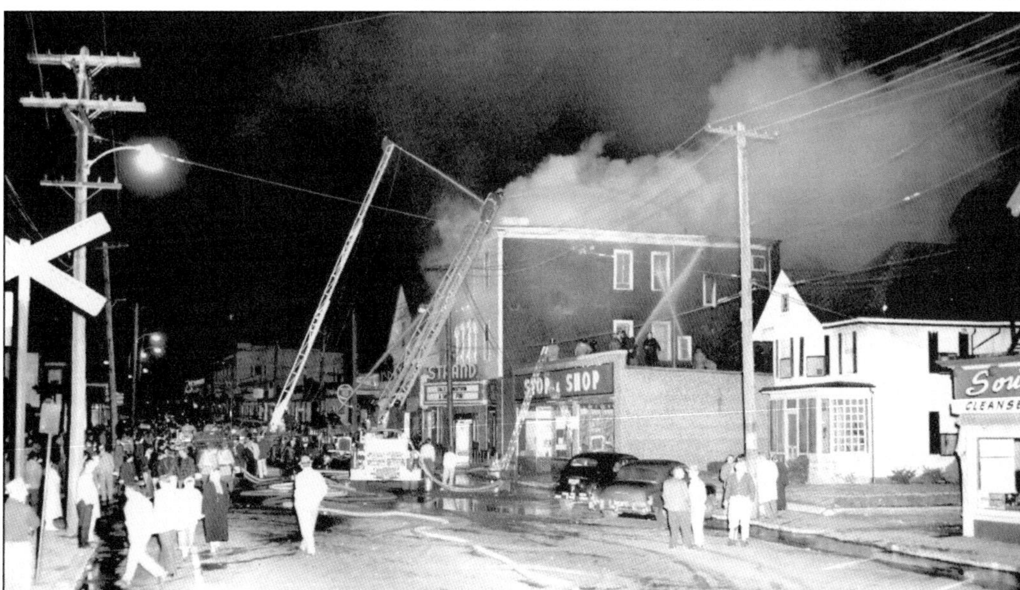

By 11:00 p.m., the fire had built itself into a raging inferno. All of the movie-goers escaped safely and quickly, as trucks from Rockland, Brockton, Whitman, and Abington responded to the alarm. Overtaken by smoke inhalation, Rockland Fire Department driver William Mullen retreated to his car for some rest. When friends came to check on him, they found him sitting dead in his front seat. With damages totaling approximately $80,000 to $100,000, the title of the Strand's last movie, *A Day of Fury*, eerily remained on the marquee.

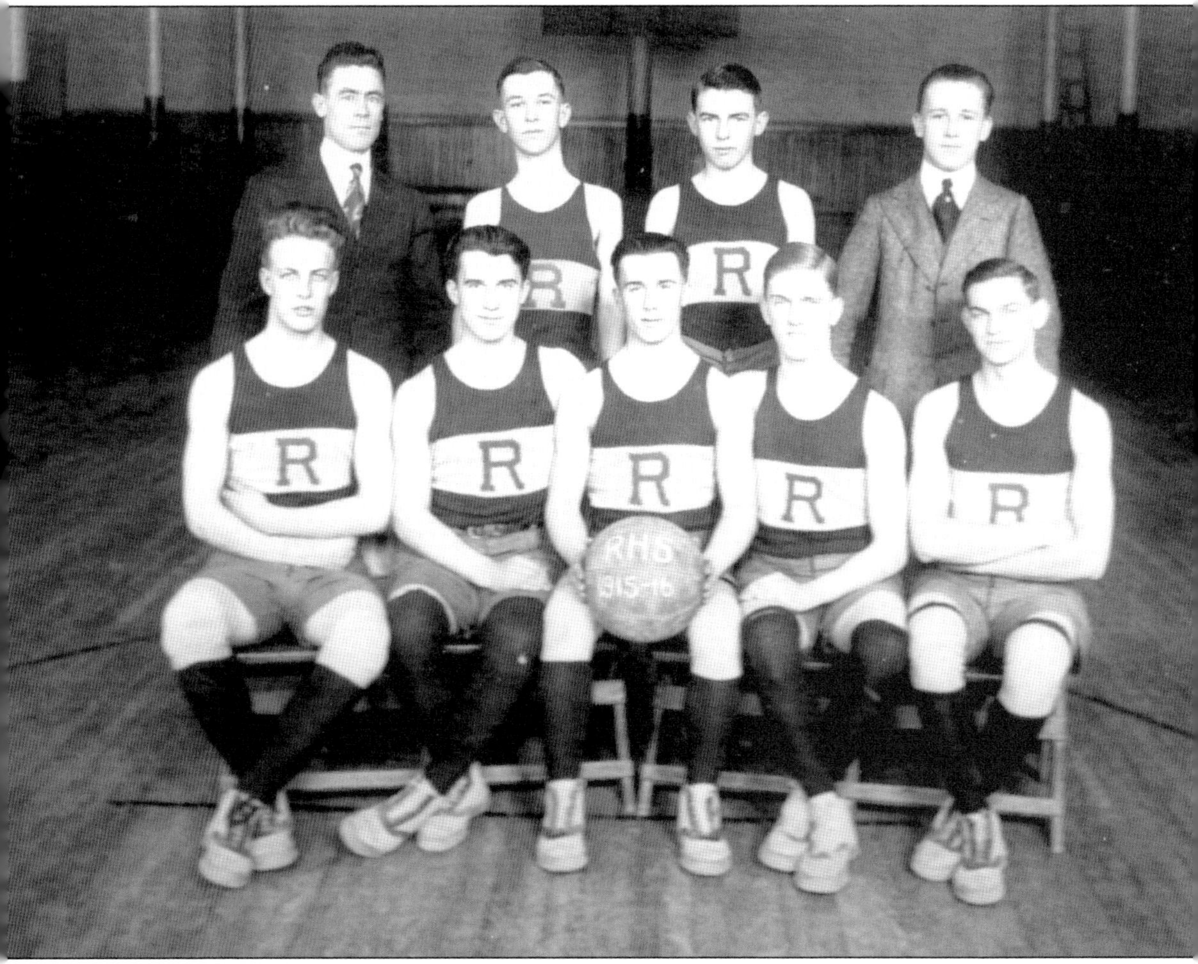

Rockland has always been a place for athletes. Several future major-league baseball players honed their skills as part of the local Old Colony League team that played at Hartsuff Park in the first decade of the 20th century. Those players included Eddie Ainsmith, who came to Rockland to play catcher for $1.50 a game, and shortstop Walt Lonergan, who had 26 at-bats with the Boston Red Sox in 1911. Even homegrown athletes like pitcher William Vargas had "cups of coffee" with professional teams. Many of them got their starts at Rockland High School. These strapping young lads of the 1915–1916 Rockland High School basketball team were defenders of school pride long before the adoption of the bulldog as the team mascot and symbol. Unfortunately, these boys currently remain anonymous, as the authors have been unable to locate a 1916 yearbook to identify them. This lack of information illustrates the importance of the historic preservation missions of organizations such as the town library, the Dyer Memorial Library in Abington, the Rockland Historical Commission, and the Historical Society of Old Abington.

Seven

Familiar Faces
Rockland's Movers and Shakers

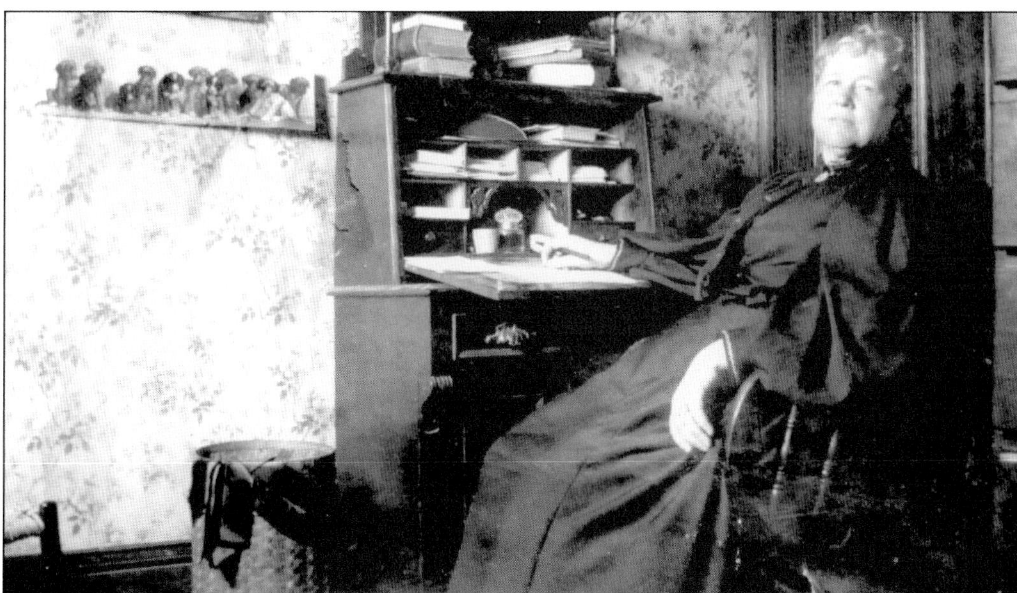

Sometimes their names appear on street signs. Other times, their names can be found memorialized in parks or on buildings. Yet some of Rockland's most famous citizens have disappeared from modern memory, relegated to dusty rarely seen town reports, club minutes, or high school yearbooks. Some have nothing more than tombstones to pass on their memories. Many past citizens helped to shape the community in which Rocklanders live today. They wrote the words that set the laws, spoke out when opinions were called for, and acted in times of emergency. Some, like Victorian novelist Maria Louise Pool (above), earned fame far beyond the borders of the town. At one time, they were the familiar faces that made Rockland famous.

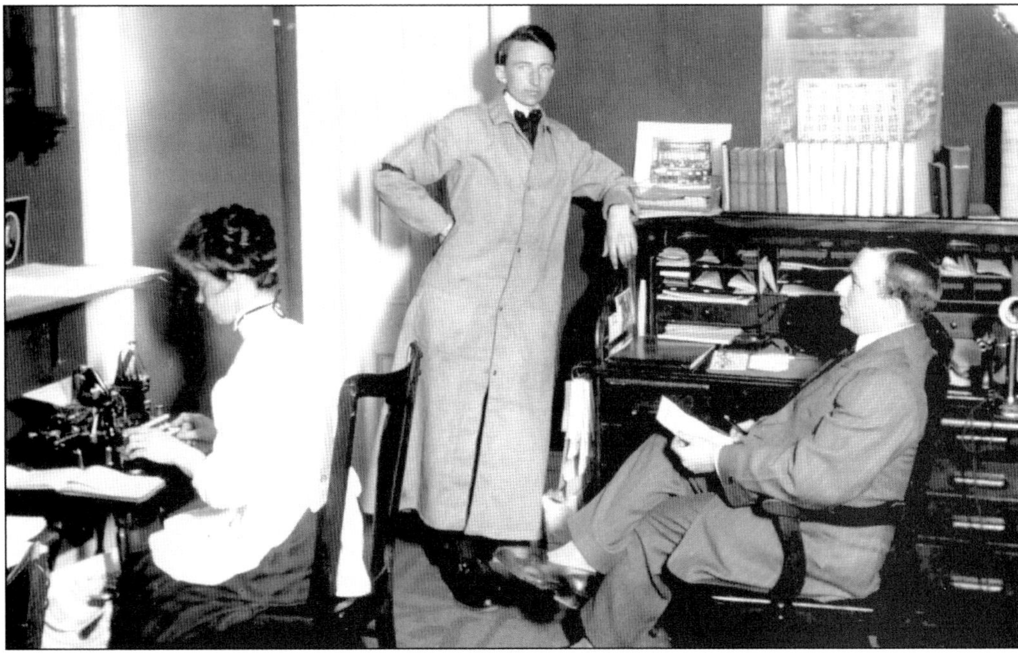

While Pool played in fiction, other writers in Rockland chose to make their mark in the newspaper trade as journalists. William T. McCarthy (standing) became a familiar presence in Rockland through the written word, first as editor of the *Rockland Independent* and later through his reminiscence columns in the *Rockland Standard*. McCarthy was one of the town's first historians.

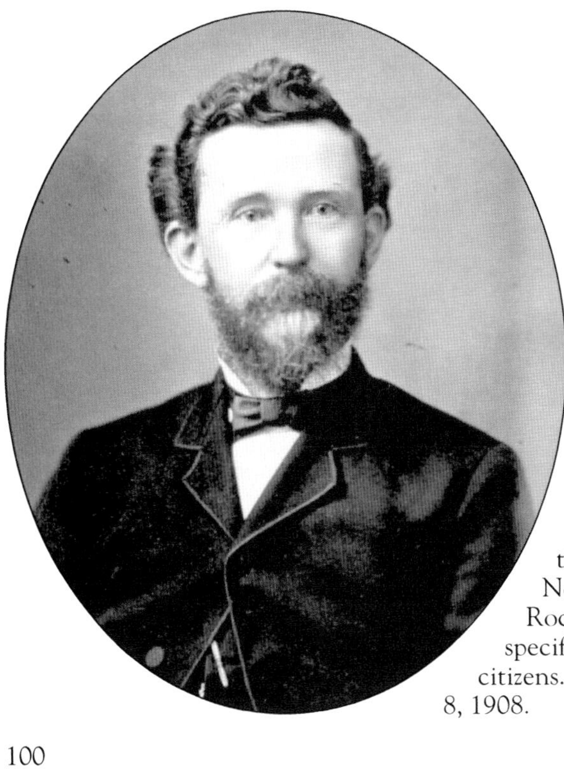

Lorenzo D. Perkins served as an historian of the moment. Born in West Hanover on October 12, 1836, Perkins made his way to Rockland via jobs in shoe factories, groceries, Gideon Studley's box mill, furnishings stores, and music stores before finding his true calling as a writer. Penning columns for the *Standard* under the pseudonyms Polly Ann, Isaac, Mrs. Noah Newcomb, and Ossa, Perkins has left Rocklanders several important neighborhood-specific essays on everyday life and blue-collar citizens. He passed away unexpectedly on December 8, 1908.

Huldah Barker Loud stood out in the crowd. The irrepressible Loud went from school teacher to editor in 1884, when job printers E.C. Osborne and W.J. Barry founded the *Rockland Independent*. Five years later, when she purchased the paper, Loud announced that she had done so "to help save the world," and that the paper would be a "medium through which she could convey her best thought to the world, unhampered by worldly interests."

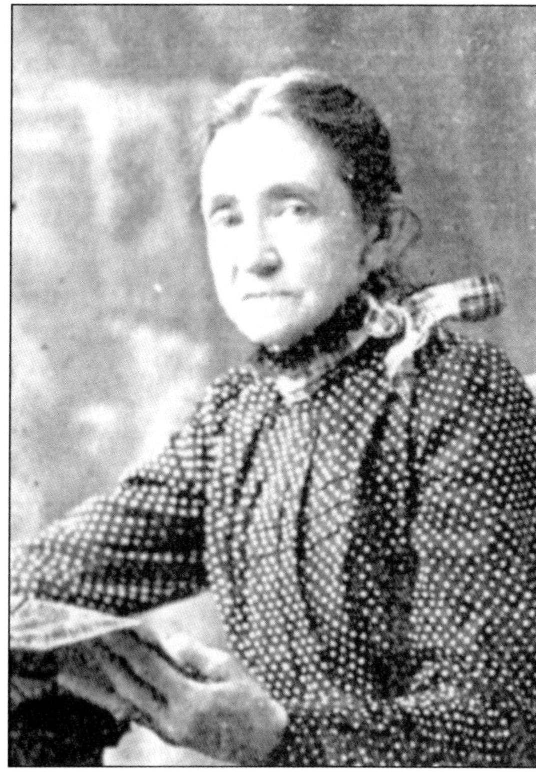

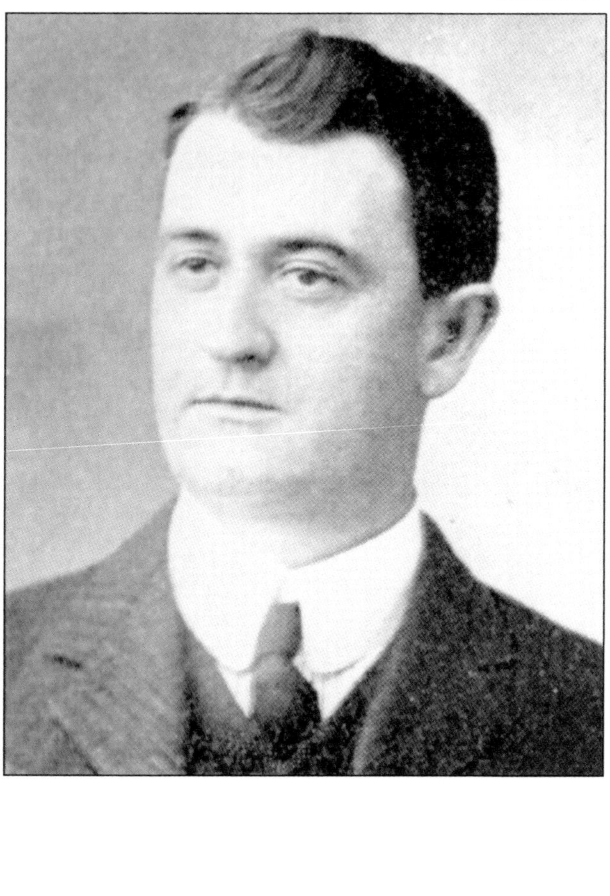

Frank S. Alger, born on August 3, 1871, in Salisbury, owned and published 12 newspapers in and around Rockland, including the *Rockland Standard*, and served as the local correspondent to the *Boston Herald* and *Brockton Enterprise*. An 1888 graduate of the Hanover school system, Alger worked for the *Plymouth County Journal* for two years before taking a job as office boy at the *Standard* office. With perseverance, he eventually rose to co-owner and then owner of the paper, building himself a small publishing empire.

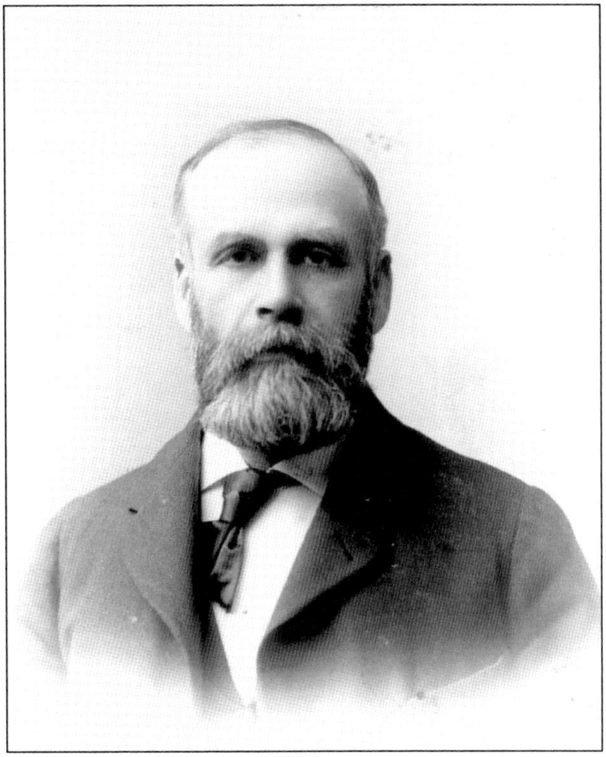

In 1901, the First Congregational Church of Rockland embarked on a 100-year project when they compiled the contents of their century box. The box was inventoried every year at the Rockland Savings Bank until the day came for 21st-century parishioners to open it and shake hands with the past. Photographs and other items saw the light of day for the first time in 100 years at a public opening at the church. Businessman Henry E. Fuller was there with a story to tell about life in Rockland at the beginning of the 20th century.

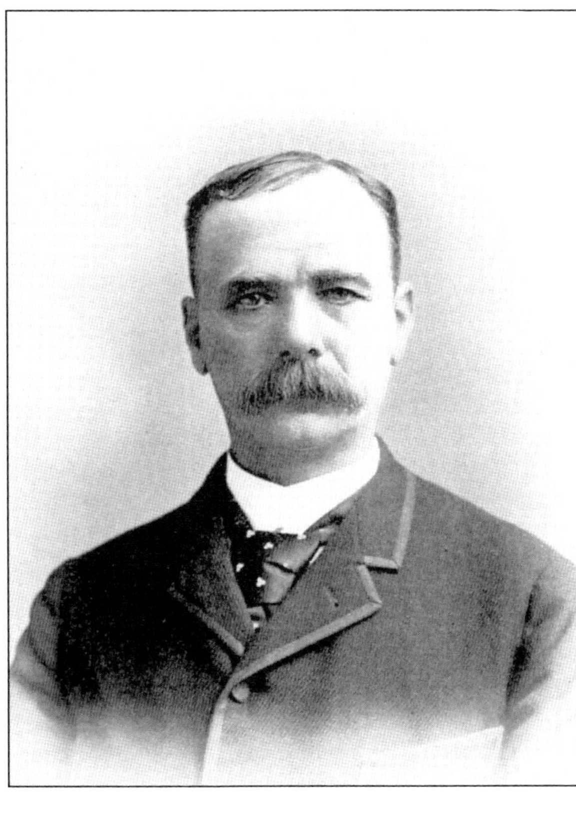

Civil War veteran William H. Bates was born in East Abington in 1837, but, when he was one, he moved with his family to Hanover. In 1862, he enlisted with the 38th Regiment Massachusetts Volunteer Infantry, his clerical skills earning him a position on the staff of Gen. William H. Emory. After the war, he entered the shoe business, eventually rising to president and manager of the Rockland Company, formed from the firm of W.E. Putnam & Company.

Born in 1838 in Vermont and reared on a farm in upstate New York, Albert Culver made the most of his few available hours of self-education. Breaking away from the farm at age 18, he joined his brother John in North Abington in the feed and coal business, before taking other local jobs. His bookkeeping skills led to important positions with the Hanover Branch Railroad. He eventually owned his own firm, dealing in coal, wood, hay, flour, and grain. His warehouse at Union Square was an unmistakable landmark until it burned in 1945.

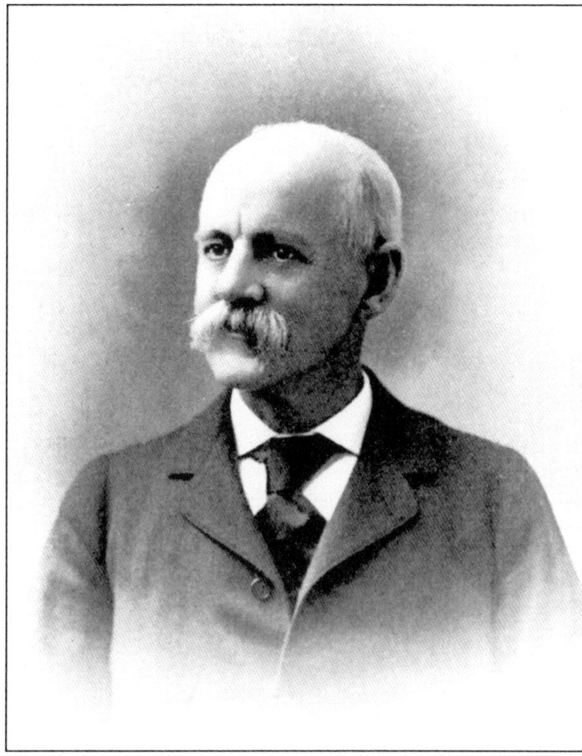

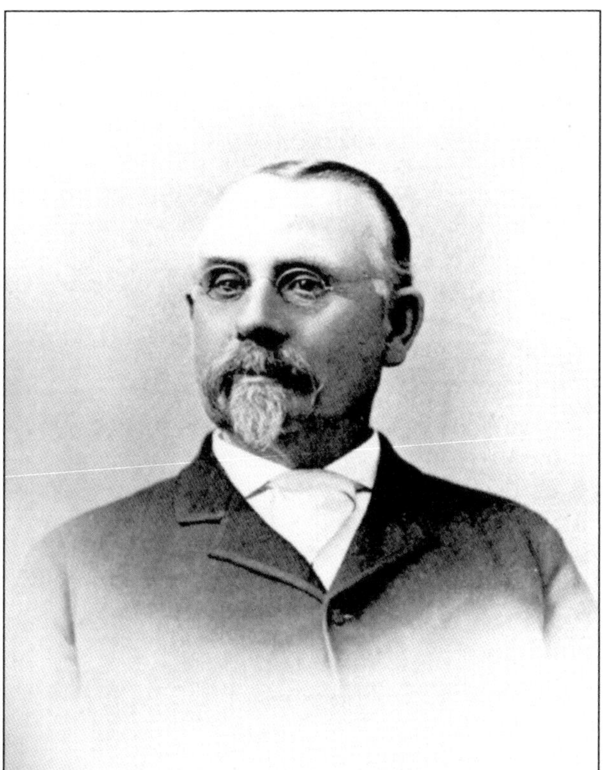

Edwin Whiting, born in Hanover, opened the first clothing store in Rockland in September 1862. Going to work at an early age as a shoemaker, shortly after his father's death, he eventually rose to become one of Rockland's most respected citizens. Whiting sold his business and retired in 1897.

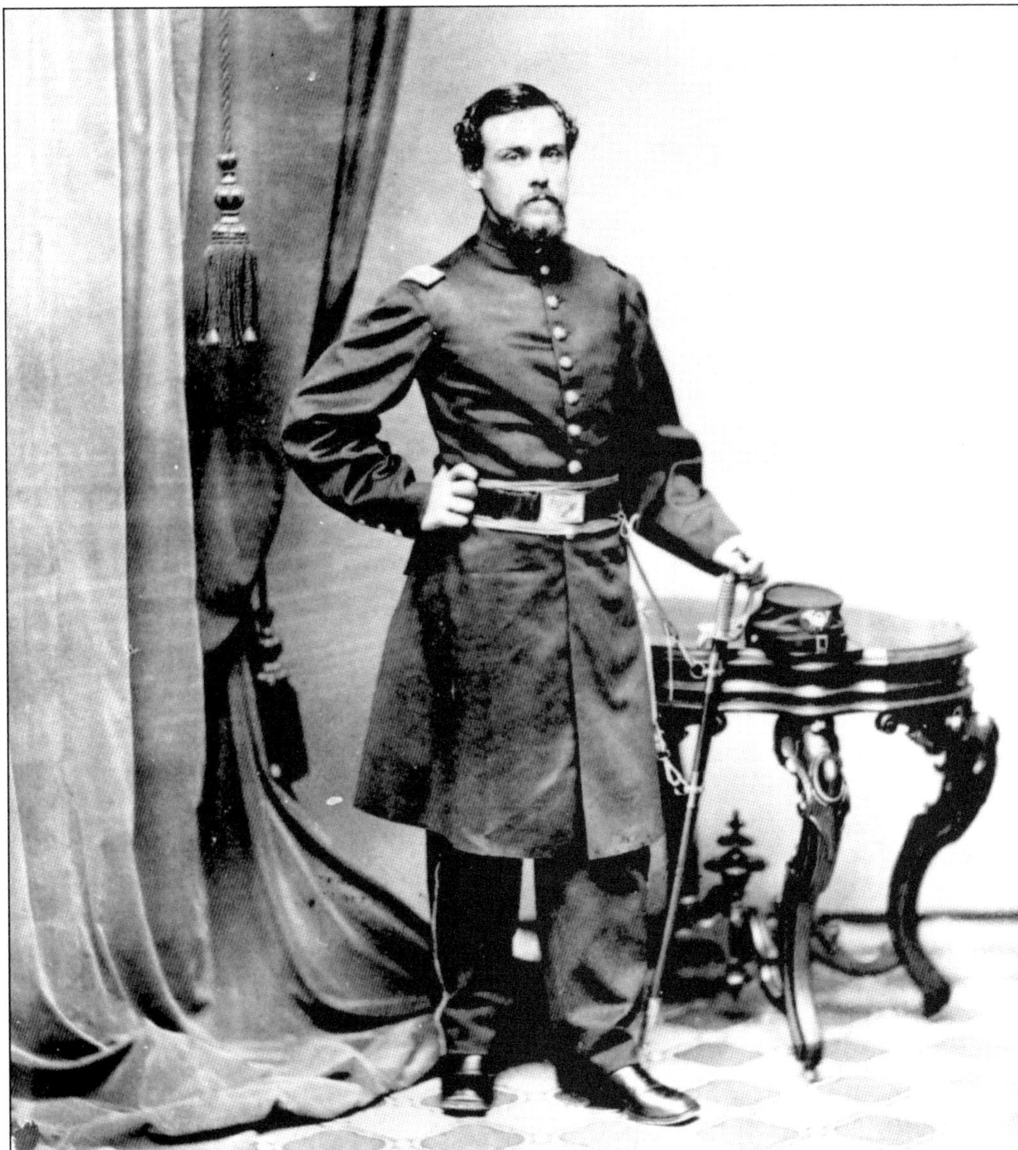

According to his November 5, 1925 obituary in the *Rockland Standard,* Capt. Lewis Reed may have held the record for longest service in the Civil War of any enlistee from the town of Old Abington. He signed up to fight from East Abington on April 28, 1861, just a few short weeks after the firing on Fort Sumter. He remained in service until August 1865, four months after the end of the war. Along the way, he served with the 12th Regiment Massachusetts Volunteer Infantry (the Webster Regiment) and as an officer with the fighting 54th, the African American unit formed by Gov. John Andrew, made famous by the movie *Glory*. Wounded at the Battle of Antietam on September 17, 1862, Reed had also fought at Cedar Mountain and Second Bull Run. After his recovery at Chancellorsville, where the Confederate general Thomas "Stonewall" Jackson died, he fought at Gettysburg. Nine days after Robert E. Lee surrendered to Ulysses S. Grant to end the war, Reed was involved in a skirmish at Boykin's Mills, South Carolina, neither side having received word that the war had ended. He passed away at age 83 in his home on Highland Street.

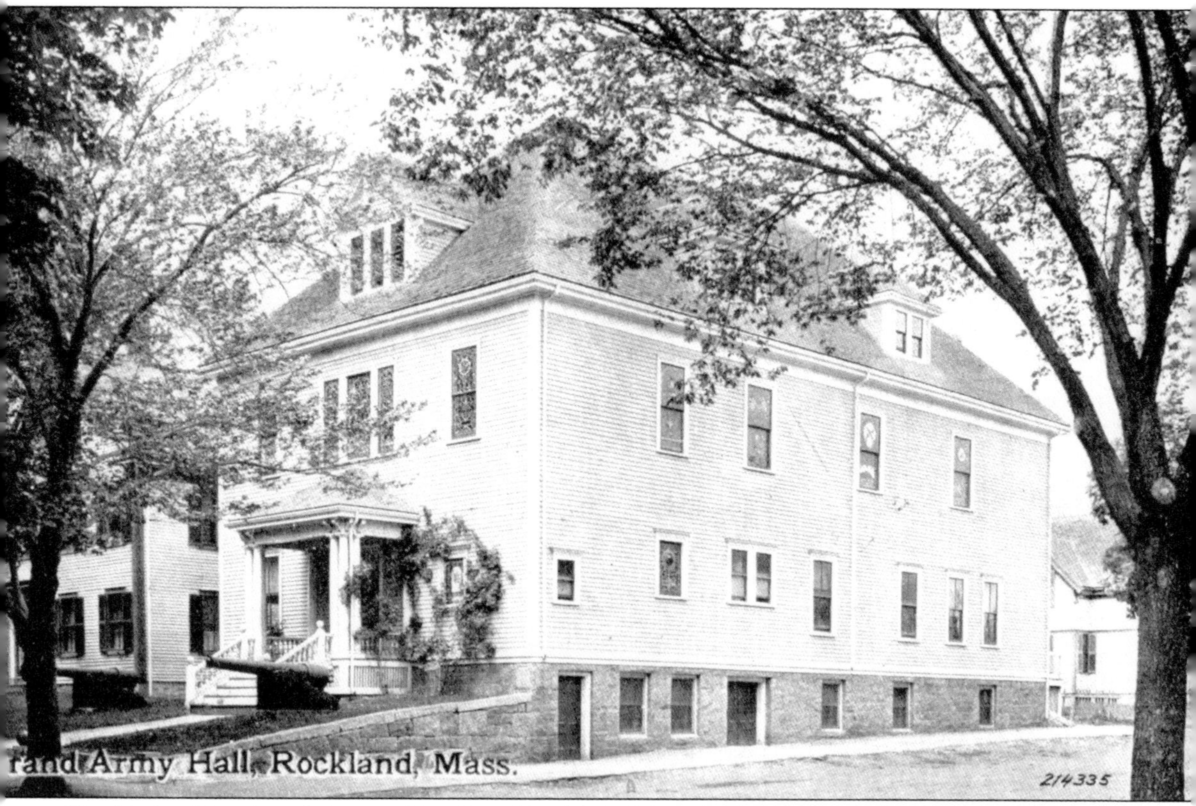

The birth of the Grand Army of the Republic (G.A.R.) took place in Decatur, Illinois, in 1866. That year, G.A.R. founder Dr. B.F. Stephenson traveled from Springfield to Decatur with plans for a secret society similar to the Sons of Malta, a popular men's organization of the time, but with rituals tailored to an all-Union military veteran membership. Although the organization struggled through its early years, it grew in earnest from 1875 onward. In 1890, the G.A.R. reached its peak, with 490,000 members in chapters nationwide. Although it claimed not to be a political organization, members held strong influence over national politics. Five G.A.R. members even ascended to the presidency of the United States. Over the years, as the veterans passed on, the organization lost its clout until finally, in 1949, the six remaining members of the G.A.R. permanently shut down the organization. Rockland's Hartsuff Post No. 74, chartered on January 11, 1869, met in the impressive Grand Army Hall on School Street. One can only imagine the war stories that have been shared in that hall.

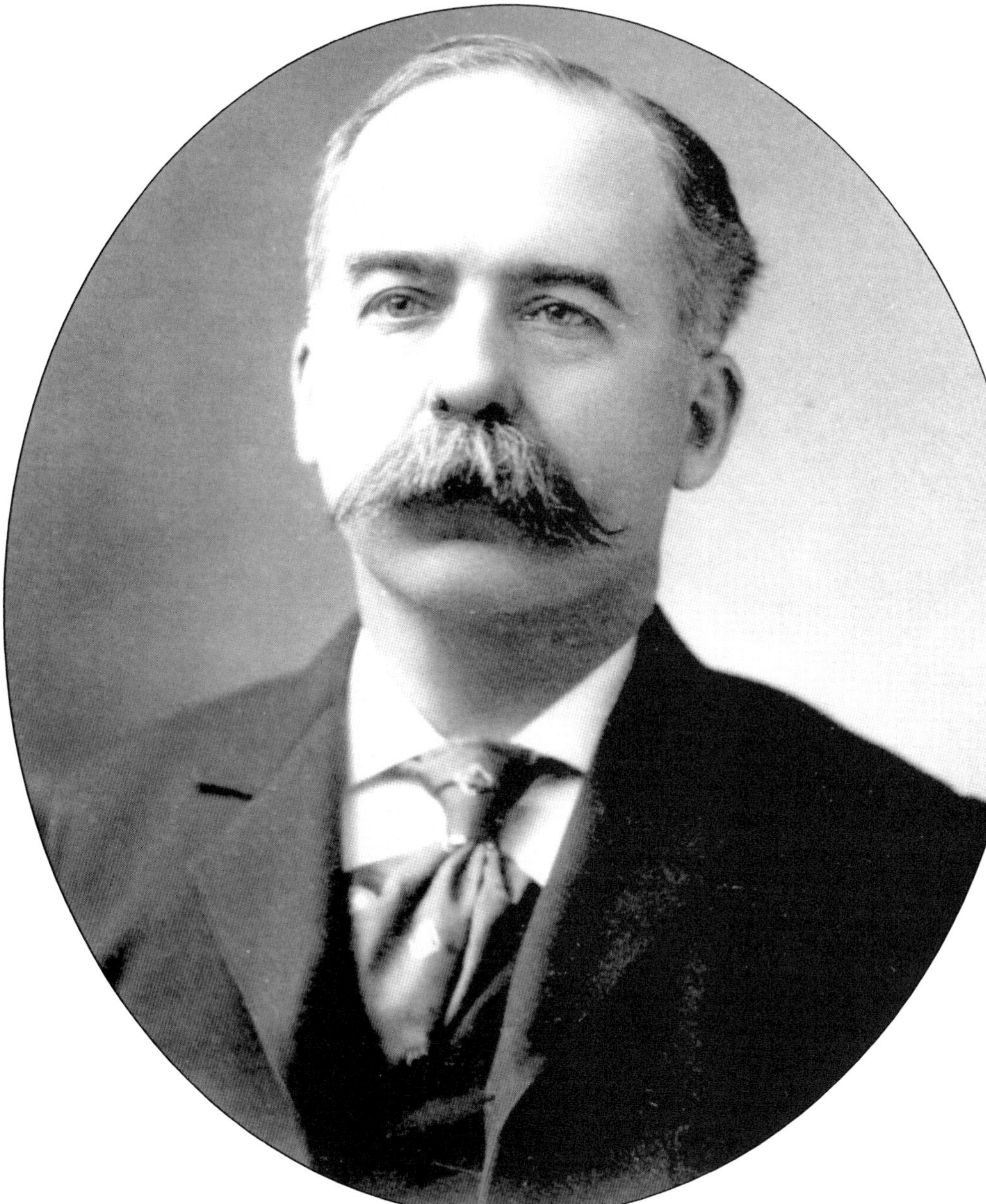

Theodore H. Farr served as the principal of Rockland High School from 1885 to 1903. Born in Franklin, he was working as the principal of the high school in Altoona, Pennsylvania, when he was chosen as the most qualified of 100 candidates to take the Rockland position. He began at an annual salary of $1,260. In the early fall of 1887, he resigned temporarily to take a similar position in Boston, but a $40 per year raise lured him back to town. During his tenure, Rockland had its own superintendent, then the position was shared between Rockland and Abington, and later Rockland and Whitman. Attendance rose from less than 60 to nearly 200 students in his 18 years at the school, and he worked hard to convince the townsfolk of the need to build new school buildings. Outspoken on many topics related to education, his pages in the annual town reports make for some interesting reading. Farr took a leave of absence in 1903 and never returned.

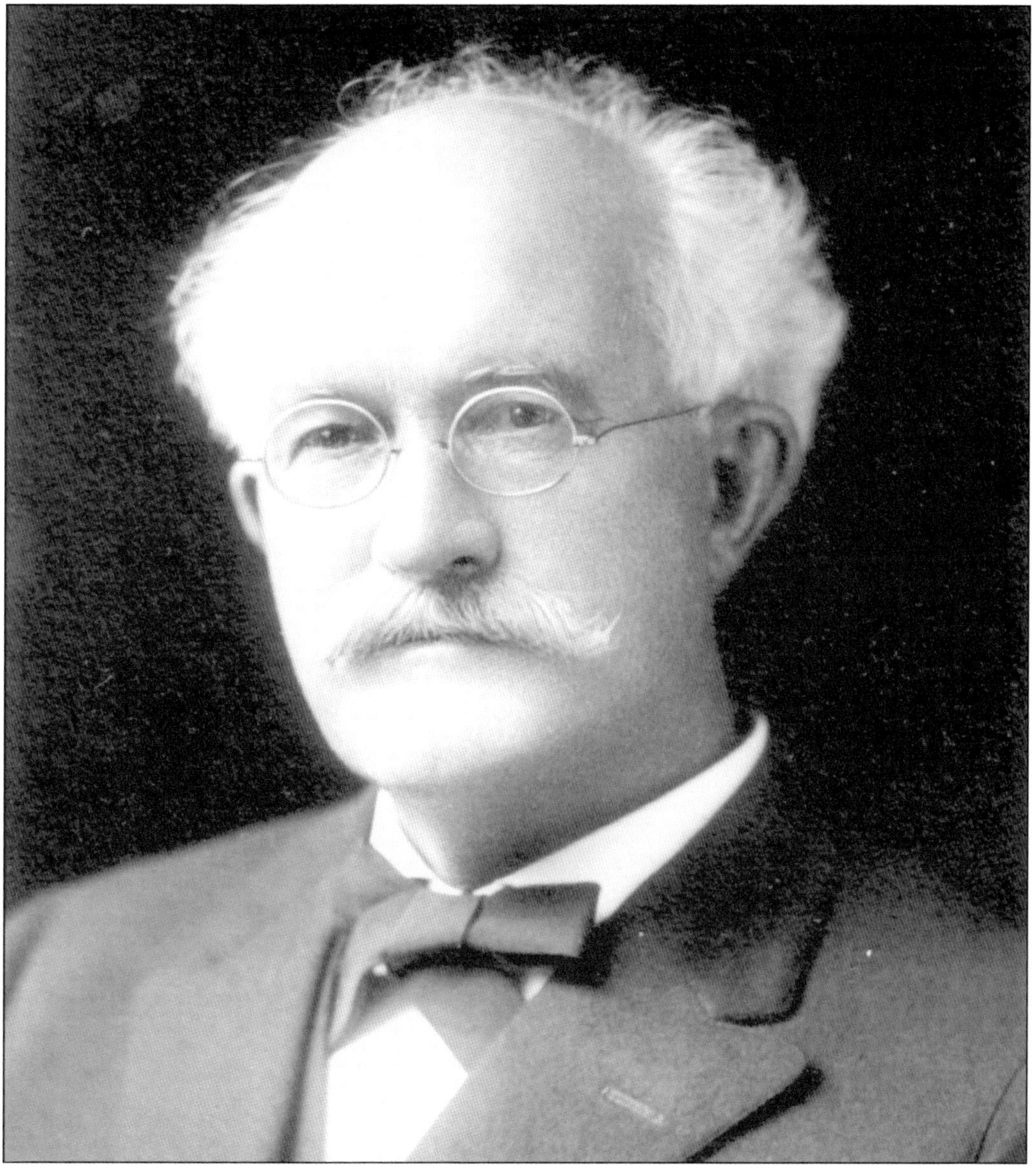

Born in South Braintree on September 20, 1851, Judge George Washington Kelley moved to Rockland to practice law in 1876. He stayed for the rest of his life. While serving as justice of the second district court from 1883 until his death in 1926, Kelley worked to improve the community in which he lived. He served on the school committee from 1877 to 1886 and as chairman of the library trustees from 1879 to 1881. He even compiled the first card catalog ever used at the Rockland Memorial Library. Kelley chaired the water commission, was director of the Electric Light and Power Company of Abington and Rockland and the Rockland Trust Company, and was a founder of the Unitarian church in town. When unions tried to block a young boys' band from marching in the 1905 Fourth of July parade, Kelley organized his own parade for the boys, riding on horseback at the head of the column and drawing thousands of people to Rockland for the spectacle. The *Brockton Enterprise* reported, "Judge Kelley's parade will go into Plymouth County history on the same shelf of the hall of fame with Sherman's march to the sea."

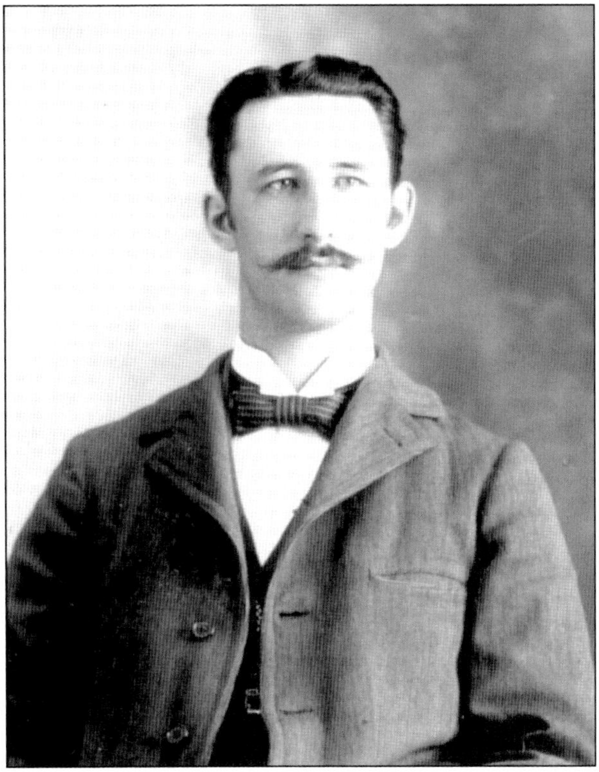

Herbert W. Hunt caught genealogy fever along with many others at the turn of the 20th century. The approach of the year 1900 created nostalgia, causing Americans to look back through time to their New England roots and the stories of their forebears. After compiling a Hunt genealogy, he followed the natural progression to the descendants of other intermarried lines and helped them in their research, particularly the well-established Stetson Kindred of America. His diligent work aids researchers even today.

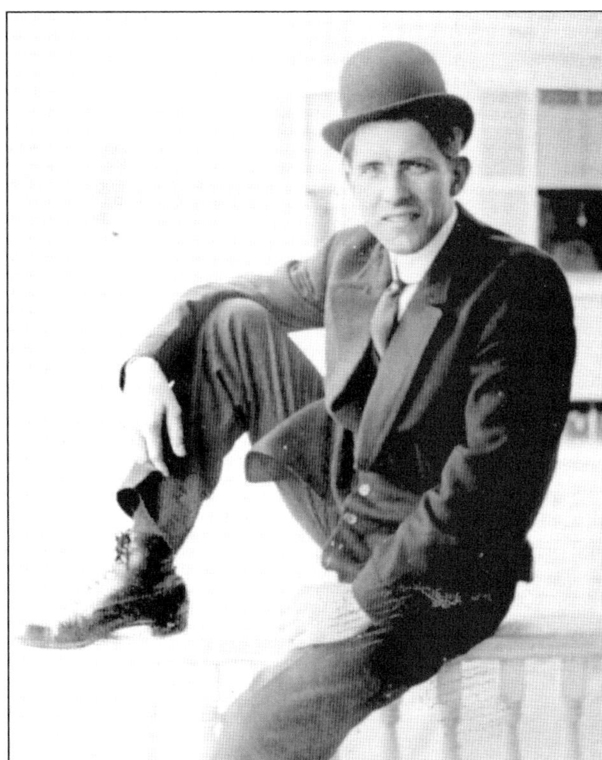

Photographer John Hannafin, who took several of the photographs that appear in this book, took a moment to step out in front of the camera for this pose. Apart from being a prolific chronicler of Rockland life, Hannafin had a day job working at the same shoe factory from his teens into his nineties.

In 1836, E. Payson Torrey, just three years old, moved from Hingham to East Abington with his family. Starting out driving cattle for his father, he simply could not be held down on the farm. At 19, he opened a general store in the Randall Block on Union Street selling groceries, carpets, housewares, furniture, and more. From 1870 to 1889, he sold shoes with partner James Gurney.

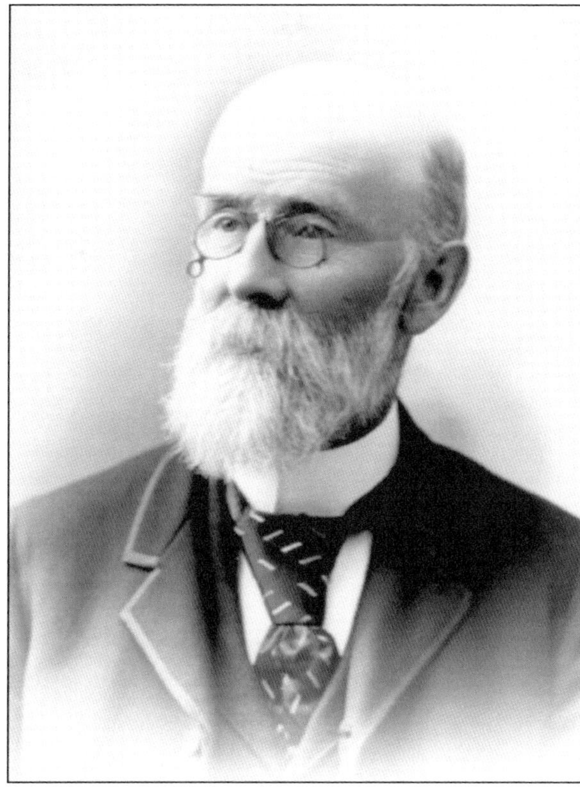

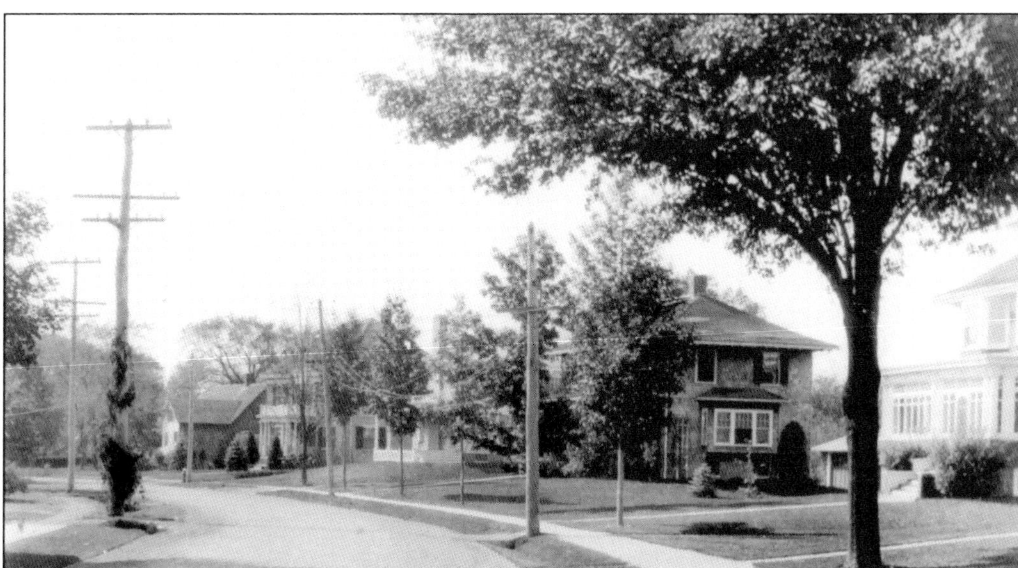

Torrey's business interests earned him enough money to build the Payson Block and the Grace Block on Union Street. He also laid out Arlington Street and Payson Avenue (above), and built many of the homes on those roads. In 1888, he helped form the First National Bank of Rockland. Torrey died on January 27, 1919, after a long, productive life.

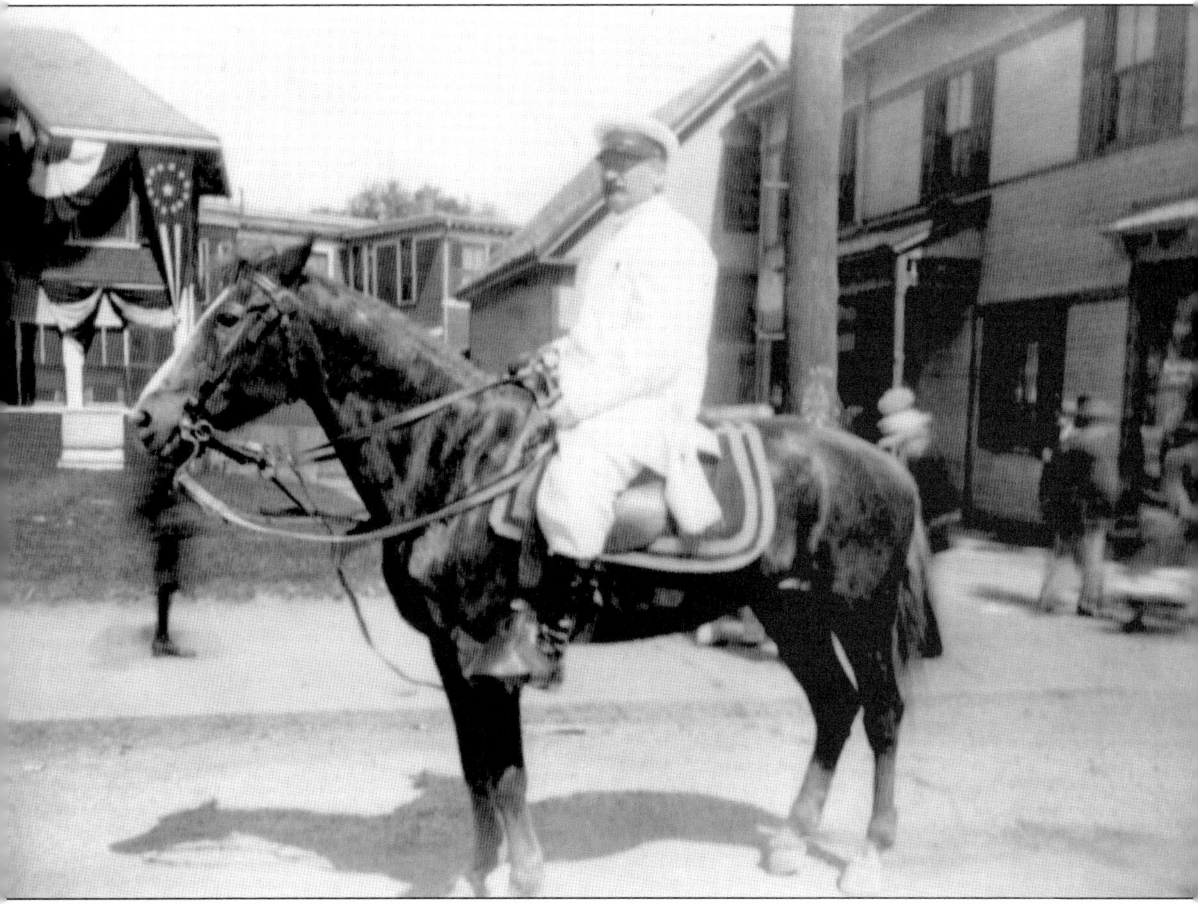

Dr. Gilman Osgood was born in Abington on February 26, 1863, and graduated from Abington High School in 1880, helping his family by taking a job as a shoe cutter before heading off to Bellevue Hospital Medical College in New York. Earning his M.D. in 1886, he worked at the King's County Hospital for the Insane on Welfare Island in the East River. He served as assistant superintendent there for two years before returning to Rockland to open a local practice in 1890. From 1898 until his death in 1934, he served as either the medical examiner or the assistant medical examiner of Plymouth County. His interests ranged from the legal side of medical practice to mental health to oral hygiene.

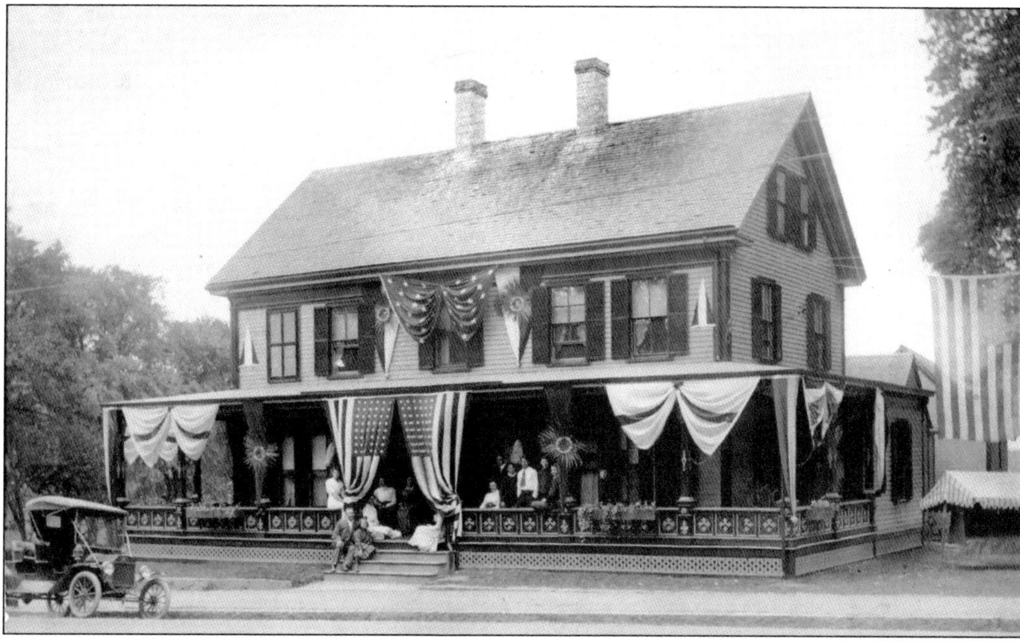

In his free time, Osgood dabbled in local history. Proud to be a citizen of Old Abington when Rockland, Whitman, and Abington celebrated the ancient town's bicentennial in 1912, Osgood decorated himself and his home at 258 Union Street, located on the corner of Goddard Avenue where the gas station next to Rockland's town hall is located. He also wrote an article on the history of the Abington schools for the celebration and headed the bicentennial exhibition committee.

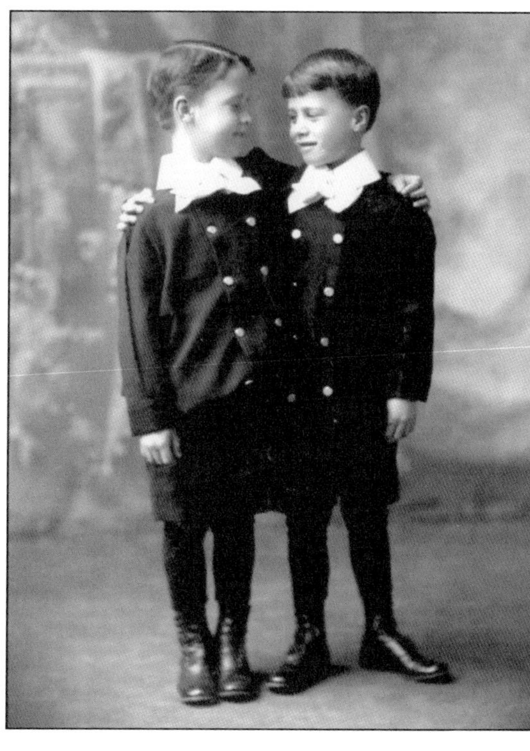

Perhaps just as well known as the good doctor were his twin sons, Foster (left) and Russell (right), who were born on December 13, 1899. Two of the five children of Gilman and Mabel (Russell) Osgood, both boys graduated from Rockland High School with the class of 1916 and served with the U.S. Navy in World War I. Foster is buried in Arlington National Cemetery in Washington D.C.

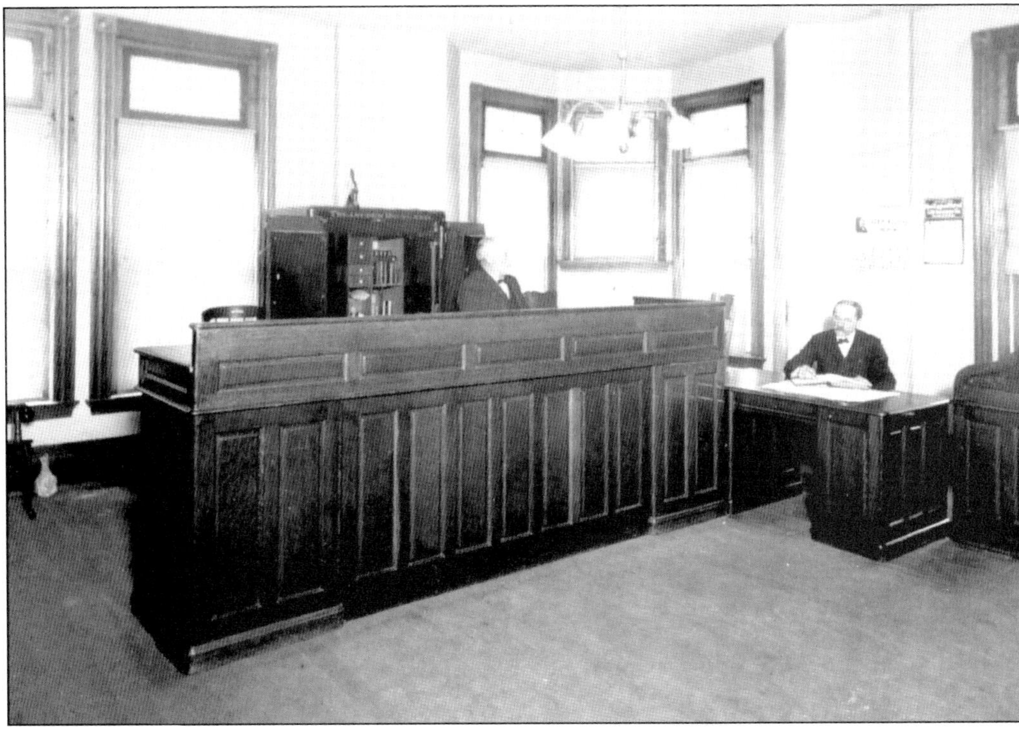

A lot could get done at the town offices in 1904. Open for business in this picture are selectman Charles A. Townsend, behind the counter, and longtime treasurer Joshua Gray, behind the desk on the right. A Civil War veteran and a member of the Hartsuff Post G.A.R., Gray retired as treasurer in 1929 at 88 years old.

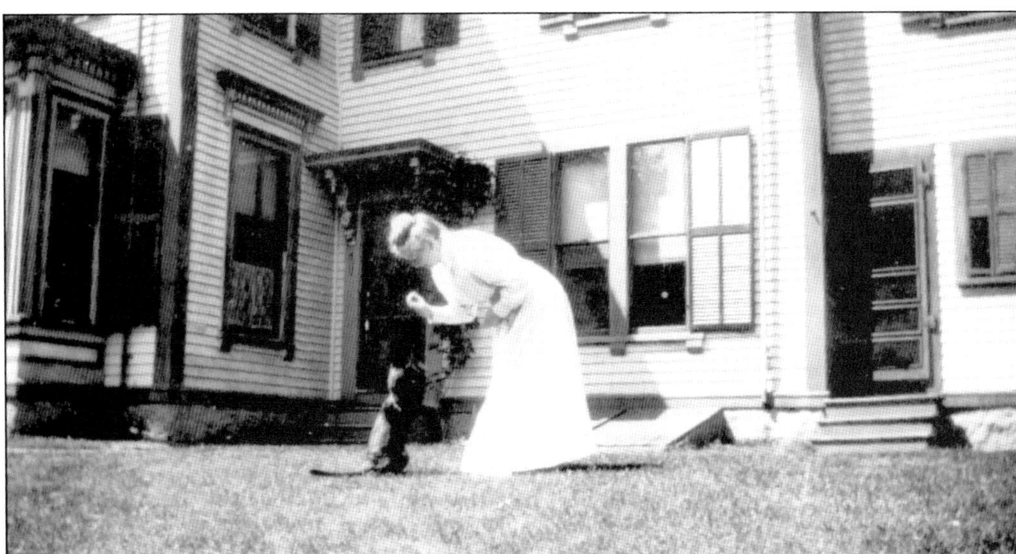

Gray and his wife, Sarah, lived at 37 Linden Street and were feted with a large banquet upon his retirement. A musical talent and gifted accountant, Joshua Gray was a member of the Union Glee Club, the Rockland Choral Society, the Stoughton Musical Society, and the Grand Army Quartette.

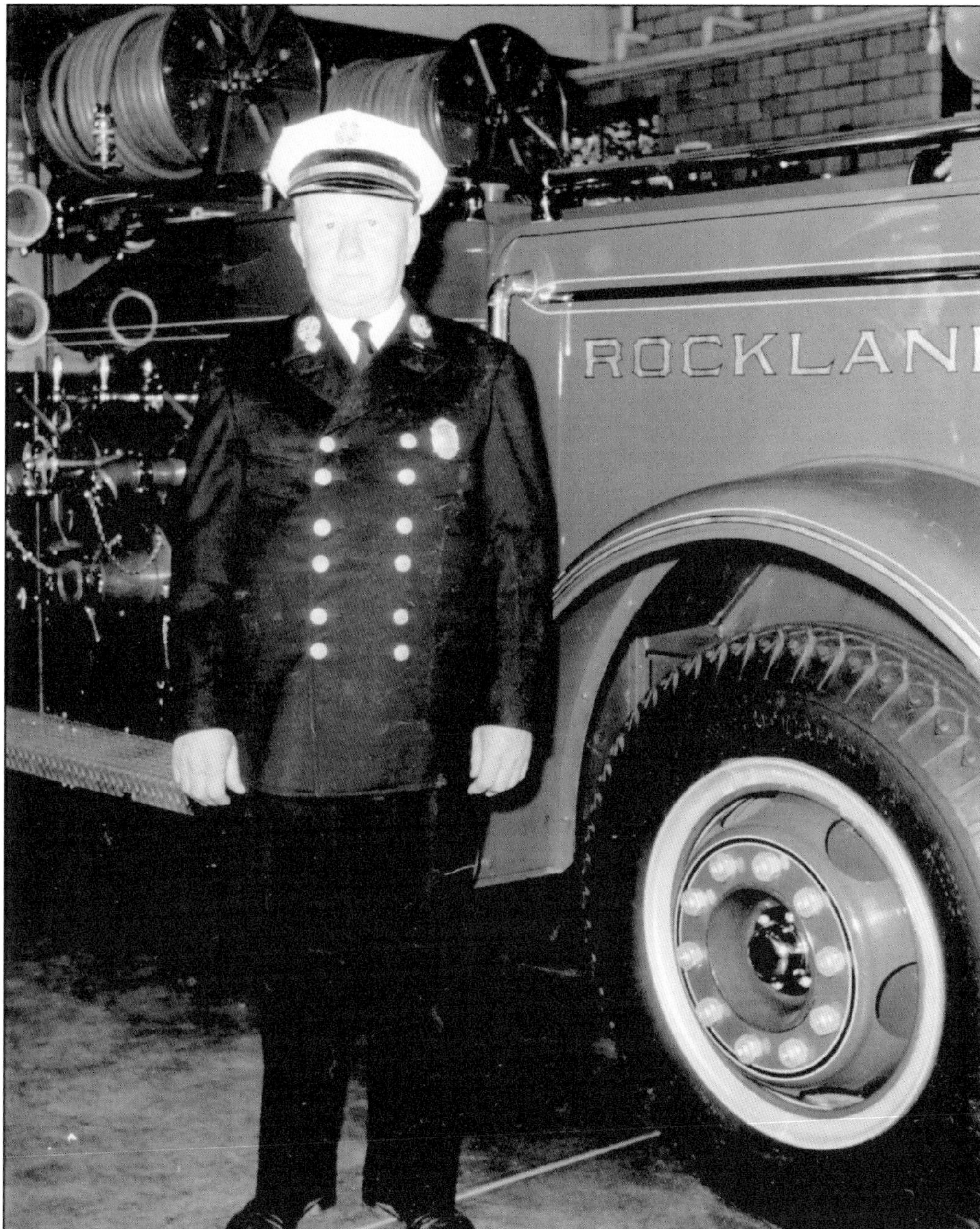

Clyson Inkley worked at the Hatherly fire station from 1910 to 1915. He worked on the town's board of engineers from 1915 to 1920. In 1920, he filled the vacancy created by the resignation of Fred Chapman as chief and never looked back. When he started in that position, the town had one permanent on-duty fireman. By 1945, there were four full-timers and 40 on-call men. Inkley was on hand for many of the famous fires that plagued Union Street in the 1920s, 1930s, and 1940s, including the fires at the Webster Building in 1923, the Standard and Phoenix Blocks in 1929, and the big Gladstone Block conflagration that gutted the town offices in 1941.

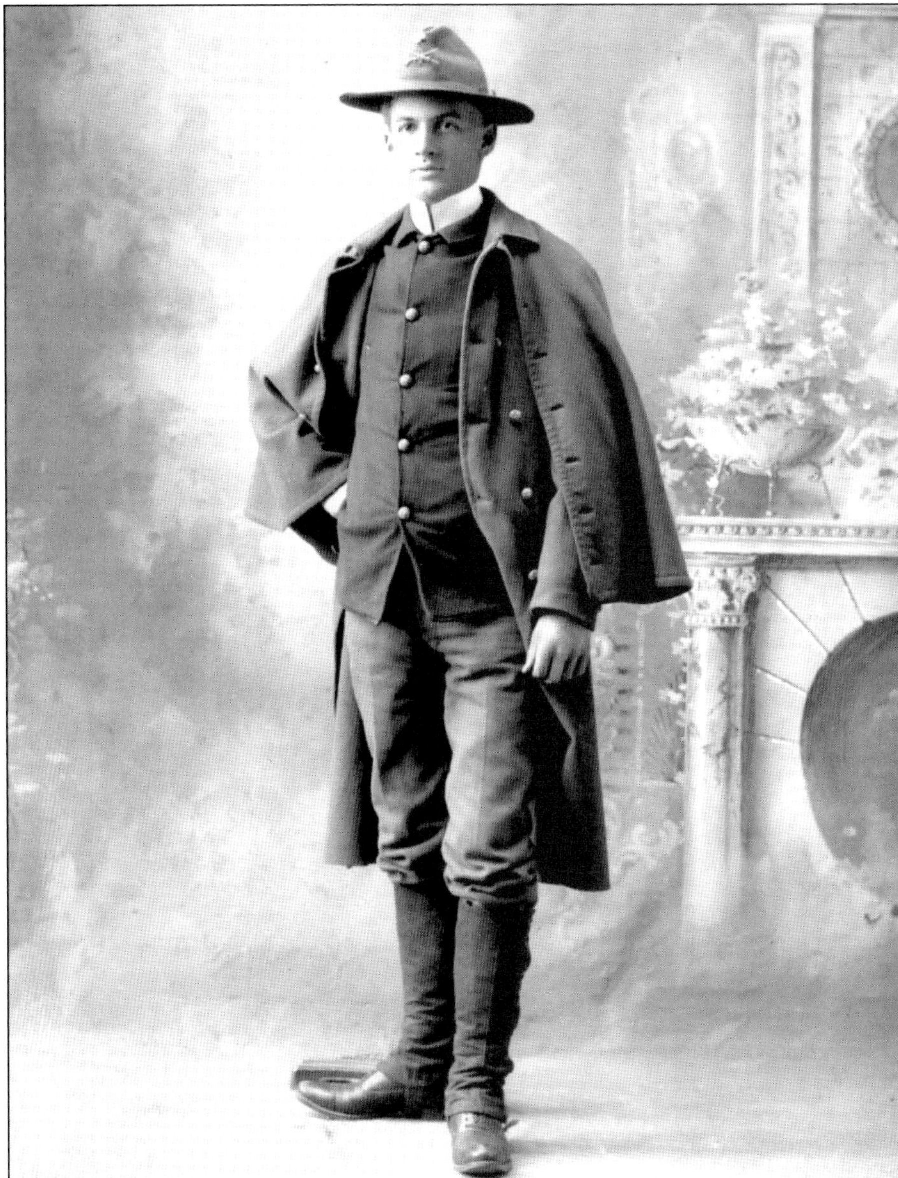

Harold Studley served as the first commander of the Peter A. Bowler Camp 63 United Spanish War Veterans when it formed on March 26, 1922, two decades after the war ended. At first, meetings were held at Temperance Hall. They were later moved to the Grand Army Hall on School Street. Although the post was supposed to be named for the first local man to die in the conflict, Bowler was not the first Rockland man to do so. Joseph Sullivan of the 9th Massachusetts Volunteer Infantry died at Fort Myer, Virginia, on September 1, 1898, while in training. Bowler died two days later at Massachusetts General Hospital of a fever contracted before Santiago, Cuba. Patrick H. Mahoney died of yellow fever at Siboney, Cuba, on July 26, 1898. On October 13, 1900, Frank Maguire also died of a disease contracted in service. In all, 16 Rockland men enlisted to fight in the war in the infantry, heavy artillery, marines, and hospital corps. Luckily, thanks to photographs such as this one, the memories of the Rockland men who fought in this long-forgotten war will not be lost.

Eight

Shoes for America
Rockland's Shoe Factories

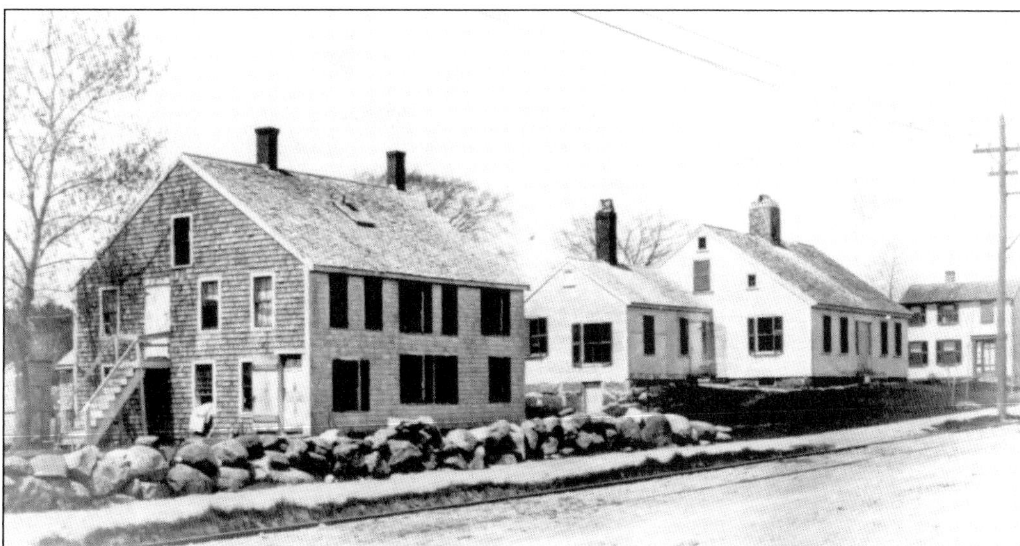

Long before Rockland was known as Rockland, the community was known for its high-quality shoemaking industry. The industry had humble beginnings. Capt. Thomas Hunt, who set up shop near the Weymouth line in 1793, began what would become Rockland's most significant industry when he told friends and neighbors that he would thenceforth be available to make shoes for payment. Early shoemaking establishments were simple 10-by-10-foot shacks in back and side yards, known as ten-footers. As demand grew, factories were built. The house on the left, on North Union Street, was the shoe factory of Hunt and Loud.

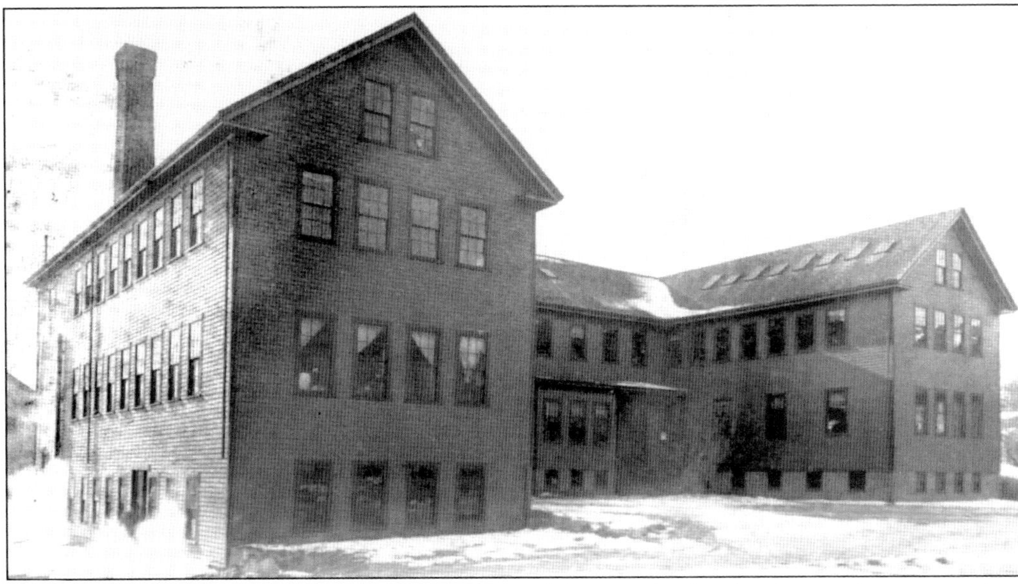

William H. Bates's Rockland Company, makers of shoes and other leather products, grew from W.E. Putnam & Company when two of his associates, W.E. Putnam and H.S Jenkins, retired from active work and purchased stock in his new concern. According to an 1897 biographical sketch of Bates, "The new company erected a factory which is a model of completeness and convenience – an attractive building without and within – and moved into their new quarters on January 1, 1896. Their business . . . amounts to over half a million a year."

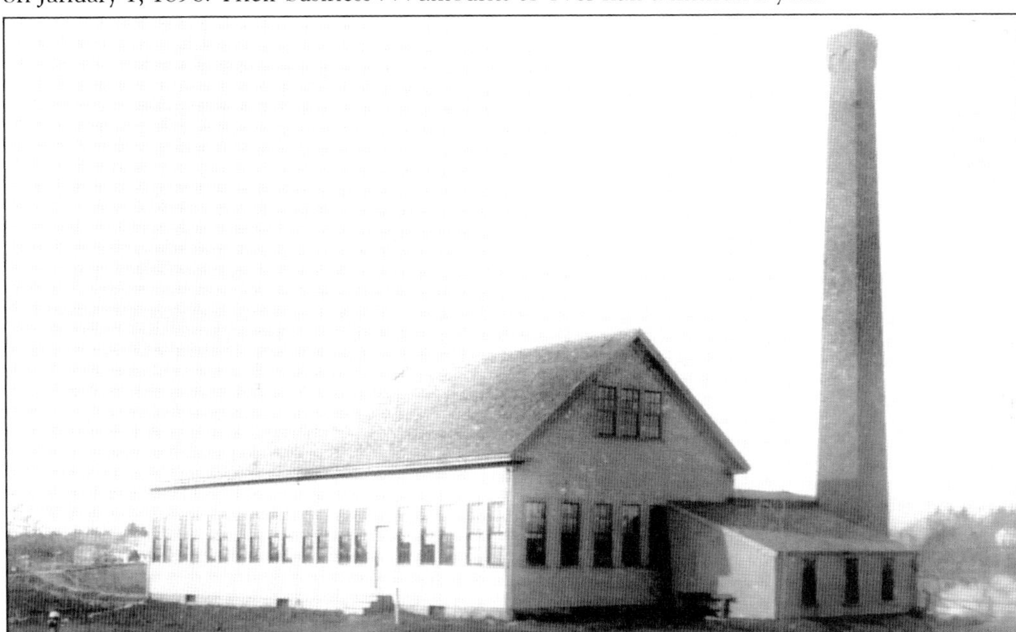

As footwear evolved over time, so did the complexity of its designs. While some manufacturers dealt only in the production of finished products, others opted to create some of the vital components needed to make them, from the lasts on which they were made to the glues that held them together. On Grove Street, partners French and Hall owned a factory, shown here, that specialized in making tacks.

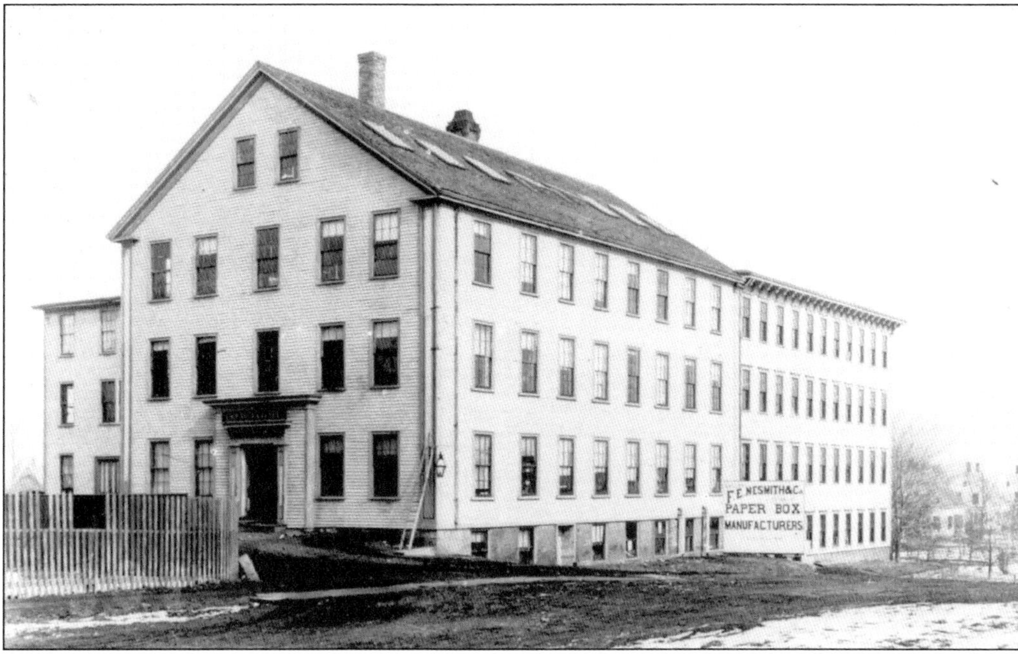

Joseph French and George Hall went into business together in 1881, building a four-story factory and employing 75 people in the manufacture of boots and shoes. According to historian Charles F. Meserve, "The special line of trade for which this house is celebrated is the manufacture of fine- and medium-grade hand- and machine-sewed calf boots and shoes, a department in which it stands second to none for excellence and durability of this class of goods."

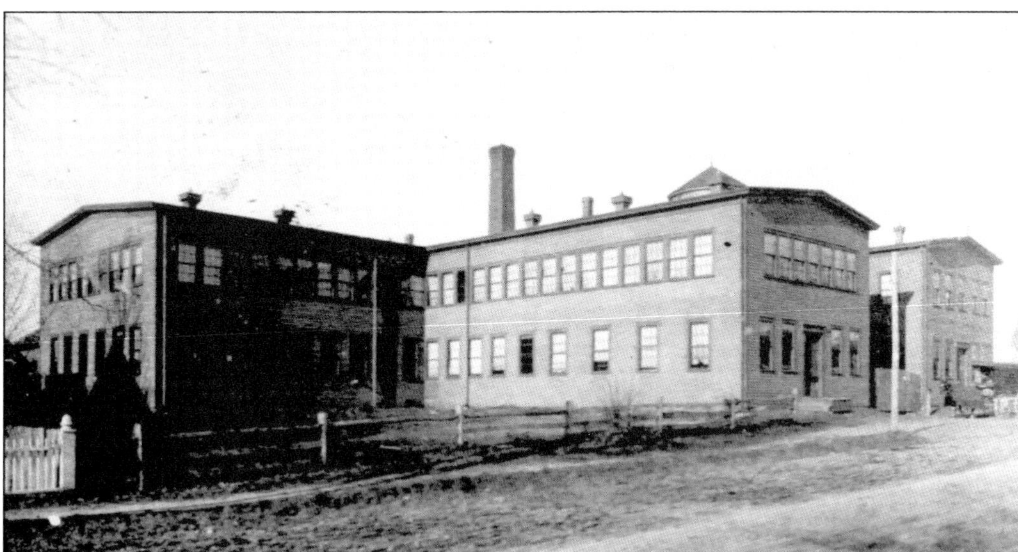

The J.S. Turner Boot and Shoe Manufacturers opened its doors for business in 1865 under the name Studley & Turner, but Mr. Studley passed away in 1873, leaving the entirety of the concern to his partner. At its height, the Turner factory employed approximately 250 people. In the 1880s, it produced an annual income of about $350,000.

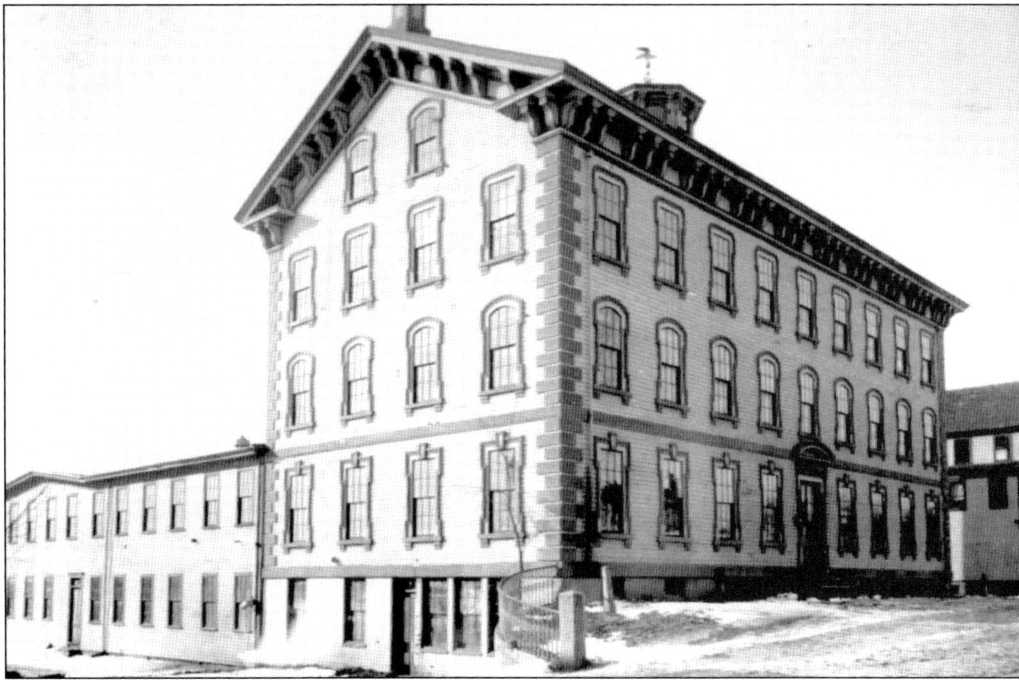

As the shoe economy boomed in Rockland, factories, such as this one owned by Jenkins Lane, grew not only in size but also in architectural style. Standing at the foot of Union Street, this building features a fancy cupola with an eagle weathervane, quoins, and other classic motifs. The extension off the back, though, is more utilitarian, reflective of changing economic needs and later architectural styles.

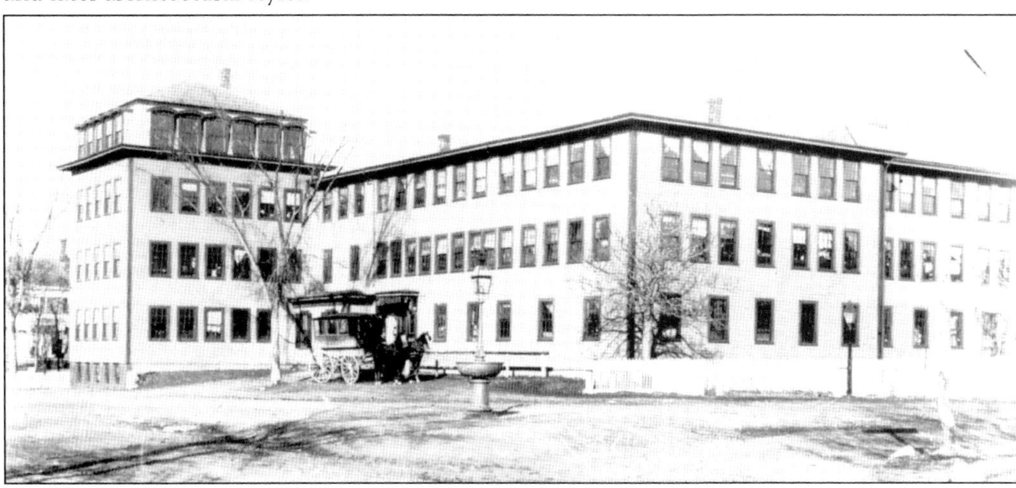

In this age of buyouts and name changes, when cable companies and long-distance providers seem to turn over on a monthly basis, one may look back and wish for simpler days, when a company chose a name and stuck with it. However, in 1872, L.J. Loud and B.E. Burrell formed a business that they thought would stand forever, the proud shoe manufactory known as Loud & Burrell. Less than three years later, Bernie Burrell bought out his partner and changed the name to Burrell & Company. In 1878, he invited a Mr. Houghton to join him, forming Burrell, Houghton & Company. Houghton later went into business himself, under the name Houghton & Company.

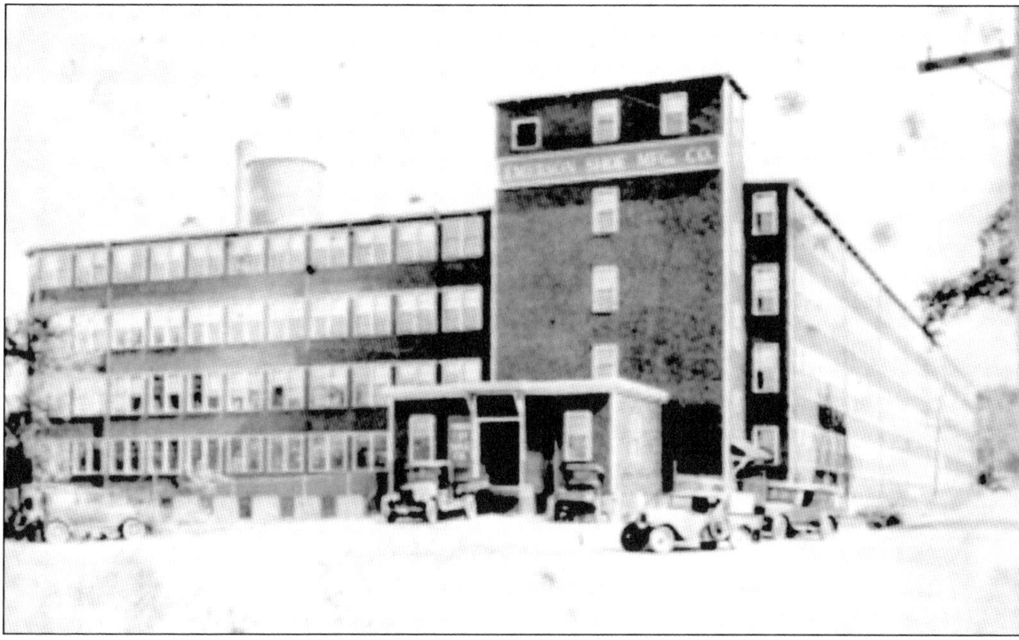

Rockland's first shoemakers walked out to their backyards and opened the doors to their personal shops to start their day's work. Later, when the first larger factories were built, they traveled on foot, horseback, or by coach to get to and from work. When the electric trolleys arrived, workers lucky enough to live near the line could hop a ride each morning. On a good weather day, they might have ridden bicycles. After 1900, the car became the transport of choice to factories such as Emerson's, one of the larger concerns in town.

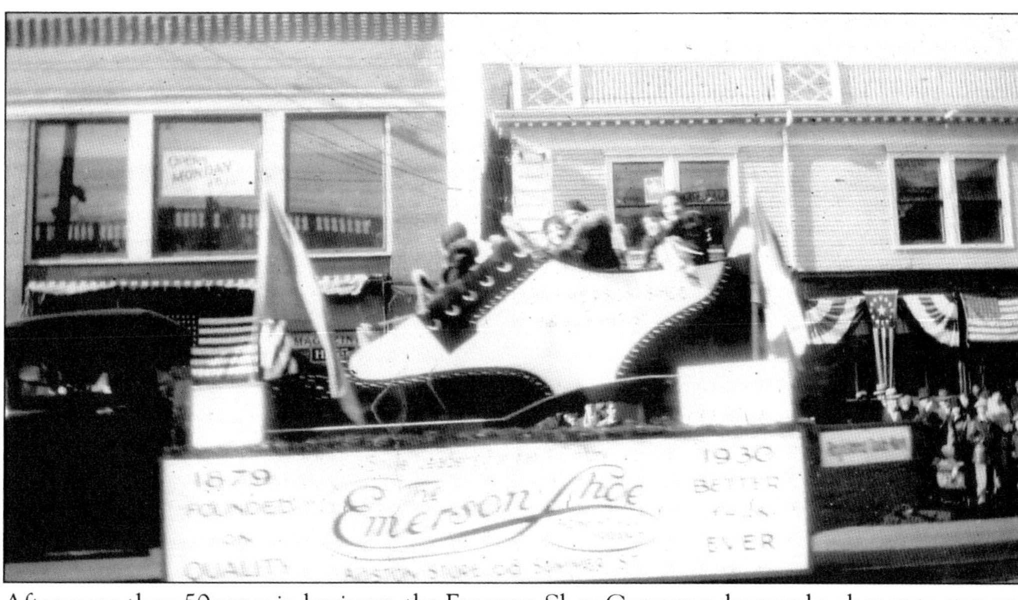

After more than 50 years in business, the Emerson Shoe Company deserved a chance to step out in style. Although the Depression had begun by the time of the parade in this 1930 photograph (which was rescued from a negative that had not seen the light of day for decades), Emerson Shoe Company was still going strong.

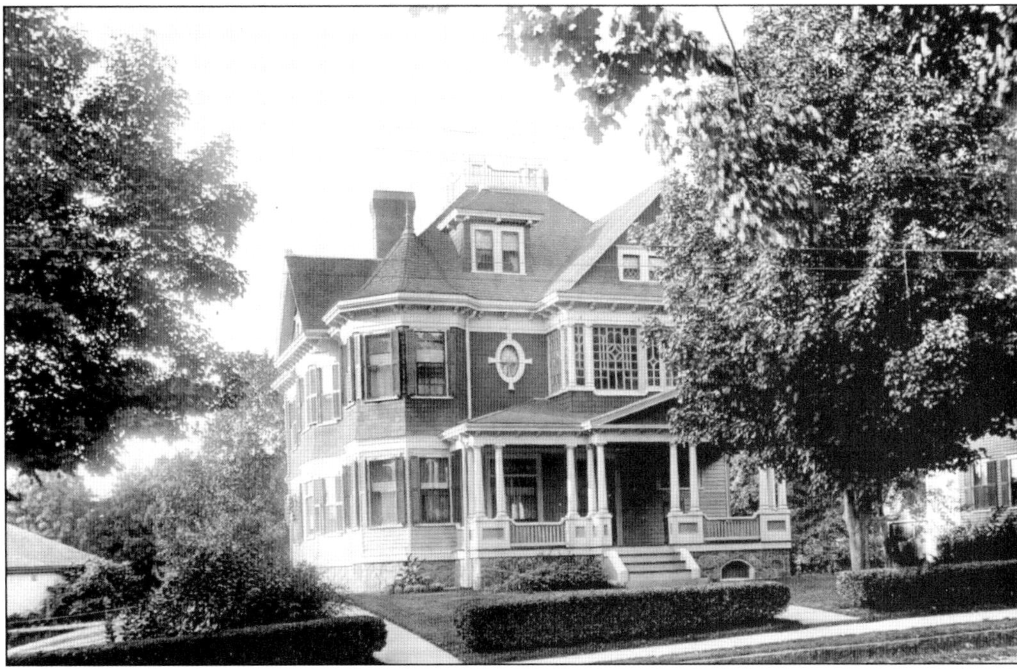

With success in business came privilege. While most of the workers connected to the Hurley brothers' factory lived in smaller homes, William F. Hurley's talents earned him enough money to own this house, located at the corner of Plain and West Water Streets. The home is recognizable today by its distinctive decorative front windows.

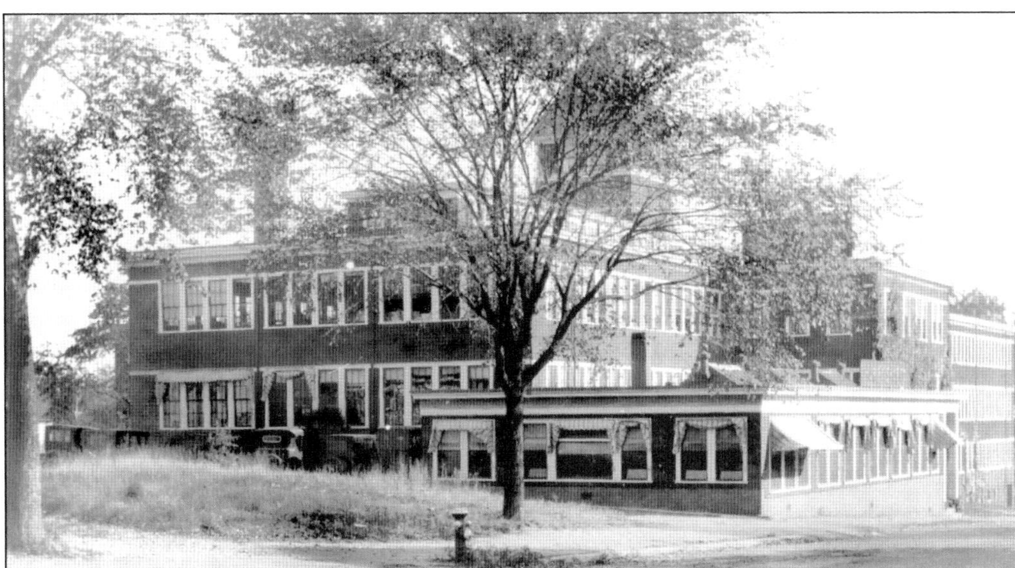

The Hurley brothers were born in West Hanover. John, William, George, and Edward went into business together in 1893, creating one of Rockland's most recognizable brands, the Hurley Shoe. As late as 1928, a biographer of William Hurley wrote, "They are known to the shoe trade throughout the country, and there are many of their retail patrons who insist upon having the Hurley shoes or none." The Hurley Shoe factory still stands today on Church Street.

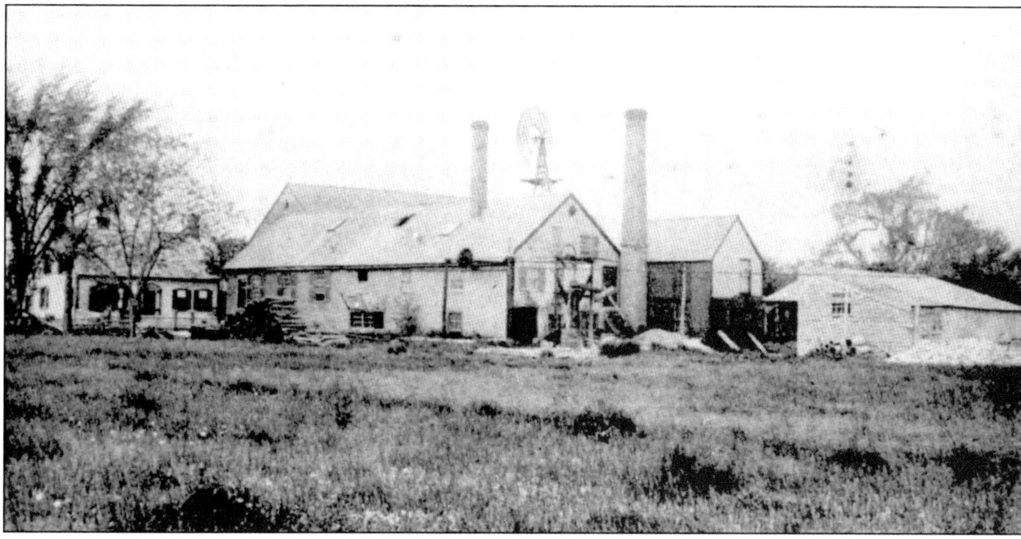

Not every factory in Rockland produced shoes. At 423 Market Street, the Torrey family manufactured soap. Unfortunately, the smells from the boiling animal fats used to make the product gave the neighborhood quite a reputation, although no one doubted the value of the item being made. Josiah Torrey, who was born in 1798, at first farmed the land he owned and then moved into the soap-making business.

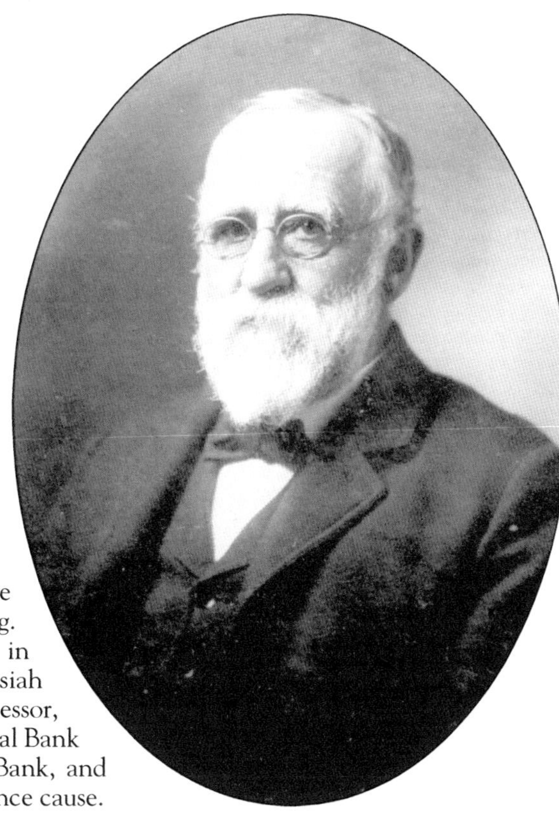

Josiah's son Josiah A. Torrey carried the business forward after his father's passing. He had been made a partner at age 21 in 1856. One of 13 children, the younger Josiah also served the town as selectman and assessor, worked as director of the Rockland National Bank and president of the Rockland Savings Bank, and stood as a strong supporter of the temperance cause.

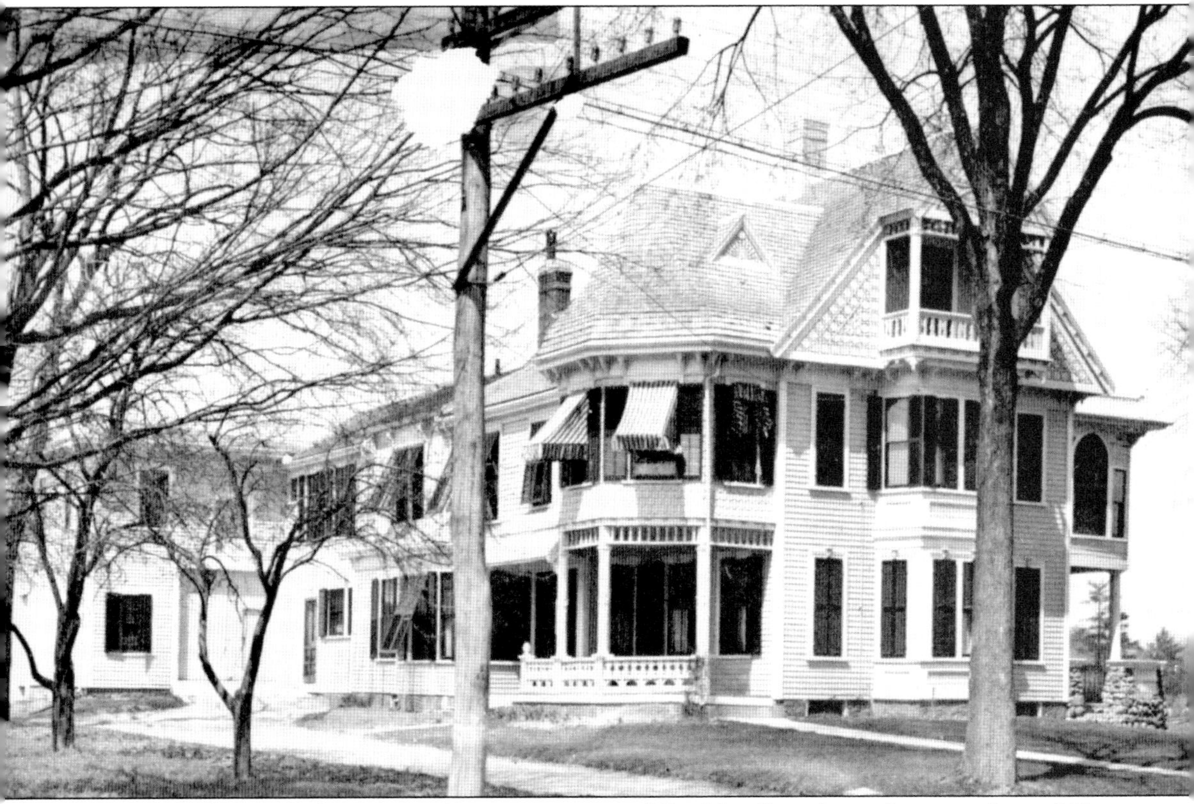

Perhaps the most dramatic and inspiring story of Rockland's industrial past is that of Elwin T. Wright, whose Webster Street home is pictured here. Wright was the later owner of E.T. Wright & Company. At age 13, Wright, born in Plympton, left school to learn the shoemaker's trade. At 24, he vowed to become a manufacturer and the owner of his own line. In 1876, he set up a small shop on Water Street adjacent to the railroad station in the newly incorporated town of Rockland. By 1896, business was so good that he admitted a partner, Alfred W. Donovan, and by 1906, Wright put his faith in his friend to run things while he served merely as treasurer. His world-famous arch-preserver line made him, according to one 1928 biographical sketch, "probably the dean of all shoe manufacturers in the United States." In support of his adopted community, he served as state representative for two years, a state senator for two years, and chaired the Rockland public safety committee during World War I.

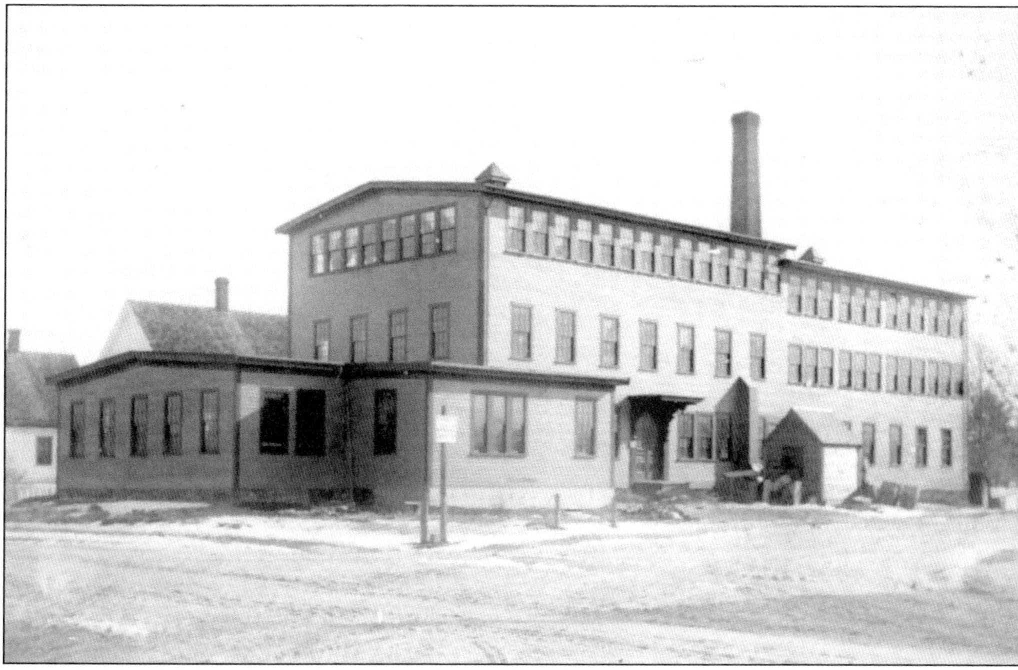

From the one-room shoe shop grew a business that could only be contained by a 100,000-square-foot factory operated by approximately 800 employees that turned out more than 3,000 pairs of shoes a day.

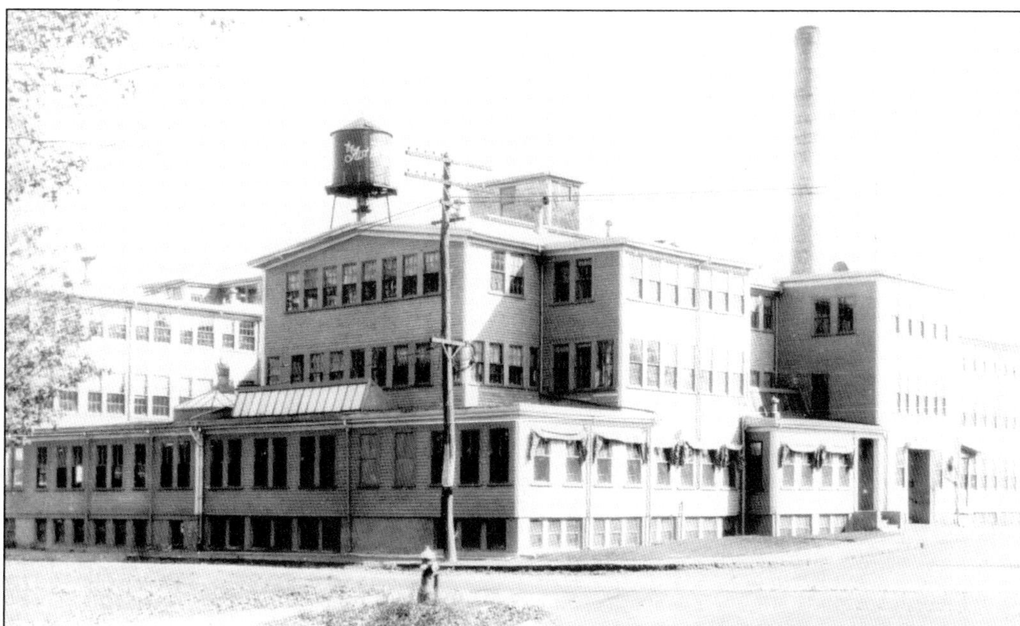

As demand increased, so too did the bounds of the Wright building. Pavilions built out from the main frame of the original building added needed floor space for machines, offices, and an increase in people in all facets of the work. Although electric lighting had arrived by the time of this photograph, natural lighting was still cheaper, and the high number of windows around the factory attests to that fact.

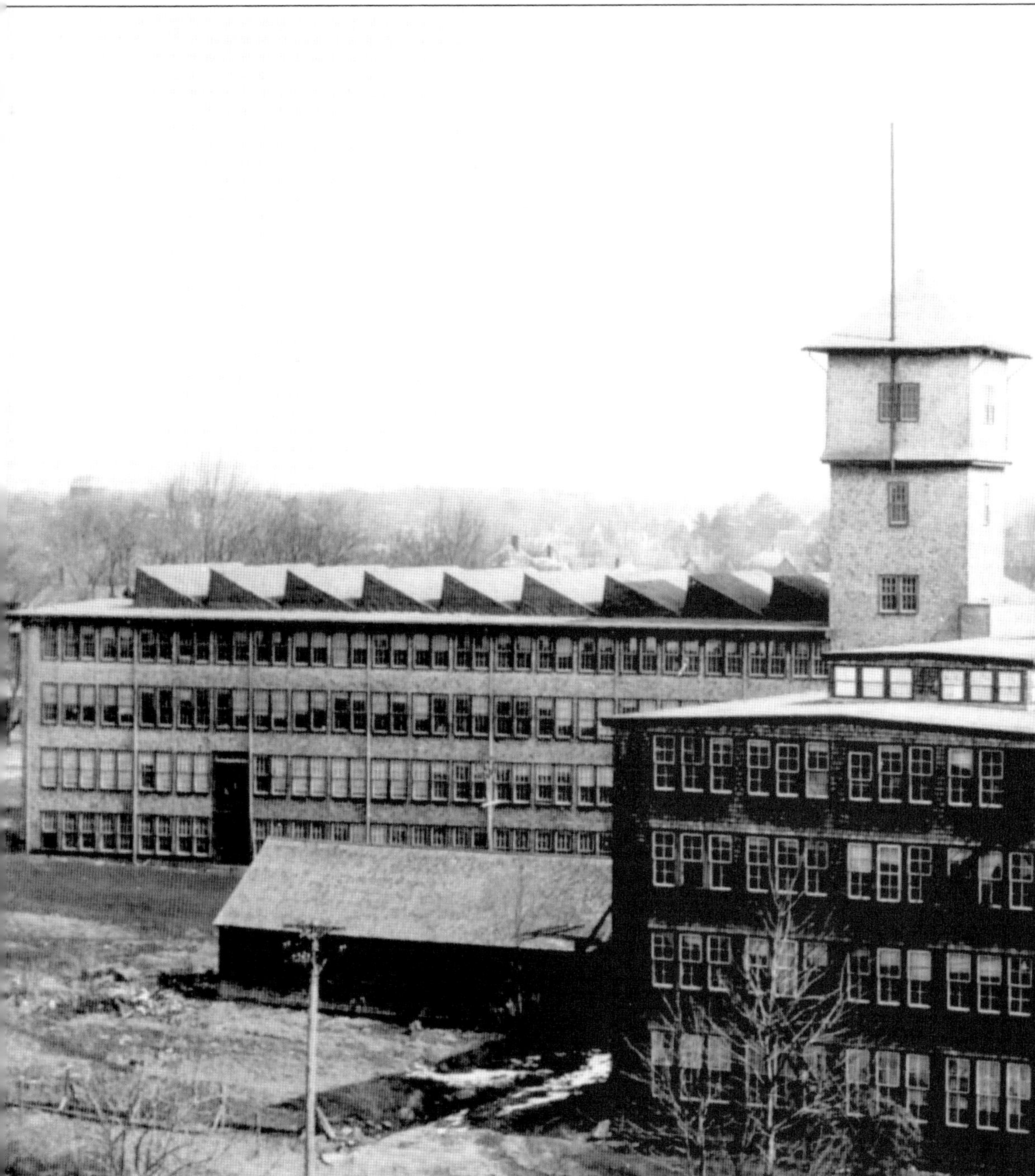

By 1928, 56 factories in seven Plymouth County towns manufactured shoes. Massachusetts turned out 72,000,000 pairs annually. The factories produced about one quarter of all of the shoes in the United States: 24.2 percent of men's shoes and 27.7 percent of women's shoes. The state's factories employed about 80,000 workers, and 10,000 more worked in related industries. The people of Rockland could look back—perhaps from the windows of the mammoth Rice and Hutchins factory as they watched trains pulling up to its front doors—to a time when Thomas

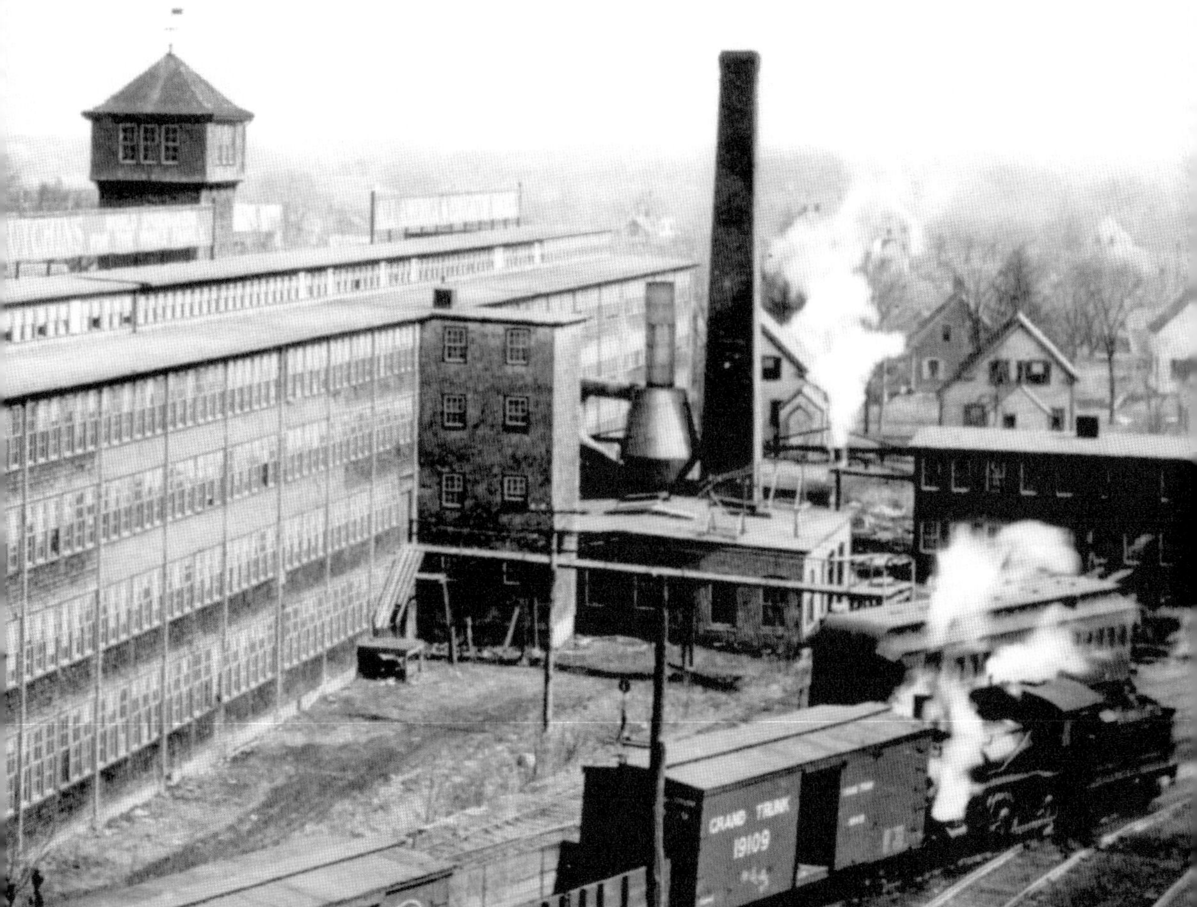

Hunt set up his ten-footer on North Union Street and "put out his shingle" for the first time in a time without electricity, without railroads, without even running water, and be proud. In less than a century and a half, Rockland had gone from a small east-end village to an independent community to one of the world's most renowned shoe manufacturing centers. As stated in the *History of Plymouth, Barnstable and Norfolk Counties*, "Brockton and the South Shore District set the style and furnish the cream."

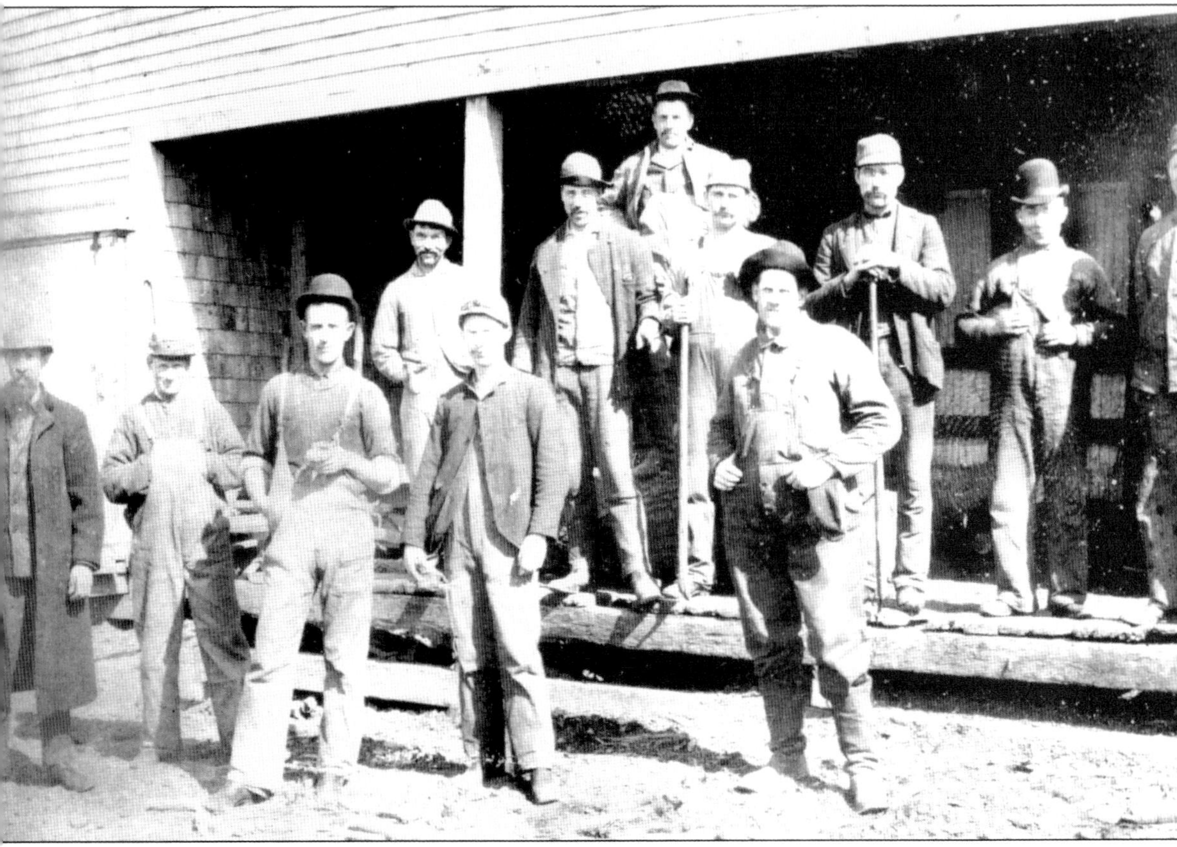

The history of Rockland, while driven by such visionaries as E.T. Wright, William H. Bates, and the Hurley brothers, was built on the backs of hundreds of laborers who have passed more or less anonymously into the abyss of time. For every E.T. Wright, there were a dozen shoe cutters; for every William Bates, there were 100 sewing machine operators; for every Hurley brother, there were hard-working Rocklanders such as these men who worked on the crew of the Gideon Studley box mill. History is written and recorded by those with the time, means, and privilege to do so. Often, that history can be incomplete. Each life is a story, and each story deserves to be told.

ACKNOWLEDGMENTS

The authors would like to dedicate this book to all who have worked hard in the past to preserve and protect the history of Rockland, including Cyrus Nash, Peg Donohue, Lorenzo Perkins, Herbert W. Hunt, Clyson Inkley, Rose White, Burton O. Estes, William T. McCarthy, Katherine Gilbride, Bernie Monahan, Martha Campbell, Dr. Gilman Osgood, and Raymond Smith.

The authors would like to thank the following individuals and organizations for their roles in helping to create this book: Ken Taylor and the directors of the Historical Society of Old Abington; Joice Himawan, Pam Whiting, and the trustees of the Dyer Memorial Library; Beverly Brown and the staff of the Rockland Memorial Library; the Rockland Historical Commission; Al Smith; Jean Holland; Dwight Swanson; Northeast Historic Film; Marge Bryant; the First Congregational Church of Rockland; Michael Stoddard; Kathy Peters; Carole Mooney; Amos Phelps Insurance Company; Helen Keeler; Sylvia Duhaine; Deborah and Donald Springhetti; Dean Sargent; the Rockland selectmen; A.W. Perry, Inc., and John "Jack" Spurr; Kevin Bird and the Rockland post office; the *Rockland Mariner*; and Amy Sutton, Jill Anderson, Jessica Engstrom, and the staff at Arcadia's Northeast office.

Special thanks to Janet Cann and Debora Babin Katz for help and support.

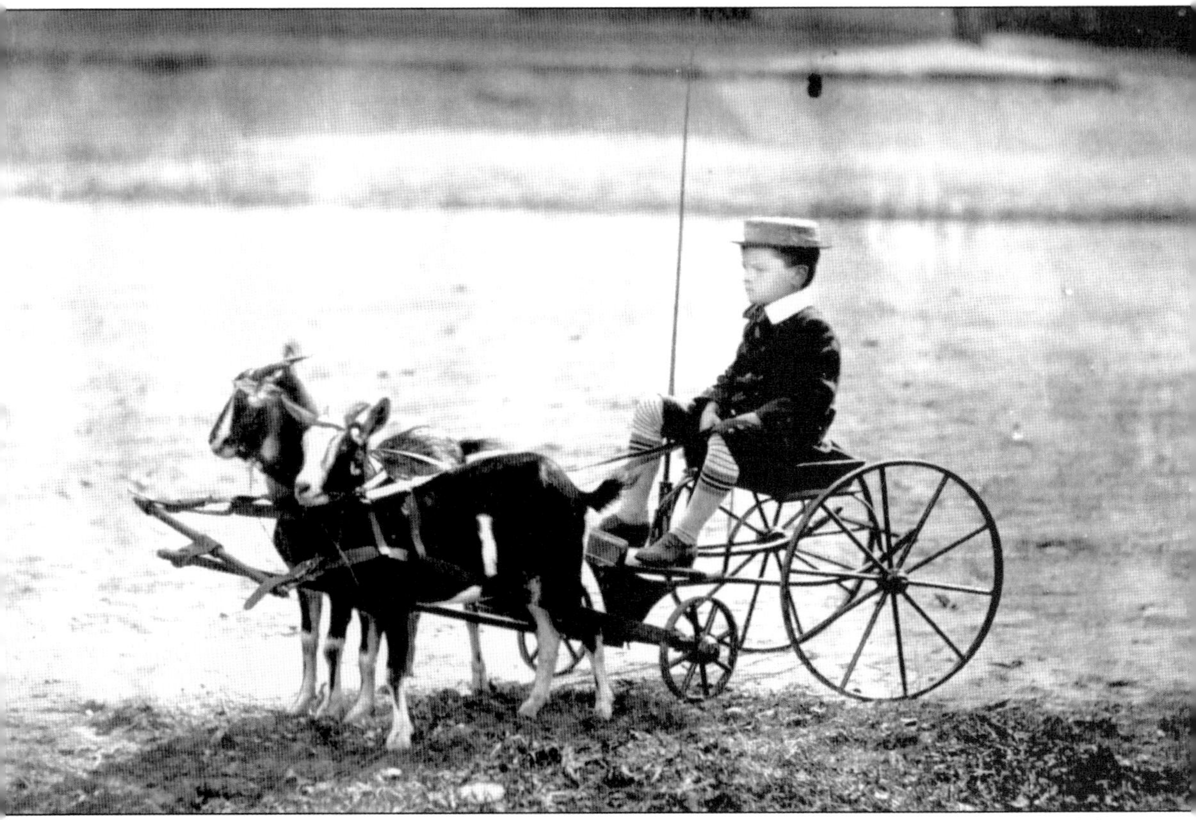

It may sound cliché, but while conducting the research for this book, the authors realized that there are thousands of words for each photograph. Take, for instance, George Rockland Hunt and his personal sulky. At six years old, Rockland's first citizen had trained a pair of goats to pull him around town. Would anyone actually believe that story today were it not for the existence of this amazing photograph?

Sadly, along the way, the authors also found that several photographs, and indeed entire collections, had been lost to time. Wonderful story-telling photographs had either faded, destabilized, or crumpled due to sunlight, moisture, or insect damage. In order to prevent Rockland's history from disappearing any faster, the authors will contribute equal portions of the proceeds from this book to both the Historical Society of Old Abington and the Dyer Memorial Library for the preservation of historic photography.

In order to further protect the future of Rockland's past, we urge you to donate to these local nonprofit institutions and to consider the Dyer Memorial Library as the final repository of your family's historic photographs of Rockland.

For more information, contact the Dyer Memorial Library, 28 Centre Avenue, P.O. Box 2245, Abington, MA 02351. Telephone: (781) 878-8480.